Witness

Witness

Sakshi Malik
with
Jonathan Selvaraj

JUGGERNAUT BOOKS
C-I-128, First Floor, Sangam Vihar, Near Holi Chowk,
New Delhi 110080, India

First published by Juggernaut Books 2024

Copyright © Sakshi Malik 2024

10 9 8 7 6 5 4 3 2 1

P-ISBN: 9789353456221
E-ISBN: 9789353452605

The views and opinions expressed in this book are the author's own.
The facts contained herein were reported to be true as on the date of publication
by the author to the publishers of the book, and the publishers are not
in any way liable for their accuracy or veracity.

All rights reserved. No part of this publication may be reproduced,
transmitted, or stored in a retrieval system in any form or by any means without the
written permission of the publisher.

Typeset in Adobe Caslon Pro by
R. Ajith Kumar, Noida

Printed at Replika Press Pvt. Ltd.

For my dada and dadi.
I wish they could see me achieve all that I did.

Contents

1. End of the Line — 1
2. Growing up in Rohtak — 12
3. Starting *Kushti* — 26
4. First International — 50
5. Camp Life — 60
6. *Dangal*s — 75
7. Brij Bhushan — 81
8. No Place to Hide — 88
9. Making My Way Past the Seniors — 95
10. The Fight before the Fight — 104
11. Satyawart — 113
12. Making It to the Olympics — 122
13. My Olympic Journey — 138
14. Returning Home a Champion — 163
15. Body Talk (A Small Digression) — 172
16. Fighting for Satyawart — 176
17. Post-Olympic Struggles — 191
18. My Struggles Continue — 203

19. The Final Hurrah	218
20. How the Protest Started	224
21. The Committee Fails Us	244
22. Second Protest	256
23. Aftermath	274
24. Cracks Start to Appear	277
25. *Dabdaba Tha, Dabdaba Rahega*	284
27. Why I Continue to Fight	294

1

End of the Line

Wrestling is the art of moving a body against its will. When it came to being pushed around or pushing, I thought I knew all the moves. But on the morning of 28 June 2024, I learnt a powerful new technique that no coach had ever taught me.

It was the thirty-seventh day of the protest against the Wrestling Federation of India and its president Brij Bhushan Sharan Singh. I, the other wrestlers and our supporters had decided to march from our protest site at Jantar Mantar in New Delhi to central Delhi, where the new Parliament building was being inaugurated.

But we must have barely covered a hundred metres when a swarm of police personnel descended on us. I tried my best to keep marching while the police tried to pull me into a bus. There were several hands grabbing at me. I'm sure they had plenty of experience with this sort of thing, but I was an Olympic medallist, after all. It's hard to drag me out of position. Every time the policewomen pushed me, I'd readjust my stance or grab the bus doors or handrail. I could sense I was starting to frustrate them.

Finally someone behind me yelled, 'Tickle her!' I was probably stronger than all those policewomen, but once you are tickled, you become helpless. My strength evaporated, and before I knew it I was bundled into the bus.

In the chaos, I lost sight of my companions. My fellow wrestlers Bajrang Punia and Vinesh Phogat were bundled off in a separate bus. My husband Satyawart was also put in another bus. The police were sending each of us to a different police station, and they kept driving in circles so we couldn't get our bearings. In my bus there was no one I knew. Apart from me, there were two men who were part of the protest, whom I didn't recognize, and a couple of constables. Nor did I have my phone with me. Satyawart had kept it in his pocket at the start of the march so that it wouldn't get misplaced.

The two other protesters were sitting in the front of the bus and I was sat a couple of rows behind them. A woman constable was behind me. She had her hand on the seat in front of me, to keep me from moving.

I really didn't want to be by myself. I kept pleading with the police to put me in the same bus as my husband, or at least with someone I knew. The longer we circled around, the more I started to panic.

In tears, I begged and pleaded with the police. Feeling sorry for me, one of the men from the protest gave me his phone and I managed to call Satyawart. When my husband heard me bawling he couldn't take it.

He broke the back door of his bus and jumped out of the vehicle. On the phone he shouted to me to send him my location. He was coming to get me. I too decided to jump out of the bus. It was a crazy thing to do. I know now that detention doesn't mean arrest. You are eventually released a day later. But I knew little about protests and protesting. Until a few months ago, I was someone who would avoid confrontation at any cost.

Perhaps if I was sitting with my husband, or with Sangeeta or Vinesh, I might have been calmer. I might have thought through my actions. On that day though, everything was happening too fast. When Satyawart kicked open the door of his bus, I decided I would do the same.

I started moving to the front door. The policewoman tried her best to hold me back, but of course this wasn't a ten versus one, as it had been on the grounds. There was just one of her, and her grip wasn't anything I hadn't dealt with before. I just shook her off, pushed the door open, jumped down and started to run.

As I took off, with two police constables chasing after me, I felt a familiar twinge in my left knee. It didn't hurt, although it made me run a little funny. Just a little reminder of a ligament torn and patched multiple times and a career in wrestling that was on the verge of ending.

I didn't get very far. I dashed into a lane and then turned into another, which, unfortunately, turned out to be a dead end. In front of me was a building that was under construction. If I hadn't turned into the dead end I would probably have escaped because damaged ligament or not, I was still pretty quick. I might have called an autorickshaw, found out where Satyawart was and gone to him.

Instead, as I stood in front of that building, trying to figure my next step, I realized that one of the construction workers was staring at me. I tried my best to hide. There was a staircase just outside his line of sight and I squeezed myself next to it. Of course he had already seen me. He'd also seen the two police constables who were running towards us. He asked me why I was hiding and why the police were after me.

Before I could answer him the police caught up with me. I didn't have the heart to run again. The fight had gone out of me, as quickly as it had come. Now, as I walked back to the bus, I couldn't stop my tears. In fact I was hysterical. People in the lane peered out of their windows in curiosity at my wails, watching this crying woman being led off by the police. I hoped no one recognized me as the Olympic medallist Sakshi Malik.

Eventually, I ended up at the police detention centre. My mother-in-law also joined me there. We were detained at the police station until the evening, when they decided to release me. They took me to a hospital for a check-up. There were scratches all over my back and neck where the constables had grabbed me. I was in pain, but to avoid being held up any longer I told the doctor that I was fine. Besides, I was a lot more hurt emotionally.

Once Bajrang and Vinesh were released too, I started coordinating with them. Our protest had been stopped, but we weren't done. We decided to meet at 11 p.m. to decide what we would do. That night, at our lawyer's office, all of us talked around the table.

We all had very mixed emotions. The adrenaline we felt earlier in the day was wearing off. I was proud that we had fought and raised our voice, but now we were feeling very low, like we used to feel after a defeat on the mat. Bajrang had been one of the last to be released, and his wife Sangeeta was still in tears. We tried to cheer each other up by making light of what had happened. My escape and recapture by the police got a few laughs, but there wasn't much else to smile about.

We had been on the streets protesting for nearly forty days, and now we had nothing to show for it. Our protest had been ended violently. Our protest site had been torn down. There didn't seem to be many options. But we had to move fast. Our protest had become a movement and had captured the imagination of thousands. But if we delayed our next action, many would lose interest in the movement.

We thought of going back to the protest site, but that had already been cleared out by the police. Another idea was to go on a march to Rajghat, but that was also dismissed. A third was to somehow restart our protest. We needed to make some gesture to show we were continuing our fight.

That night we decided we were going to immerse the medals we had won over the course of our careers into the Ganga at Haridwar. The way our protest site was demolished, the way we had been dragged by the police into a detention centre made it very clear to us that our reputation as international athletes had counted for nothing. In such a scenario, what was the point of all the medals we had won?

We had originally planned to immerse all the medals that we'd won, but we decided to just immerse the medals that meant the most to us. Bajrang brought the Olympic bronze medal he had won at the Tokyo Olympics. Vinesh brought her two medals from the world championships and a gold medal from the Commonwealth Games. That night I fetched from Rohtak the bronze medal that I had won at the Rio Olympics.

That medal meant the world to me. Ever since I'd first won it, it hadn't left my side. Sometimes I'd take it out of its box and just admire it. Sometimes I'd put it on and look at myself in the mirror.

It was beautiful. I've won medals at the Commonwealth Games and Asian Championships, but the Olympic medal was different. It looked like nothing else I had. The other medals had a thin silk ribbon. My Olympic medal had a double-layered, sea-green ribbon, which felt soft and almost cushion-like against my neck.

After I got married and moved to Satyawart's home, I decided to get it framed. I got it done in such a way that one side of the square frame had a photo of me winning the bronze and the other side the medal itself. I had it hung on the wall of my bedroom, right next to my Padma Shri medal and my Arjuna award.

Now I was going to lose it.

I took the frame with my medal off the wall and stuffed it into a bag.

Bajrang and Vinesh would carry their medals loose in their hands, but I didn't take my medal out of its frame. I wanted it to stay inside, all shiny and clean.

I slept fitfully that night in New Delhi and got up early the next day. My mother-in-law was staying with us, and she made some dal and roti for breakfast. I couldn't eat anything beyond a few bites. I didn't bathe either. I just wanted to get through that day. My mother-in-law then made some *churma* with ghee, sugar and shredded chapattis. It's the sort of thing mothers in Haryana make as a comfort food. She knew what we were planning and that I was going to be in very low spirits that day.

At night our decision felt like the right thing. In fact, it felt as if there was no other alternative. But I began to waver as the day came and we began planning our journey. The idea of losing the medal forever felt very painful. It was the same for Bajrang and Vinesh.

We had initially planned to immerse our medals without any fanfare, inform the media after the act was done and then restart our protest. But then, just before we left for Haridwar, Bajrang suggested we post messages on social media to say what we were going to do. It was a six-hour drive from New Delhi, and we hoped that it would be enough time for perhaps the sports ministry and the government to feel that things had gone too far and, out of necessity, agree with our demands. We were hoping against hope that we'd get a message on our phone that read, 'Kids, this has gone far enough. Don't get rid of your medals. We will listen to your demands.'

So we each posted a message on our social media accounts about half an hour after we left Delhi. All of us posted the same message. We said that we were immersing our medals in the Ganga because only the river had the ability to wash away all sins. Once we had done this, I felt maybe this wasn't the best idea. But I didn't realize just how bad it was going to get.

I was travelling with Satyawart, my mother and my mother-in-law. We met with Vinesh and Bajrang near Sonepat after they had picked up their medals from their homes. We wanted to travel in the same convoy and keep moving so that we couldn't be stopped by the police before we got to Haridwar.

I had tried not to look at my medal. I just put it in a bag, which I kept in the boot of the car. I knew that if I saw it I would start to cry. But try as I might, I couldn't not think about it. I talked about it constantly. Satyawart tried to change the subject, but we'd circle back to that Olympic medal. For the five hours that we were on the road, the only thing I remember thinking was that I was going to lose my medal.

Because we had already publicly declared what we were going to do, I started getting a lot of calls. People were telling me not to get rid of my Olympic medal. This was the fruit of my labour of so many years. They told me the government didn't really care, so I shouldn't give up something that was so important to me.

The mood inside the car swung between determination and despair. I'd tell myself – what's the big deal about a medal? It's more important to win this other fight. I had to get rid of an evil man. But almost immediately I'd start thinking that if I lost the medal, then what would I have to show for all my years of struggle?

I was hoping against hope that a miracle might happen and the government would come around and tell us they'd agreed to all our demands. I just wanted my medal to be saved, somehow. I started thinking all kinds of absurd thoughts. Perhaps the International Olympic Committee had a policy of replacing medals that were lost, so I would get a duplicate of mine?

My family in the car was as emotional as I was. About halfway to Haridwar, my mother-in-law suggested we could still back out – she could see I was a wreck. But then I'd remember the goal. I kept thinking back to how I'd been pushed into a bus, had run away, got captured again and then detained in a police station for six hours. There was no other option. After the humiliation that I had felt two days before, it had become really important to get a win.

We reached Haridwar by around 6 p.m. Once we reached the bus stand near Har ki Pauri ghat, I got out of the car. It was a five-minute walk to the ghat. I held the frame with my medal close to my chest as I walked. There were already a lot of people, including the media, waiting for us.

All the wrestlers who had brought their medals went and sat along the ghat even as a crowd surrounded us. While we were sitting there, someone came and took Bajrang away, saying Amit Shah wanted to talk to him. The rest of us were instructed to wait until 7 p.m. because there was a 'big' meeting going on between Bajrang and Amit Shah. We sat there on that ghat for half an hour, hoping against hope that Amit Shah would actually call Brij Bhushan and dismiss him. Simultaneously, we also got word from Naresh Tikait, a senior activist who was known to all of us as one of the leaders of the farm rights agitation from a year ago and whom we respected as an elder of the Jat community we belonged to, to wait until he could speak to us.

I'd always imagined that one day, when I became a mother, my daughter would point to the wall, to my framed Olympic medal, and ask me what it was. And I would open that frame and show it to her. I might be older and out of shape by then and my kids might think I was just a boring mom, but I'd tell them what that medal was. I'd tell them the story of how their mom won it. I'd tell them the story of how she met their dad. How she was something once, a long time ago.

But instead, I was on that ghat, about to throw that medal away, all because I'd tried to fight for a cause I knew was right, hoping against hope for a favour from a politician that might stop that from happening.

As the crowd got bigger and bigger and tighter around us as we waited, my heart started to sink. I knew that we were being backed into a corner. And then, suddenly, from the midst of that crowd, Naresh Tikait emerged. He unwrapped the safa on his head, walked up to each of us, took our medals and placed them in that cloth. He told us the medals were the pride of the country and he'd make things all right.

Then he walked away from the ghat, leaving us there by ourselves.

Within a couple of minutes we realized what a tremendous mistake we had made. What was supposed to be a great act of defiance had turned into a complete farce. Not only had we not been able to get Brij Bhushan Singh out of the federation or give up our medals, but we had also broken our word to the people who had supported us.

All of us sat in a car in a state of complete bewilderment. We were crying. Vinesh had started hitting herself. I was just blank. When animals face a predator, they either run or fight. And they say the same applies to us humans. For me it is neither. I just freeze. When I am faced with something traumatic, I just switch off. My mind stops working. I start thinking everything will get better. It's wishful thinking, I know. Of course things don't just get better by themselves.

When we had recovered somewhat, we thought we would go and take back our medals from Tikait and throw them in the Ganga as we had first planned to do. It was too late for that, of course.

Even as we were sitting in our car, some of his supporters had gathered around us. We were told we were to go with them to Tikait's house and sit with him while he addressed a press conference. And just to make us more inclined to agree with them, they mentioned that the police were coming to arrest us.

We went to Tikait's house and sat silently next to him while he addressed the media and took credit for being the man who had stopped India's medals from being lost. It was his moment to shine. As for us, we had been completely dishonoured.

Later, people would tell us that Tikait, for all his image of confronting the government, had a history of selling out movements he had been part of, and he'd done the same to us. I don't know the truth about that, but the fact is that the mistake of actually handing over the medals was made by us. The kindest explanation I can give for myself is I was so swayed by the emotion of the moment that I wasn't thinking clearly at all.

Until then, I had always felt I could turn things around in the protest. That had been how I had wrestled too. I was known as someone who would pull off comebacks from the direst of situations.

But there was no comeback here. We couldn't have been beaten more thoroughly. There was nothing I could do to turn this around. It was a shock of a kind that I've felt just a few times in my life.

The last time I'd felt that helpless was when I was a little girl, when my grandmother died. That was the first time I learnt that sometimes there's no salvaging a bad situation. Sometimes things are final.

2

Growing up in Rohtak

I was extremely close to my grandmother, Chandravali Devi. It was she who raised me the first four years of my life. About two weeks after she gave birth to me in Mokhra – my father Sukhbir Malik's village – my mother Sudesh returned to work. She would come to the village every few days to be with me, but for a very long time it was my dadi whom I would call my mother.

I didn't miss my mother, and I don't blame her either. My brother was two years older and she had to take care of him as well. I don't think it would have been possible for her to take care of a two-month-old child or to bring her to work every day.

My mother worked as a supervisor at an anganwadi, a government child-care centre, in Rohtak. There they would cook meals for children, conduct vaccination drives and give them polio drops. While my mother was looking after the health of other children, I had a major health crisis of my own.

One day, when my mother had come to Mokhra and was feeding me, she discovered red rashes on my body. No one knew what they were, but within a few hours I had swelled up to twice my size. My mother rushed me to a doctor in Rohtak, who in turn insisted I be taken to Delhi immediately because he was sure I had been bitten by something venomous. No one really knew how I got bitten or by what, but by the time I was taken to the doctor the poison had spread through my body. I am told I nearly died.

My father borrowed a car and I was rushed to Delhi. I was admitted to the hospital, where the bite that caused my rashes developed into an open wound that pus leaked out from. I was in the hospital for a month and doctors had put me on an intravenous drip as I wasn't able to feed normally. I still have a scar on my neck from whatever bit me. After I recovered, I was taken back to the village. They say that such an early illness leaves kids extremely weak, but that's never been the case with me.

Despite that crisis, I had nothing but happy memories of my early life in Mokhra.

There was a canal that flowed past one end of the village, and all the kids would go there to play. If we weren't there, we would be playing in the fields. We'd play the entire day. And then, when the sun would start to set, my grandmother would call us back indoors because there were no street lights, of course.

Our house was like most other houses in the village. It was made of brick and mud without any plastering. The floors were of mud too. Our house was quite small and most of the household activities took place outside. All the cooking was done in an open chulha outside the house, and next to the gate was an open space called *bagad*, where the men would smoke their hookah pipes. Next to our home was a buffalo shed where, like every family in the village, we kept our cattle and the fodder-cutting machine with which we would cut their fodder for them.

There were no bathrooms in the village. We used to go to a *kurudiya*, which is just an open outhouse behind our home, to relieve ourselves. Since I was a kid, I'd be able to get up and go with all my cousins whenever we wanted to, but the women in the family would go there early in the morning before anyone else had woken up.

My grandmother was in her fifties when I was born. She looked exactly like every older lady in Mokhra. Women of her generation weren't allowed to wear their hair loose, and she was also expected to have her head covered at all times. She wore her hair in what we call a *choonda*. She would weave strips of cloth into her hair and braid it all together into a single plait, which she would cover with a dupatta so that not a single strand of hair could be seen.

Dressed in a kurta and salwar, she was always busy feeding or watering the buffaloes or cooking on the open-fire chulha. Cooking on that chulha caused her to develop a persistent, hacking cough. I'd always be scared when I had to run and find her her asthma pipe when it got too bad. But she would always pacify me. She'd tell me in Haryanvi that it was just a normal cough.

Despite how close I was to my grandmother, I didn't share a lot of activities with her. When I was little, she'd allow me to cut fodder and feed our buffaloes. I'd bring water for the buffaloes too. Since I was very small I could carry only a small bowl of water at a time, but my grandmother always let me bring that so I'd feel I was helping. My favourite memory is of sleeping next to her on our cot. I almost never went out of our home with my grandmother because at that time it was very rare for her, as for any married woman of her generation, to leave the home. Her world revolved around the house.

My grandfather, Chaudhary Badlu Ram, on the other hand, would always take me out. Although I was close to my grandmother,

I think my grandfather had an especially soft corner for me. When he'd go to the fields he'd always bring some fruit for me. If it was the watermelon season, he'd get me a ripe watermelon, and he and my grandmother would watch with a big smile as I worked my way through that fruit over the course of the day.

It wasn't just that. He always let me have a little extra freedom, compared with what other girls my age had. When my grandfather would light up a hookah with his friends each evening, he'd let me play around them. At other times, he'd take me to our fields where we grew sugarcane, wheat and cotton. While he'd work, he'd pluck tufts of cotton and give them to me to play with.

I was never given the impression that I was a girl so I had to behave a certain way. In contrast to the other girls of my age who would always be dressed in salwar-kameez suits, I'd be the only one who wore shorts and T-shirts.

I enjoyed going to the fields, but what I loved most of all was going to weddings. If you were a girl, you weren't allowed to go to a wedding if you weren't related to the family. But as the village sarpanch, my grandfather had to attend them. When my grandfather would get set to leave, I'd cry and say, 'Dada, please take me,' and he'd sigh and take me along.

Going to a wedding was the highlight of a kid's life in the village. You always knew that you'd get something special to eat there. At home we'd only get to eat bajra roti, or if we were especially lucky maybe wheat rotis. But at a wedding we would get to eat puri or even rice. You would get laddoos and jalebis. There was no chance we'd get to eat anything like that at home.

There was a samosa shop in our village, but samosas cost two rupees each, unaffordable for a little girl like me. Sometimes my grandfather would buy me a samosa and I'd live off that memory for weeks. So, to have a day when I could eat all the jalebis, laddoos and samosas I wanted was like going to heaven.

That wasn't the only way my family wasn't like other families in the village. My grandmother was very different from other women of her generation in the village. In her time, it wasn't just men who made life hard for women. Mothers-in-law would treat their daughters-in-law very cruelly. They wouldn't give them anything to eat. They'd wear the *ghunghat* (veil) themselves and enforced *ghunghat pratha* (culture of ghunghat) in their homes too.

Women weren't allowed to step outside their homes, take up a job or have an independent source of income. The culture back then was that the daughters-in-law would be all but locked inside their homes, where they'd have to cook and clean and look after the cattle. If there was milk to drink, the mother-in-law would dilute her daughter-in-law's share for no other reason but to lower her self-worth. The mindset was that the mother-in-law had been been treated like dirt in her time so she would treat her daughters-in-law the same way.

When I was older, I'd often ask my grandmother about her childhood and youth. She told me that her mother-in-law didn't treat her well and subjected her to all sorts of petty humiliations. But rather than inflict the same torments on my mother and aunts, she said she'd wanted to try to change that pattern of behaviour.

My mother would tell me later on that she had never met someone as open-minded as my grandmother. She had three sons in all, and each of their wives went out and worked. My grandmother never expected anyone to wait on her. Instead, my mother told me, she'd wake up earlier than the rest in the morning and cook breakfast for her daughters-in-law.

When I was four years old, my parents took me from Mokhra to live with them in Rohtak. I hated it there. I hardly recognized my parents and I missed my grandparents desperately. I cried constantly, asking to go back to Mokhra. Even though Rohtak is a relatively small city in India, it was completely alien to me. In my first year there, I couldn't wait for the weekend to arrive. That's when I could go back to Mokhra. If it were up to me, I'd have stayed there.

My grandparents had enrolled me in the government nursery school in Mokhra. I enjoyed going there with my friends. Once I was brought to the city, my parents wanted me to get a good education in an English-medium school, so they got me admission to DAV School.

Although I'd already gone to school for a few months, I had to restart my education all over again in Rohtak. The two schools were entirely different in culture. For one, girls at DAV School wore skirts. In the village school we wore shorts. At DAV, Rohtak, not only did the girls wear skirts, they were also properly dressed up, in shirt and tie. It was an English-medium school, after all.

The food we ate and even the way we spoke were different. Even something as simple as asking, 'What are you doing?' marked me out as a stranger. In Haryanvi you say, '*Ke kara se?*' In Rohtak, I was expected to say, '*Kya kar rahe ho?*' in Hindi.

Speaking Hindi was the least of my challenges. My family wanted me to study in the best possible school, and that meant an English-medium school. If Hindi was hard to adjust to, English was harder still. I'd try to adjust, but I'd still slip. Once in my first grade, I badly needed to relieve myself, so I raised my hand and yelled across the classroom, '*Muthey aun?,*' in Haryanvi, instead of 'May I go to the toilet?' My teacher was shocked that I was using what she considered as uncouth language.

I had to adjust. I learned to say all the standard lines expected of me, 'May I come in, ma'am?', 'May I go to the toilet?', 'May I drink water?'

Today I can speak both Hindi and Haryanvi when I have to, but if I really have to express myself, then the words that come out of my mouth will be Haryanvi. I won't speak in what we call *'prabhavi'* Hindi. If I'm talking to reporters, I'll speak in English or Hindi and ask them *'Kya kar rahe ho?'* But if I want to ask Satyawart what he is doing, it will always be the Haryanvi *'Ke kara se?'*

Even though my mother had brought me to the city, I still didn't see too much of her. She had to leave for work at 8 or 9 a.m. after packing our school breakfast and lunch. My father would leave for work at 4 a.m. They weren't around at home when school finished and I'd get back. My brother and I would be let in by an aunt, the wife of one of my father's younger brothers, who were staying as tenants in one of the rooms of our house.

Although I felt lonely, with both my parents working, there wasn't any other option. Neither of my parents could support our family on a single income. My father worked as a DTC bus conductor in Delhi. He made only around four thousand rupees a month at that time, and our family needed the second income. Dad would leave for the Sheila Bypass bus stand near our home at the crack of dawn. He'd reach Delhi by 7 a.m. and begin his work as a bus conductor. He'd work a full shift and then leave for home to reach by 4 p.m.

We were always told to watch out for my dad, to finish our homework by the time he came back and not make a noise. But he was generally an easy-going man.

Occasionally, on a Sunday or whenever he had a holiday, he would make us omelettes. My brother and I would get an omelette made of two eggs each. These days I just eat the egg whites and throw away the yolks, which seems so wasteful. But back then we'd eat all of the egg, and love it. Sometimes my father would make us egg curry. He'd stand in the kitchen, chopping onions and tomatoes and cracking eggs and frying them.

That was always a special treat, and not just because my father was cooking for us. At that time it was really unusual for us to eat eggs because we were supposed to be vegetarian. In our neighbourhood there must have been only a couple of families who ate eggs. I always thought that we were doing something very illegal.

There wasn't a lot to do in Rohtak in the late 1990s, and so sometimes my father would take us on little outings to Delhi. We'd mostly go and see monuments like the Red Fort and the Lotus Temple. Sometimes we would visit the international airport. I loved that far more than the monuments and the temples. It was so exciting to see the planes from up close! I was obsessed not just with the planes but also with the people who would sit in them. I used to wonder just how rich those people who could fly in the sky must be.

While most of our neighbours were working class, there was one who had started to make some money in the property business. I really enjoyed going to his house because his son had wonderful toys. My eyes would grow wide at the sight of his remote-controlled cars and action figures. I'd think, 'So, this is how rich people live.' During Holi, I'd feel a little jealous of that boy because he got to play with the fancy plastic pichkari while I only had the simple metal one. But I knew I couldn't get the plastic one because I knew my parents were just about making ends meet.

My mom's job was to manage four or five anganwadis in the villages around Rohtak. She had to keep track of the rations coming in, how many workers were employed and how many daughters and sons were born in the village. Counting the number of newborn girls was a big part of her job. She had to make sure that the ratio of daughters in the area didn't drop too much. If it did, she had go to the village and try to explain to them to treat daughters and sons as equal. That was a big issue in rural Rohtak at the time.

I was lucky that my parents never treated me with any unfairness as a child compared to how they treated my brother. But in the society I grew up in, I understood that there was a general preference for boys. My tau, for example, had two daughters. No one said it overtly, but I could pick up from conversations that they were trying really hard to have a son. I remember my mother telling my tau's wife that it would be nice for them to have a son too. She didn't say this directly, but couched it by saying her two daughters needed a brother. Otherwise, whom would they tie a rakhi to?

I sensed that my mother's family too seemed to prefer my brother over me. I didn't enjoy going to their home on vacations. Children can pick up very quickly when they are being ignored. I might have been a little naughty, but that didn't explain why they would ignore me or try to belittle me. They'd rudely ask me to leave the room I was in. Or if we were eating fruit, they'd give the bigger piece to my brother. Or they'd give him something nice to eat and not give me anything. It seems a bit petty to complain about this, but as a kid you really understand that it is unfair, and you remember these incidents.

I much preferred going to Mokhra. We'd go there almost every weekend on my dad's scooter – a Bajaj Chetak. The four of us would squeeze onto the scooter, with me standing in the front of the driver's seat and my brother squeezed between Dad and Mom.

We'd make up games while travelling. Dad and I used to make up one team. And Mom and brother the other. Sometimes the game was to count red tractors, and whichever team counted the most by the time we got to the village would win. I was extremely competitive. I'd have to cover for my dad, because he was of course driving the scooter and paying attention to the road. But I'd still manage to win. There were no prizes for winning, but the best part of that journey was that we'd get to spend two perfect days with my grandparents.

My mother's side of the family would often tease me for my preference for my paternal grandparents. Some of them would lie to me, saying my grandmother had died, just to make me cry. One day they told me my grandmother had actually died. I was about nine years old at the time. I thought they were trying to prank me again.

I began to realize something was wrong when they took me on a scooter to Mokhra. We reached my grandparents' home, and there was a pile of footwear outside. That's when it hit me. When I saw my grandmother's body, my relatives tried to calm me down by saying they were just dressing her up. I knew that was not true. When they took grandmother for the cremation, I begged them to let me come with them too. But as a girl I wasn't allowed to be part of the cremation. I kept insisting until finally one of my relatives slapped me to keep me quiet.

One of my greatest disappointments was that my paternal grandparents never got to see my success as a wrestler. My grandfather saw me win a few medals as a junior, but my grandmother didn't even see that. I'd often think how special it would have been, had my grandmother been able to see me at the Olympics. Would she have been able to fathom just what I had accomplished? I was a girl from a village playing a sport, and travelling across the world for it. I think she would have loved it. I'd have taken her on a plane with me, maybe, to one of my tournaments.

Of course, back then I had no idea I was ever going to be a wrestler. It was enough of a struggle for me just to cope with being the odd girl in Rohtak. I was very conscious of the fact that I wasn't nearly as well off as the girls I went to school with.

I had a huge inferiority complex.

I'd always be thinking my school bag was looking cheap or my clothes weren't looking good or my books weren't as new as theirs. My bag was a flat, rectangular one made of cloth and had metal clips. I'd feel jealous of the girls who brought backpacks made of shiny, synthetic material with multiple zips. I'd feel embarrassed about bringing out my steel lunch box while the other girls had plastic ones with cartoons printed on the cover.

I knew even then that I couldn't ask my parents to get me any fancy school kit. Sometimes they'd give me two rupees for the canteen. Very rarely, I'd get five rupees. And that was party time.

I was very conscious of what I was bringing to school for lunch too. The other kids would be bringing things like pasta, sandwiches or chocos, and I'd have roti and sabji like okra, potatoes, cauliflower and pickle. Sometimes, if I was lucky, my mom would cook Maggi noodles, which felt modern and special. On those days I wouldn't even wait until lunch time to open my lunch box. I'd just gulp down my noodles as quickly as I could between the first and second period of school.

But for the most part I was envious of what the other girls would bring for lunch. One day, I remember a girl taking out a slice of bread from her lunch box and then opening a piece of plastic and taking out a yellow square thing and put it on the bread. That was the first time I'd seen a slice of cheese.

Another girl brought something else, which I learned was called pasta. I'd never ever seen anything like it before. I knew what Maggi noodles were and I guessed it must be some kind of fancy Maggi. Someone else would bring sandwiches with cheese slices and egg. I'd think, wow, what are these things? I guess that's what rich people eat.

My mindset back then was that others had so much and I nothing, so it did not matter if I took something from them. So, on some days, when there was no one watching the classroom, I would open someone's bag and take some of the money they had brought to buy things from the school canteen, and buy food for myself. I can see how wrong it was and what a shock it must have been to the person I had stolen money from to find some of it missing.

I might have wanted to be like all of my rich classmates, but very few of them ever gave me much attention. There was one girl named Nitika, whose approval I craved the most. She was the daughter of one of the school teachers, and I thought she was the coolest girl in school. But the more I tried to be friendly with her the more she'd talk down to me. She always had that air about her – that she was better than me.

Even after I'd won the Olympic bronze and led the wrestlers' protest, she never followed me on Instagram. I'd check her out on social media and wonder why she never followed me. But I've come to terms with it. God has given me enough, anyway.

There were also times when I wouldn't be ignored. Sometimes the other kids would make fun of me because I would bring milk to school. That was seen as a very village thing to do. They'd tease me about how I spoke Haryanvi. Sometimes the teasing got to me. I was ready to fight with anyone. In the second grade, I stabbed one of the students with a pencil because she mocked my English, which I was very conscious about. I had gone from a completely Haryanvi environment to an English-medium one. I was not going to become a madam overnight, was I?

My parents were called to school after the 'stabbing'. I was probably an inch away from being suspended. My mom didn't have any sympathy for me. I simply got slapped and scolded. I can understand just how frustrated she was with me when I was that age.

I was a complete terror. I'd get into fights with kids not just in school but in my neighbourhood as well. I had a reputation for being completely vicious. I'd be playing with someone and get into a fight with him, and then I'd come home with a handful of his hair in my hands.

If there was one child I would do anything for, it was my elder brother. I adored him. I'd follow him everywhere. I'd accompany him when he went out to play cricket, and also when he'd visit the video game parlours where we played games like Mario and Tekken. More than playing myself though, I liked to watch him play.

Playing those games cost money though, and slowly I started stealing money for it. If my aunt left her purse unattended, I'd steal a few coins from it. At other times I'd pick up money that was lying around. I would hide my stash under the seat of a bicycle or under a staircase or bedcover.

I would give the coins to my brother and say I found them lying around. Then I'd suggest we go and play video games, and I'd watch as he played.

Eventually I was caught.

Growing up in Rohtak

One day, when I was about six, after I'd stolen some money and gone to the parlour with my brother, we lost track of time and my father showed up looking for us. He asked us where we had got the money to play video games at the parlour and my brother said I had got it. I lied, saying I found the money under the cycle seat. Of course my father didn't believe me. I finally confessed and got a solid thrashing.

When I think back to that girl who stole money and 'stabbed' people and pulled their hair out, I just can't recognize her or relate to her. And in a way, that girl was someone else. After all, I wasn't Sakshi Malik back then. I was called Sofia at birth. I've no idea why my mother gave me that name.

Because I wasn't born in a hospital, I only got my birth certificate when I was in my fourth grade. Around that time, my brother got close to a classmate called Sakshi, and he started calling me by that name. My parents too started using it, and so that's the name they entered in the birth certificate. I still like the name Sofia because it was the name I grew up with. That's what all my relatives and friends from my childhood still call me today. I might be Sakshi on paper, but I was always Sofia to them. But Sakshi's not a bad name either. When I think about how my life has played out, I don't think my parents could have chosen a better name. Sakshi means witness.

Sofia and Sakshi Malik are very different people. Sofia was an absolute nightmare of a girl. Sakshi is the complete opposite. I can't stand confrontation today. I've a reputation for being someone who won't take any unfair advantage of another. When it comes to money, I get paranoid if someone leaves their money with me. But this change didn't happen by itself. I think wrestling made me more mature. It changed my personality. I started behaving less aggressively with people I met. I became more disciplined and hard-working.

3

Starting *Kushti*

I was always playing as a child. If I was in the village I'd be climbing trees or just running around. After I moved to Rohtak we played games more suited to the lanes of our neighbourhood, like *pithoo* or *stappoo*. But these were all games that only kids cared about.

Cricket was what the grown-ups preferred. As a child I'd want to watch cartoons on TV, but I'd always have to make way if there was a cricket match on. At that time Sachin Tendulkar and Virender Sehwag were really popular, and although I didn't know much about cricket, as I sat and watched TV, I could tell that the grown-ups were especially interested in these two. Of the two though, there was a different kind of craze for Sehwag.

He was from the Jat community, which we belonged to, so there was a lot more interest in his achievements. If he was batting, the entire family would drop what they were doing to come and watch. The discussion in the room was never as to whether India would win or not; it was about how many runs Sehwag would make or if he would get to a century.

He was the first person whom I saw as a star. I wanted to be just like him. I'd dream of shaking his hand. It wasn't as if I wanted to play cricket. I used to watch cricket; my brother would play it in the streets, and although I'd tag along and play a little bit, I never wanted to be a cricketer myself. I just liked the idea of being someone who would appear on TV, whom people would watch and praise.

We had a sports period at DAV School, where we got to play athletics, kho-kho, basketball and table tennis. Every sports class, our physical education teacher would have us form groups – one for those interested in running, another for those who wanted to play table tennis and another for those who played basketball. I picked up table tennis fairly easily, but I never stuck with it. It wasn't as if I was not interested in that sport, or in basketball for that matter, but there was just a limited number of bats and balls and I didn't like having to wait for my turn to play.

Athletics was one sport where you didn't need a lot of equipment. I was always faster and stronger than most kids my age, so I'd always choose the running group. If we had races I'd always finish in front. Running seemed fairly simple. When you were told to go, you took off. There was no need to think. You just had to run.

One day, when I was in the fifth grade, I was told I'd been chosen to compete in an inter-DAV School sports meet to be held during the summer vacations. I'd travelled with my family out of Haryana before, but that inter-DAV tournament was the first time I'd be travelling without family, and as an eleven-year-old I couldn't have been more excited about it.

I was looking forward to travelling on the school bus to a different state and running in my first proper sports competition. I felt like a proper sportsperson going on an adventure. I couldn't keep quiet as my mother packed my kit – a change of clothes, a towel and a pair of Gold Star canvas shoes.

At the competition venue in Jalandhar, I found out I was going to be running four laps of the school field, or about 800 m in all. I'd only ever run 100 m before in Rohtak, but that didn't bother me. I was very confident I would win, and more than that I was just thrilled I was taking part in a competition.

When the race started, I burst forward with all my strength, and by the end of the first lap had gone well in front of the other runners. This was easy, I thought to myself.

What I didn't know was that I was supposed to pace myself. Neither did I know nor did I have anyone to tell me how to do that. Our school didn't have an athletics coach, just a physical training, or PT, teacher. Forget any specialist knowledge of running an 800 m race, he had just a beginner's understanding of athletics, as any elementary PT teacher would.

Now I know that you are supposed to have a sprints coach for the 100 m and a middle-distance coach for the 800 m, but at that time my PT teacher had to do everything. He just told me to run fast, and keep running fast. So, while I had a huge lead in the first round, I started feeling my muscles burn towards the end of the second. By the third I could see that the others were gaining on me. By the fourth some of them were leading me. By that time my legs felt like jelly and I knew I wasn't going to win. But I only remember thinking, 'Just don't come in last.'

I just about managed to come third in the race. And then, as I crossed the finish line, I collapsed on the track. Someone tried to give me water, but I couldn't drink it because I was coughing so hard I couldn't put my lips to the bottle. My legs were dead under me, so I couldn't even get up. I was just lying on the ground, coughing. I thought I was going to die. I remember thinking, 'Please God, just let me be able to breathe again.'

Starting *Kushti*

Finally they got me up and gave me the medal, but I was totally out of it. I just wanted them to let me lie down and be able to breathe and to drink water. It took a couple of hours before I recovered somewhat and could breathe normally, but for the rest of the day my throat felt completely sore and dry.

I've experienced that sort of feeling later in my wrestling career as well. It happens when you put in so much effort that your body shuts down on you and stops responding to commands. Over the course of my international wrestling career, I might have experienced that bodily shut down maybe five or six times.

But I was experiencing it for the first time in that inter-DAV race. I exhausted all my love for running that day. I know that if I'd had an even slightly less unpleasant experience in my first race, I'd almost certainly have become a track-and-field athlete.

Although I hated the race itself, I enjoyed every other part of being in my first real sports competition. We were put up in one of the classrooms of the school we were competing in. There were mattresses on the floor and just a common washroom that all of us shared. The facilities were very basic, but I was excited to be a part of the tournament. I was very proud of the bronze medal that I won too. It was just a third-place medal in a school-level competition, but I treasured it. I've kept it with me all these years. It lies next to all my Nationals, Junior Worlds and Asian Championships medals.

Although running was not for me, I knew I wanted to play sports. I kept pestering my mother to allow me to, and she finally agreed to take me to the stadium after school.

The Sir Chhotu Ram Stadium was a place that was at once both mysterious and accessible. It was just a few hundred metres from our house and I'd pass by it on my way to school. As a kid, I'd sometimes gone there by myself or with my neighbourhood friends to play catch on the grounds next to the running track. I'd seen children come to train in a group of buildings in one corner of the track, but I was too shy to go over and see what they were doing.

It was only when my mother finally agreed to take me to the Sir Chhotu Ram Stadium that I finally explored the buildings to the side of the athletics track. There were four buildings with children training in a different sport in each of them. In one there was a hall where children were learning judo, and in another a bunch of girls practising gymnastics.

It was gymnastics that first caught my eye. I saw little girls balancing on a thin beam and doing cartwheels. I immediately told my mother I wanted to try that. But although I tried the sport for a few days, I didn't enjoy it. There had been a coach there, which was why the girls who were training there knew what they were doing, but he had stopped coming just around the time I joined. With no one to learn from, I tried to copy what the other girls were doing. It was a recipe for failure. I tried the vault and the balance beam, fell off both and decided gymnastics wasn't for me.

With my attempt at gymnastics going poorly, I wandered off to one of the other buildings and peeked through the door. There I saw a hall with a giant blue, yellow and red mat inside. I wasn't intrigued so much by what the children were doing on the mat as by the mat itself – it was almost as wide as the whole hall. I wondered just how they had managed to fit such a huge mat in there through such a small door.

Once I walked in, though, I was smitten.

The children inside weren't just jumping and doing cartwheels. They were picking each other up and throwing them on the mat.

Starting *Kushti*

Every time someone landed, it made this huge crash. There were some forty students inside that room, all throwing each other. The room was filled with the sound of crashing bodies. Now, that was a real sport.

Unlike in the gymnastics hall, there was a coach in the wrestling hall. I asked my mother to accompany me as I walked up to him and said, '*Mujhe bhi kushti karni hai.*'

He told me the timings and that I would have to come in twice a day. My mother told him I wouldn't be able to attend the morning sessions because I had to go to school, but that I would come for the evening training.

I started my education in wrestling in July 2004, when I was twelve years old, but I didn't get to do any of the crashing throws that so impressed me for a few months.

Before I could throw people, I first needed to learn how to stand. The wrestling coach, Ishwar Dahiya, showed me how to 'make a stance', as the phrase went. First he made me get into a crouch with my left leg slightly in front of my right. Then he had me bend my elbows and extend my arms forward, as if I was preparing to catch a football. For the first couple of months, all I did for an hour and a half each day was learn to stand in this position.

Building a stance is the foundational step in wrestling. '*Sher jaise bano,*' coach Dahiya would tell me. I had to stand like a lion! Wrestlers begin a match by standing in the middle of the ring in a stance. Even when they start moving they stay in that same crouching position. It's a pose that at once allows you to make yourself as small a target as possible, and also defend with your hands and step back should you need to, while staying low enough to explode in an attack when you have to.

It's a lot harder than you think, to hold that semi-lunge position with your arms in front of you. How long can you stand on one leg and place all your weight on it? After about a minute or two, there's a huge amount of stress on your lower back. If you haven't trained for it, you will instinctively pull yourself upright. When you stand up to relieve that stress, you are open to being attacked. Maintaining your stance is all about your core strength. I'd maintain my stance for two minutes, relax for a bit, drink some water, look at what the senior girls were doing, and then make that stance once again. I'd keep increasing the duration of my stance. At first I could maintain the stance for a minute at most. I increased that to two minutes, and then two-and-a-half minutes. I'd eventually manage to hold that pose for fifteen minutes at a time before my whole body would start to shake. I'd take a break for a couple of minutes and then get back to it.

In those early days of training I never wondered why all I was doing was making a stance. The coach had told me to do it, so I did it. I was interested in wrestling, so I tried my best to stay frozen in place while sneaking glances at the other side of the hall where the girls and boys were throwing each other on the mat.

Finally, after two months of learning to stand still, Ishwar Dahiya told me he would teach me a *daav*, or what is called a technique. The first technique I learned was the double-leg takedown. It would be my favourite technique all through my career.

I was taught almost everything in Hindi, of course. All the different wrestling techniques have English terms too. The *dhobi pachad*, where you toss an opponent over your back and out in front of you, is called an arm throw. The *kalajang*, where you get control of the arm and leg of the opponent and physically lift her on to your

Starting *Kushti*

back before flipping her over, is known as the fireman's carry. The leg lace, where you interlace your opponent's legs with your arms and roll her over on the mat, was known to us as *fitley bandhna*. Even 'wrestling' was a word I learned much later. We just called it kushti.

The one technique which I learned using an English term was the double-leg takedown. I don't know if there is a Hindi term for it. These days the coaches are incredibly technical. They'll explain where your head should be, where your arm should be. They'll explain the angle you need to have your upper body at when you attack. There was none of that for me. I was simply told to pull my opponents' neck down, '*ghus jao*' (get inside) and shoot for the legs. Very simple. I learned a very basic technique of the double-leg takedown. There are so many variations of it – *dasti* (in which you control the wrist), and others where there is no contact with the opponent's arms.

If I had a coach who taught me better technique, how to change angles, how to move my weight, then maybe I would have been a better player. But I was just told to 'explode out' towards my opponent! 'Pull down' and 'get inside'.

I can't blame my coach for that. There wasn't a lot of wrestling knowledge back then. I couldn't have expected anything more. India had not won any major international medals at any level at that time in the sport, and coach Ishwar Dahiya was neither an Arjuna award winner nor a Dronacharya winner.

A few weeks later, I bought my first wrestling costume. Dahiya Sir told me it was time I got one. My parents took me to Delhi, to the Shiv Naresh store, to buy my first pair. It wasn't the synthetic ones that fit flush on your body. Instead, I bought a pair of shorts and a loose singlet, like the ones the boy wrestlers wore. I'd also wear a T-shirt underneath the singlet because it was cut so low. I wrestled in that style of costume for a few years until I started competing at the state and national levels, when at last I had to buy the skin-tight costume that all the top wrestlers wore.

Even though the costume was very modest and I always wore a T-shirt underneath, not everyone in my family approved of it. Some of my uncles asked my parents why I was being allowed to wrestle. They'd comment on my costume. They'd ask my parents if the neighbours had said anything. To their credit, my parents didn't think about all this and never let me think about it either. I only heard about this chatter much later.

While my first costume wasn't perfect, I nonetheless felt a sense of pride every time I wore it, a feeling that I was becoming a real wrestler. Six months after my first class, Dahiya Sir entered me in my first competition. I really felt I was a proper wrestler now.

A school tournament is the absolute first step in the career of any Indian wrestler. Every one of us starts with an interschool competition and then progresses to competing in a zonal competition, then moving to a district-level meet, then the state championships, then the national championships and, finally, if you are good enough, making it to the national team.

There was no expectation that I'd do well. After all, I'd only been wrestling for a few months. I should have been happy and excited to wrestle, but I felt my stomach sink before my first bout. That sense of dread heightened as my foot sank into the soft synthetic plastic mat. It peaked as I crossed the red border of the nine-metre-wide circle that I'd have to fight inside for the next six minutes. It's a fear that I've carried to the end of my career. I've never enjoyed the actual act of confrontation.

Starting *Kushti*

I think some amount of fear is normal. Many wrestlers have a little bit of nervousness before their bout starts, which helps them get focused for the contest. I have also come across contestants who tell me they are excited before a bout. They enjoy that feeling of getting into a fight. I've never experienced that. I've always been afraid, sometimes almost sick with worry. It's like the feeling of dread before you write an exam, but it's amplified a dozen times. When I took a test in school, I was not very interested in how I did in it. It didn't really matter to me how I did in studies. But I was a lot more invested in my wrestling. I loved it so much that I couldn't bear to have to lose.

My first bout took place in the wrestling hall where I trained. My opponent was a girl named Chhoti. She was my age and had at best trained a few more months than I had. But I could tell that she was serious. You could tell that because she had what we'd call a 'boy-cut' hairstyle. That's how you knew a girl was really serious about wrestling.

I too had short hair, but I was an exception because I wore my hair short even before I started wrestling. My grandparents used to get my hair cut that way, and my parents were even more extreme. Their logic was they didn't want the mess of dealing with long hair, but I hated it. Once, just before my class-five school maths exam, they got my hair trimmed to almost a buzz cut. I started crying and refused to go to school because I knew all the other girls would make fun of me. They dragged me crying into the school bus, and I wrote that exam in tears too.

In wrestling the logic not to have one's hair long was two-fold. The first was that long hair would make it hard to wrestle. It would get dirty during training and it could get in your eyes and there was no way to tie it back in place in the middle of a match. An opponent could also grab hold of it and use it as leverage.

The second reasoning was that long hair was a gateway to all things forbidden. Anything other than short hair would result in an interest in fashion, and that would lead to an interest in boys. If you got into all those distractions, you would not pay attention to your training. So the best solution was to make you look like a boy. That was how it used to be in the past, and that's how it still is today. You almost always see Indian girl wrestlers wearing their hair short.

We were all conditioned to believe that long hair couldn't go with wrestling. Since we compete in weight categories, I sometimes wondered if long hair was extra weight too. I asked some of the girls who did grow their hair long if that was the case. I assumed that if you had waist-length hair, it must weigh at least be 200–300 g. But they told me, their hair weighed just about 50 g.

Not wearing one's hair long as a wrestler wasn't about weight. It was to do with a mindset – that if you grew your hair you would get distracted. But later I realized that it was just a lot of nonsense.

The only good thing about my parents cutting my hair short from the time I was a child was that I was already used to any taunts about it by the time I became a wrestler. As a girl I always felt a little hurt to have to have 'boy-cut' hair. Kids at school could be cruel, and they'd taunt me, saying they did not know if I was a boy or a girl.

Even though I hated having short hair, I never thought of growing my hair long. I too bought into the idea that if I had long hair I would have a boyfriend and that would mean the end of my wrestling career.

But while both of us might have had short hair, my opponent was much better than me on the mat. We were wrestling in the 48 kg category. The bout would consist of three rounds, each two minutes long. But I didn't even make it past the second.

The ultimate goal of wrestling is to force your opponent back on to the mat, which we call *chit karna* (to pin). If you do that, you automatically win, but in Olympic wrestling there are other ways to win too. You score points for either controlling your opponent, rolling her such that her chest is exposed to the sky, throwing her or forcing her off the red-ringed playing area on the mat. Score enough points and the bout will be stopped.

That's what happened in my first bout with Chhoti.

All through the fight she would catch my foot or wrist and just pull me to the ground, or go behind me. Every time she got me to the ground and got on my back, she scored a point. Fight as hard as I might, she kept finding a way to get behind me. She kept scoring points against me. In no time she had gone up 6-0 against me in the first round, winning it. Despite my best efforts, the second round went no better. In less than a minute she had taken another 6-0 lead, after which the bout was stopped and my opponent declared the winner.

If I dreaded just stepping on to the mat, I dreaded losing even more. I was crying even as the referee raised my opponent's hand. I felt I'd let my parents down because they had let me wrestle but I had lost my first bout. My coach tried to console me. He told me it's okay to lose. He kept saying that it was only my first bout. He kept saying I had to keep going and that I still had to come for training the next day. He tried to console me, saying I was still very small – although that other girl was just about as small as I was.

That was always what stood out for me about Dahiya Sir. He might not have been the most technically knowledgeable coach, but he was always very supportive. He had been a wrestler himself many decades ago before becoming a coach and was only a few years away from retirement when I started training with him. Most coaches of his generation are of a conservative mindset. They wouldn't even have anything to do with coaching girls, but Dahiya Sir never once discriminated between the girls and boys training with him.

He wasn't the most imposing figure either, physically or personality-wise, and he wasn't garrulous and talkative like some of the other male coaches I've worked with. I only rarely heard him raise his voice. But he was always someone who kept telling me to keep working hard and kept motivating me, like he did the day I lost my first bout.

While I'm sure he was just trying to make me feel better, he must have had some belief in me too. When my parents asked him if I had any potential as a wrestler, he would tell them there was nothing to worry about and that he saw me winning an Olympic medal one day. He wasn't just saying that to make a parent happy, as some coaches would, or repeating a statement he had ready for every anxious parent. He absolutely believed it, even when no reasonable person might have felt that way – forget winning a medal at the Olympics, no Indian woman had even qualified for the Olympics in 2004.

He told me later that he hadn't said this to any other parent.

He had to try really hard to convince my parents about his opinion of me because I was an exceptionally slow starter in wrestling. I won my first bout only after nearly two years of my first stepping on a wrestling mat. It wasn't that I didn't have any physical skills. I was always one of the fastest and strongest girls at my coaching centre for my age. But I never developed the fearlessness you needed for a fight. I would always get very nervous before my bouts.

At the national level, the two competitors before a match are usually introduced by an announcer. He'd say something like '*agli* kushti Sakshi Malik in red costume *aur* (whoever my competitor was) in blue costume!' The moment I heard these words, I would feel my heart thumping inside my chest. I'd just want to run away from the stadium. It didn't matter to me whether I was going to win or not. I just wanted to run away from my bout. I think that's one of the reasons I lost matches for as long as I did. It just took a long time for my other skills to improve to the level where they were able to compensate for that deep-seated fear.

It helped that although I was terrible when it came to competition, I loved going to train at the *akhara* (wrestling school). It was like nothing I'd ever done before.

The Chhotu Ram akhara wasn't like the traditional akharas of Indian wrestling. Most akharas have a pit of soft, processed mud in which wrestlers traditionally practise. Before the popularization of Olympic style freestyle wrestling in India, and even to a large extent today, training and competitions, which were known as *dangal*s, always took place in the mud pit.

My akhara didn't have a mud pit. It was a part of a modern sports stadium. And we trained on a synthetic, plastic mat. I had already learned, to my great disappointment, that the mat at my training centre wasn't a single giant one, as I first thought, but three regular mats placed next to each other and then covered with a giant plastic sheet. But they were still the same kind as were used in international competitions.

The biggest difference between my akhara and the traditional ones in Haryana was that the Chhotu Ram akhara taught women. Most Indian akharas were men-only spaces. Women weren't supposed to even enter them.

In 2004, women's wrestling was still relatively new in India. These days, if you go to any akhara where women train, you will see at least forty or fifty girls training. When I joined, there was a total of four women wrestlers at the Chhotu Ram akhara. We weren't even around the same age group. At twelve, I was the youngest of the four. One female wrestler was twenty and another twenty-five. A few months after I came in, the sister of one of the girls I trained with also joined.

Because there were so few girls, that too at completely different stages of training, there was no option for us but to practise with the younger boys. I've always found that strange. Because although we were raised in a culture where boys and girls were supposed to keep away from each other, there was this one sport where you were expected to put your hands on each other, grab and pull at what you could, and no one thought anything of it.

Although our akhara was modern in some ways, in other matters it was indistinguishable from any other in Haryana. Just to the side of the door was a small temple with a Hanuman idol. Hanuman-ji is the god of wrestling and you will see his statue at every akhara. Before we started our wrestling training, we would first sweep and swab the hall thoroughly. Then our coach would have one of us light a diya and an agarbatti (incense stick), and we would say a prayer in front of the temple, then take the lit agarbatti around the mat. We'd pray that we would train well and that no one would be injured.

There would be some days when we didn't have enough ghee to light the diya or we ran out of incense sticks. On those days we might just say our prayers and train anyway. And invariably, someone would twist their ankle or hurt their knee. That only reinforced our belief in our ritual. No matter what our personal beliefs, our sport was challenging enough as it was. There was no shortage of ways in

Starting *Kushti*

which one could get injured. It was best to stay on the right side of the almighty.

This ritual is performed even now at every akhara in Haryana. It doesn't matter how modern you have become. There are still some things you can't compromise on. You have to light that agarbatti and pray for everyone's safety at the start of both the morning and evening sessions. You then take that agarbatti all around the room so its smoke enters all the corners of the room before you return it in front of the statue of Hanuman-ji. The agarbatti stays burning throughout the session.

Before I began a training or fight, I'd put a hand on the mat and then bring the hand to my head, and I'd repeat the same ritual once the session was over. I did this almost instinctively. I don't harbour many superstitions, and I don't count this as one, either.

I have so much love and passion for wrestling that I see the akhara as my place of worship. I have to keep it as clean as possible. I have to be neat and clean myself when I go to the akhara, just like I would have if I were going to a temple.

I might even go to my school without having a bath, but I would never step on the wrestling mat without bathing. I've never stepped on a mat without having bathed earlier that day. I used to think that the more purity with which I go to the mat, the more I treat it as a place of worship and keep it clean, the more I will get back from it.

I don't think the new generation of wrestlers believes in all the things I did. Their mindset is to just stick to their training, because that's the only thing that matters before a competition. They don't pay as much attention to cleanliness as I did.

I believed in Hanuman-ji a lot during my days as a wrestler. Today, every god is equally important to me. I pray to Shiv-ji or bow to the Guru Granth Sahib. I respect what people believe in, but I have always felt that my god can be found on that wrestling mat or even in my wrestling shoes. I worship wrestling and everything associated with it.

I have carried that agarbatti many times around the mat. That takes just about a couple of minutes. Your real devotion consists in what you do in the two-and-a-half hours that you spend on the mat. I have to do that with the same devotion with which I take the agarbatti around the wrestling room.

When I began my training sessions, I'd go into the practice room with the mentality that no one should be able to train more than I did. I hated it if someone bettered me. If someone did 500 squats, I had to beat that number by fifty. If someone climbed the rope ten times, I had to do it fifteen times.

At Chhotu Ram Stadium, the hardest sessions were on Tuesday mornings. That's when Ishwar Dahiya coach and his subordinate Mandeep coach, as we often referred to them, used to make all the wrestlers do stair climbing. There were other tough workouts, like cross-country runs or rope climbing or *dand baithaks* (a combination of push ups and free squats) and *sapate* (burpees), but the stair runs were another kind of hard.

Those stairs were not like the ones you might have at home. At Chhotu Ram Stadium, each step was a foot and a half high. You couldn't just walk up them. Instead, you had to thrust yourself up over each step. Every time you climbed a stair it was as if you were doing a split lunge. There's a saying that 60 per cent of your wrestling strength comes from your legs, and those climbs built a lot of power in my quadriceps and calves.

It might have appeared that those stairs were randomly placed, but that was exactly how the stadium had been designed. It was a cheap way of building equipment right into the building itself. Starting at 6 a.m., I'd be clambering up those stairs for two hours on Tuesday mornings. Coach Mandeep would be standing in the middle of those stairs, waving a bamboo stick as thick as three fingers at us. If anyone slowed down, he wouldn't hesitate in bringing that stick down on us. He'd blow his whistle and all of us would race up the stairs. Suddenly there would be a loud *thwack* and some unfortunate wrestler would be rubbing his or her backside.

The sprints left your thighs burning, but that felt a lot less painful than being hit. I was lucky that I was always highly motivated, so I never got hit nearly as much as the others. There were other girls who'd get hit all the time.

By the time I ran my final sprint up the stairs I'd be exhausted, sweaty and somewhat sore on account of catching a few swings of that bamboo stick. Just completing the session felt like a major achievement.

But we weren't done just yet. I'd go to school after that morning session and return to the stadium for an evening mat workout, where I'd take part in practice matches against the young boy wrestlers of the academy.

They were obviously physically stronger than me, but coach Mandeep would insist we never let up. He constantly extended the duration of our sparring matches. I would spar for two rounds of two minutes each, which later became three rounds of three minutes each and finally rounds of five minutes at a time. I'd finish one round and I'd be made to wrestle another boy right away.

If I wanted to catch my breath, Mandeep coach would be waiting with his stick. When he felt I wasn't pushing myself, I'd get a whack. I was terrified of being smacked. Physical punishment was fairly common in the wrestling culture of my youth. I've been hit more than a few times, from the time I started wrestling all the way until I was an established international athlete who had won medals.

There were times my mother saw the red welts on my legs and asked me what had happened. I would lie and say I'd hit a door or had fallen off a chair. I conditioned myself into thinking that all this was for my own good. I didn't consider it wrong at the time. That was just how things were. You don't see it at the Indian national camps any more, but at the akharas it's still common for a coach to wave a stick behind girls.

Part of the reason I tolerated being hit was because I was always very hard on myself. I simply hated losing. When I got hit for the first time on one of the stair climbs, I was angry not at the coach but at myself. I was crying not just because I was hit but because I knew that I was being too slow.

I'm not sure if it was abuse, but that's just how my coach got wrestlers to push themselves beyond what they thought they could achieve. Nobody likes the feeling of one's hands becoming tired and one's legs becoming like jelly and one's body feeling like it's about to throw up. But you have to keep going past that mental barrier. Where everyone else reaches their limit, I have to get started.

There have been many times when I've given more than 100 per cent in a match. Where I've collapsed after the match ended because I could not move. There were matches where I had nothing left to give, where I could not breathe and my legs were in agony. That was only possible because I had done this tens of thousand times before in training. I was doing it long before I even won my first bout.

With that kind of training required for the sport, I still don't know why I was so obsessed about wrestling. It's not like football or cricket or tennis, where you can pick up the basics in a week and get good enough so that it becomes a sport you can play as a hobby.

I don't know anyone who wrestles as a hobby or because it's something you do for fun in the weekends. I've never seen kids wrestle in a playground, like they play cricket or football or badminton. It took weeks for me to simply figure out my stance, and months to gain a basic level of competence. There's no middle ground in wrestling. You are either going to quit it very early on or you are going to do it for years and years. And it never gets any easier.

Apart from the intensity of training, there were other discomforts. The Chhotu Ram akhara was part of a newish stadium, but it was really just a large hall covered by a tin roof. Apart the three mats it held, there wasn't much else in terms of facilities. There were of course no air conditioners or even a fan inside. Any evening session in the summer would feel like it was being conducted inside a tandoor.

At any point in time there would be forty or fifty youngsters training on those mats so the hall would get very crowded and the air would be thick and oppressively musky with our breath and the sweat evaporating off our bodies. It was like training inside a greenhouse. There were times I'd have to walk out into the grounds of the stadium, simply to be able to catch my breath because the air inside was so humid and sweaty.

Yet I loved to train. I was good at it, too. Some of the senior girls would be surprised to see me go to the weights room in the stadium and lift weights that even they couldn't. I loved out-training all of them. The only way to explain this inexplicable love for the sport was to accept that my brain was wired in that way. I really think it was destiny that I had to be a wrestler and that I had to go on to win an Olympic medal.

Those days, though, I had no idea about the Asian Games, the World Championships or even the Olympics. Every time a senior girl was picked for an overseas event, even for a friendly competition, I would think, 'Wow! She must be one the greatest wrestlers in the world.' Sometimes, after a training session, some of the senior wrestlers would talk to me about the competitions they had taken part in. They'd also give me advice on my training and on what to eat, how to crush almonds into milk as a high-protein recovery drink. But what I liked to hear most from them was their stories about travelling on a plane to foreign countries I'd never even heard of. I'd just listen to their tales full of marvel.

I was in awe of one of my seniors – Sunita Nehra – who competed in three international tournaments. I even went with her once to the airport to see her off. She'd gone to so many competitions that people would say, '*Usne toh plane ko rickshaw bana diya hai*. [She has made the plane into a rickshaw.]'

Although I had never stepped foot inside a plane, I was excited to see them flying in so close to the ground at the airport. I'd imagine just what it must be like to travel on a plane myself. Going abroad was still something nebulous. I had no idea what that meant. But travelling on a plane seemed very doable. I had seen those planes from up close and I could almost imagine it.

It doesn't seem like much motivation – to dream of flying one day – but just something as simple as that really helped to keep me at my wrestling journey. It was all part of a great adventure that I was lucky to be able to pursue.

Otherwise, who is to say I wouldn't have returned to gymnastics or some less oppressive sport? I even managed to convince my parents to believe in my obsession for wrestling.

Starting *Kushti*

But I wasn't just wrestling. I was still attending school. I'd sometimes have to leave in the middle of the morning training session because I had to reach school in time. I'd come back from school in the afternoon, and then, after a couple of tuition classes, I'd go and train in the evening session. When I finished my evening training, I'd return home and complete my homework. I was constantly rushing from my home to the school and to the akhara.

There were a couple of girls at the akhara who had decided to skip school altogether. They had taken a room near the stadium, and all they did each day was to train and rest. They weren't going to school like I did, so they'd just sleep in the afternoons and be able to recover faster from their morning training. I had gone to their room one day and felt very jealous that they were able to concentrate on just their training. They'd come back home after a hard practice session and then cook their own food, get some sleep and come back for a training session in the evening.

I too wanted to have that life. I told my parents I couldn't balance both my studies and wrestling. I wanted to choose just one. Of course they told me, 'That's fine. Stop wrestling.' So I didn't have any option but to balance both my studies and sports. However, things got a little easier for me when, after about a year of my starting wrestling – by the time I turned thirteen – my parents transferred me from DAV School to Vaish Public School.

Although it was considered one of the top schools in Rohtak, DAV didn't support me very much in my wrestling career. They were more academically inclined. My morning workouts would start at 6 a.m. and go on for a couple of hours, after which I'd rush to catch a bus to take to school. Despite my best efforts, I'd almost always miss my first class period of the day. I tried to get permission to skip assembly or the first period, but was refused. I thought, if I wanted to wrestle I had go to an ordinary school, not an elite one like DAV.

Although it wasn't anywhere as prestigious as DAV School, Vaish School was known to encourage sportspersons. If you were a state medallist, they even gave you a 50 per cent rebate on school fees. I wasn't close to being a state medallist at the time, but they gave me permission to miss the morning assembly and sometimes the first period too. The only challenge of studying at Vaish was that it was much farther from my home than DAV. There was no bus to take me to Vaish after my morning training, unlike with DAV, so I'd cycle the 8 km from the stadium to my school.

By the time I got to school I'd be very tired. I've fallen asleep more than once in the middle of a class, which my classmates found funny. Sometimes the teachers would get upset at me because they thought I was being lazy. One time I nearly failed my pre-board maths exam because I was just too tired to study. I tried to explain my situation to my teacher, but she shut me up by telling me, 'The first impression is the last impression.' Despite that episode, I'm still grateful I was able to find a school that allowed me to pursue my interest. I'm also thankful to my parents for allowing me to change schools because they had put in a lot of effort into getting me into DAV School.

My mother wasn't really keen on it, initially. She felt I'd get cauliflower ears, like most wrestlers do. My father, on the other hand, was very supportive. He said it was up to me to make the most of what I wanted to do. Eventually my mother agreed, but she insisted that even if I changed schools, I'd still have to study.

In that way, I was very different from most of the girls who wrestled. I must have been the only one who had actually studied. While every other wrestler would have some university degree or

Starting *Kushti*

qualification, I'm fairly certain most of them have never actually studied or given an exam to earn it. Many of them are barely literate. When they had to pass an exam, they usually got some other girl to write their papers for them and paid the test takers to look the other way. That was something I could never do.

I was good in studies and did fairly well in my class ten board exams at Vaish, getting over 80 per cent marks. Although I enjoyed maths in particular, I had to give it up and take up an arts subject, because I knew I wanted to focus on my wrestling. Despite that, I did manage to complete both my graduation and post-graduation.

It was only in 2005, after a year of backbreaking training, that I finally got my first win. I had taken part in many competitions through that year, each defeat piling upon the previous one so it all became a big blur. My win came in the state school championships. Funnily enough, my opponent was Chhoti, the girl against whom I'd lost the very first match of my career. This time though, I was just a lot better prepared and I was able to land the technique I'd been learning almost weekly – the double-leg takedown – on her. I don't remember the match clearly. I remember it being messy, but at the end of six minutes I had my hand raised for the very first time in my career.

I was ecstatic when it finally happened. Now I was ready to take on anyone. The winner in that competition would be presented a Mayur water jug, and I wanted to take that home with me, just to show my parents that I had finally won something. If I won that competition, I might even get to take part in the national school championships. But that was not to be.

4

First International

My happiness at winning my first bout lasted all of a few minutes because I lost my very next match. I burst into tears and was inconsolable. If I couldn't even win a medal at the state school-level competition, how on earth was I going to win at the national level?

Ishwar Dahiya Sir tried to encourage me, but no one could comfort me. It took me three years from when I first started wrestling to become the best in India.

During those years I'd come to train every day at the Chhotu Ram akhara and I'd look jealously at the boys and girls who came to the stadium wearing T-shirts with the word 'Haryana' printed on the back.

I used to think they were such impressive athletes, having managed to compete for Haryana in the national championships. I wondered when it would be my turn to get such a T-shirt of my own. I'd feel nauseated with jealousy and anxiety and thought I was a great failure.

Eventually though, I started winning. Competing in the cadet age group – which is for wrestlers under the age of seventeen – I claimed my first district title as a fifteen-year-old in 2007. From there I went

First International

on to compete in the Haryana State Championships. Even though women's wrestling was still only starting out, even in 2007 there were a lot more girls wrestling in Haryana than in other states. I won the state title too. That win made me eligible to compete in the Cadet National Championships at Anandpur Sahib in Punjab, and that meant I finally got my very own T-shirt with 'Haryana' printed on the back.

I was so eager to make an impression at what was my first national tournament that I ended up overtraining for it. By the time I got to the competition I came down with a very bad fever. I was really worried about how I would take part, being as unwell as I was, when one of the other girls gave me a tablet.

We used to call it *hara patta gola*. It's banned today because it has severe side effects, but it worked for me. By the time I came out to wrestle, I was much better. I beat everyone I was up against. My final was against a girl from Punjab, and although I had started feeling the effects of my illness, I was still able to beat her 7-0. Just like that, I had become the cadet champion of India. I couldn't believe I had won my first national wrestling title. I was clearly good already – anyone who came through the wrestling championships in Haryana had to be. But it was only when I finally got my first national gold medal around my neck that I really started believing I could be a good wrestler.

But even more than any self-confidence that this fetched me, it got me really excited because I knew that as a national champion I'd get to go to the national camp. Although I'd never been to one, I had heard of it. Before a team is sent out to represent India at any international wrestling competition, a number of wrestlers – usually picked on the basis of their performance at the National

Championships – are brought to a common venue where they train together for a few weeks. At the end of the camp, trials are conducted and a team is picked. I knew that if I won those trials I'd get to go for my first international competition. And even more important, I'd finally get to be on an aeroplane!

The first national camp I went to was in New Delhi. We stayed at the sports hostel at Jawaharlal Nehru Stadium and trained at the Indira Gandhi stadium some 5 km away. This would be followed by a selection trial for the Asian Cadet Championships.

When I won my selection trials, I was ecstatic. I was so close to that plane trip! That happiness lasted exactly one day. The day after I won my trials, we were informed that India wasn't going to be sending a team to the Asian Cadet Championships after all. This would happen later too. Camps would be conducted and teams organized, and then at the last minute the Wrestling Federation of India would realize that there weren't any funds for their travel. When that happened, the federation would tell us we could still go if we wanted to but at our own expense.

My family told me not to worry and that they'd fund my trip since it was my first international competition. One of the girls in the camp – Navjot Kaur – was crying because her family had told her they couldn't pay for her. She was from a very poor family. I tried to console her and said I'd arrange for her to go too. But in the end the entire tour was cancelled. The federation must have realized it looked bad to ask athletes to pay for their own travel, so they decided they weren't going to send anyone at all.

We used to take the bus from Indira Gandhi Stadium to Nehru Stadium for our training. It was on one of those rides that the announcement was made. I returned home with my bags packed but

First International

with nowhere to go. I felt as if my whole world had collapsed. Was I ever going to get another chance to go participate in an international competition?

I would, just about a year later, when I competed at the Children of Asia competition in Russia.

Before I could compete there I first had to win my second cadet nationals. If my first National Cadet Championships had seen me catch a high fever, my second in Jalandhar saw me almost forfeit the competition after picking up another injury. We'd arrived in the city a few days before the competition, and after every training we'd go to a juice shop near the stadium. I was messing about with the juicing machine and ended up badly slicing my forefinger. Once again, I started to think I wouldn't be able to would I play the nationals, but I eventually got that finger bandaged up and managed to win the tournament without letting my opponent grab that injured digit.

That national title got me a call to the selection trial for the Children of Asia competition, which I ended up winning. The Children of Asia competition was a by-invitation multi-sport games organized every four years by Russia. It wasn't nearly the most prestigious tournament I'd ever compete in, even in the age-group category. Despite that, I still remember the competition vividly.

I very nearly ended up missing that opportunity too. By this time I was a part of the senior national camp in Hisar – something I'll talk about later. A week before the Children of Asia competition, a few girls in the national camp in Hisar caught chicken pox. Worried that I would get it too, I called my home to ask my mother to pick me up. Despite my best efforts though, it was pretty obvious that I was starting to break out in those tell-tale spots.

When you catch chicken pox, you first break out in pustules, which then settle down over twelve to fifteen days. Unfortunately, I had to go in a week's time. My mother took me to a doctor and told him my problem. He gave me a bottle of ointment, which he told me to apply on my spots every time they erupted. Right until the time of my first bout, I would religiously apply that balm to my boils.

Before every wrestling competition, there's always a medical test done. You stretch your arms to the side and a doctor looks all over your body and under your arms to see if you have any skin infections or allergic reactions so you don't spread it to the other wrestlers. The doctors in India would sometimes just take a cursory look and let you compete, but that was unlikely to be the case in an international competition. If a doctor in Russia spotted anything as obvious as a chicken pox boil, there was no way I'd be cleared to compete.

I have no idea what that medicine was that the doctor gave me, but most of the pustules and all of the ones on my face settled down. Maybe I was just lucky. I'd seen other girls with chicken pox who were completely covered in those spots. I had perhaps just three or four boils on my face and maybe another five across my body and legs. And all of them started to settle after just three days. I was able to train for another three days before I left for Russia.

I was really excited to go to the airport. When my seniors from the Chhotu Ram akhara set out for an international competition, I'd always ask them if I could go to the airport with them. There would be one car taking them to the airport from their home in Rohtak or whichever village they hailed from. There would be another car just for their coaches, friends and family. Everyone would go, as if that wrestler wouldn't be returning for a year. I'd gone on many of these send-off trips. Now I was going to get to be one of those being sent off.

First International

Apart from my scare with chicken pox, the whole experience was like a dream. I was counting down each day to my flight. Three days to go, two days to go . . . Apart from sitting in an aeroplane, I also really wanted to see what other countries looked like. The internet had barely arrived at the time, and certainly there was no Facebook or Instagram back then, so I could only imagine what foreign countries would be like. I had no idea what the rest of the world looked like. I'd wonder how the people there looked, what their houses were like, how they lived. I might have been going to Russia, but I could very well have been going to another planet.

A day before my journey, I arrived in New Delhi where a send-off programme was being organized for the children who were part of the Indian team. We were given our official kit with blazers and track suits, and were hosted a dinner too. I went to the airport the next morning. At the emigration counter, I presented my brand-new passport with its first visa stamp – Russia's – on it. Now I've gone through multiple passport books, but that visa stamp was my very first one. When I finally entered the plane, I found it was full of children of my age who played all kinds of sports. There were judokas, wrestlers, athletes and boxers.

I got a middle seat. People usually like sitting next to the window or the aisle, but I've always preferred the middle seat. I never liked the aisle since you always had people walking past you down the flight corridors. I didn't mind the window seat, but I always liked the middle seat the most because I usually travelled to competitions with my friends and I enjoyed being around them. I also liked to sit with my legs spread out, and if I was with my friends I could sprawl all over them and they wouldn't say anything!

I knew many of the girls who were travelling with me. They

weren't just wrestlers but girls from other sports too. I ran into one of them, who was competing in the judo competition in the Children of Asia Games. This girl had started out as a wrestler, and that was how I knew her. But one day it seemed as if she had just disappeared, before reappearing as a judoka. I later found out that she had left wrestling after she was banned for failing a dope test. During her ban, she'd not only changed her sport but also her age. Having competed with her, I knew that she was two years older than me, but at the Children of Asia Games she'd got a new passport where her age was two years less than mine! Later she would return to wrestling and went on to medal at the world level too! It wasn't fair, but many coaches would encourage their athletes to take advantage of whatever they could, and it was also a lot easier to get a change of passport back then.

The games were held in Yakutsk, in Siberia. The most interesting thing about the place was that the sun never seemed to set there. Even at midnight you'd see the sun set only a little bit, and at 5 a.m., it would rise again. I never got tired of seeing that. I couldn't wait to tell my family that I'd been to a country where the sun doesn't set.

I'd been, more or less, a vegetarian all my life and had just started eating chicken, but Russian food was very bland. We were served lamb and chicken, but they were cooked without much by way of spice and smelled odd. So I ate rice and vegetables with ketchup every day. Even later, at international competitions, I'd mostly just stick to vegetarian food because I could never get over the smell and flavour of meat the way it was cooked overseas. I learned to mostly stick to potatoes – curried, stewed or fried – along with rice, ketchup and salad.

The training environment was different there, too. I got to train in Yakutsk for two days before my competition. Those were still the

First International

early days of women's wrestling, even in Russia, and there was just a handful of local girls training along with us. These days the level of competition is very high and Russian girls are very strong in multiple weight categories, but back then, when they were competing in the Children of Asia Games, they didn't even have the numbers to feature a full team across weight categories.

When the tournament started, I got to wear my singlet with 'India' and 'Sakshi' printed on the front and back, respectively. I wrestled my first international opponents – from Russia, Mongolia and Kazakhstan. Three bouts later, I had won the gold. I stood on the podium, and for the first time I listened to the national anthem being played and saw the Indian flag being raised in a foreign country for something that I had achieved. It was a special moment for me.

The competition itself couldn't have gone any better, but at that time I ended up thinking the Games Village was haunted because of an incident involving my roommate. I didn't know it then, but she had a medical problem and would get seizures. She would be fine one second and a moment later her eyes would roll back and her body would 'lock' and start to shake. I'd never seen anything like it. The two of us were in a strange country, and I was sure she was possessed by a ghost. It was of course a medical issue, but I was just very naive back then.

This episode happened a few times. I'd sprinkle water on her face and she'd recover and be back to her usual self, as if nothing had happened. There was one instance when, right after the wrestling competition had concluded, she had such a bad seizure that she wasn't able to wake up. I had to call the manager of the team, who in turn called an ambulance. As she was being wheeled away, she started freaking out. She refused to go into the ambulance and started saying that they were trying to kill her. She had no idea what was going on. Luckily, the tournament was over by then, otherwise it would have been impossible for the two of us to compete, given the situation.

The two of us had already won gold in separate weight divisions earlier in that competition, but rather than celebrating I stayed in her hospital room the whole night. Once she recovered, she had no memory of what had happened. A wrestler-friend tells me she is better now and doesn't suffer those attacks any more.

That incident left me shaken, but chocolate soon made up for it. In India you'd only get Dairy Milk and a few other brands in the late 2000s. Russia seemed to be a chocolate paradise. There were grocery stores near the venue that were stocked with all kinds of chocolate brands that I hadn't even heard of. I'd visit those stores every day once the competition had finished. Using my tiny daily $10 stipend, I bought the really large boxes and packets, the ones you wouldn't get in India. It cost around $6–7. I used to buy one every two or three days and finish it.

In terms of international debuts, I couldn't have asked for a better one. Even the medal I won seemed to be special. It was a circular one with a 'diamond' embedded in the middle. For a long time I really believed that it was a real gemstone in the middle of the medal. But even if its gemstone wasn't real, I felt the medal was one of the more unique ones I had won in my career. When I was going through my medals before heading to Haridwar, I saw that medal hidden amongst the pile of others. It was a bit duller than I remembered, but that 'diamond' in the centre still shone as brightly as ever.

Your perspective changes completely when you go abroad for the first time. You realize there's a bigger world out there than the one you have imagined for yourself in India. Although I didn't compete against either the Chinese or Japanese, and I wouldn't have been able to tell a Mongolian or a Kazakh player apart, I understood that there was an entire ocean of competition outside India. It whetted my hunger for more.

Just a few weeks back, my life's ambition had been just to sit in a plane. Now, though, I realized there was just so much more to want out of life. As the tournament ended and I returned home, I was very excited to tell my stories of a country with its never-ending days, its people and the medal that I'd won.

5

Camp Life

By the time I competed at the Children of Asia Games, I'd already been part of the senior national camp for several months. I was the exception in this regard. While every other girl who was part of the senior camp was there based on her performance at the senior National Championships, I'd only take part in my first senior national competition in 2009, two years after first joining the national camp.

It was Ishwar Dahiya Sir, the head coach at the Chhotu Ram akhara, who first felt I should be part of the senior national camp, even though I was still taking part in the cadet and junior competitions (for wrestlers under nineteen years of age). There was already a girl – Suman Kundu – from my akhara who had joined the national camp after winning a medal at the Senior National Championships, and Dahiya Sir had seen that I was already starting to give her a tough fight in the academy.

He knew the secretary of the Haryana Wrestling Federation, Rajkumar Sangwan, and asked him if I could somehow be accommodated in the senior national camp. He told him that I was very talented and that there weren't many women partners for me at

Rohtak. That part was true. There were just four girls in all, training with me at the Chhotu Ram akhara and only one of them was in my weight category. Dahiya Sir insisted that if I got to train against girls who were from my weight category but of a higher level, I'd improve a lot. He'd never asked for favours from anyone before this, but he did for me. Dahiya Sir didn't just say he saw big things for me in my future. He also fought for me to get the opportunities I needed. For that I will always be grateful to him.

I was a bundle of nerves on my first day at the national camp at the Sports Authority of India in Hisar. Everyone knew that the best wrestlers in India were at the national camp for seniors. These national camps were usually organized over several months at a Sports Authority of India facility – initially in Haryana but later in Lucknow – with the intention of preparing wrestlers for the year's most important international tournaments. Going there meant that I was going to be in that elite group for the first time.

I was curious about their training, diet, etc., and excited about the opportunity to train against wrestlers who were much more experienced than I was. But I also felt a great deal of fear and was overcome by shyness. I wondered if I would be able to match the level of these *badi didis*. I was just sixteen years old, not even out of the cadet-age category. Most of the seniors at the camp were in their mid-twenties, and some even in their thirties. I was the youngest by quite a margin. What would I even talk to them about? Would they even want to share a room or a meal with me?

At first I felt that my fears were going to be realized. I had joined the camp a couple of days after it had started and everyone had already chosen their roommates by the time I showed up.

As a rookie, I didn't get to choose whom I stayed with. The hostel warden just looked around to see which room still had some space for me. She found one where there were just two girls, and I was told to stay with them. I nervously made my way into the room with my duffel bag in which I'd packed a bed sheet, a blanket and a few changes of clothes. My parents had also given me a phone since I was going to be away from home for several weeks.

By the time I became a regular on the Indian team, my family's financial circumstances were no longer as precarious as they had been. My father had started a small property business and that allowed me to bring additional stuff that made my life a little easier every time I joined the camp. I brought a food processor, then an induction cooker and a fridge. By the time the national camp moved to Lucknow in 2013, I had brought along a washing machine too, so that all of us girls could wash our sweat-soaked singlets. Because I knew I was probably going to be part of the next national camp, I'd usually just leave these appliances behind at the hostel once the national camp ended so that they were in place for use at the time of the next camp.

At my first camp though, I had no idea just what to expect. I'd never been away from home for very long – three or four days at most. If I had a national championship, then I'd have to stay at a hostel for a day or so and spend another two days travelling, but I'd never known what it was like to stay away from home for weeks at a time.

My first roommates were two senior girls, Anita and Poonam. Anita would be my roommate from the time I first joined the national camp in 2007 until 2013, when she retired. Although I'd never met either of them before, they were very welcoming. They had two beds in the opposite sides of the room, but they decided to push them together so I could sleep in the middle in the little ditch formed where the two beds met. It wasn't the most comfortable bed but I was happy I was just able to get a place to stay at all.

My first session at the national camp lasted just a few days. Within a few days I picked up a freak injury, not while wrestling but while I was playing a game of basketball with some of the senior girls. I was going to catch the basketball when my foot got stuck in the ground and my weight fell on my right knee.

Although I didn't know it then, I had badly damaged my anterior cruciate ligament (ACL) and medial collateral ligament (MCL) – the two ligaments that allow you to maintain balance and stability in your knee. There was no way I would have known what had happened. Back then I didn't even know what the ACL was or what a partial tear was, what rehab consisted of and whether I needed surgery. Back then I didn't even realize I should probably have gone straight away to a doctor specializing in sports medicine. To me it was just '*goda mud gaya*', a knee that had got twisted. I just tied a bandage on it and hoped the pain would go away on its own.

When the pain wouldn't ease, my mother took me back to Rohtak. I didn't see a doctor there either. Instead my mother took me to a bone setter at the market near my house. You still see them in India – they have their shops at the town markets, usually carrying an advertisement of a muscle man with a plaster on his arm. The bone setter was completely untrained in modern science, of course. He applied oil on my knee and massaged my joint for a month. My knee did recover, likely because of the complete rest I took, and I was able to return to the camp a month later. In reality though, there had probably been a serious tear in the ligaments of my knee. Although I was able to wrestle when I came back to the camp, the injury was building up to something bigger.

When I returned to the camp I went back to the same room with Poonam and Anita. Since there was another Poonam in the camp, everyone called my roommate '*Poonam bhainso wali*', since her family owned a dairy farm. It was a funny sort of nickname, but that's just how it is in Indian wrestling. There are many wrestlers with common names. At the camp we had many Amits, Ankits and Poonams. So we would always find something to identify them by. Many of us use our village names as identifiers. Ankit Baiyanpuria, who is very famous on Instagram, takes his last name from his village Baiyanpur. Satender Malik, who would later be part of the wrestlers' protest, was always known as Satender Mokhra, after his village Mokhria, which is where I happen to be from, too.

Some others were given nicknames, and they stuck. Deepak Punia, who won a silver medal at the world championships, was known as Katli (kettle) on account of his prodigious appetite as a child – apparently because when he was very young he drank an entire kettle of milk. Meanwhile Bajrang Punia was called Bhoora (brown).

Womens' wrestling picked up that tradition, but to a lesser extent. No one called the Phogat sisters by that name. Everyone just called them *Balali wali behne* (the sisters from Balali).

There wasn't any Sakshi in the national camp, so I never got a nickname. As a kid you don't give much thought to your name, but when I started wrestling I felt my name didn't have any strength to it. I wanted a hard, strong name. I wished I had a name like Geetika Jakhar or Geeta Phogat or Alka Tomar. Those were names that sounded tough.

I didn't just wish I had a name like those of some of the senior girls, I was obsessed with what they did, too. I would observe when they woke up, how they prepared their bed, how they prepared for

Camp Life

the day. I'd observe how they trained, even how they packed their kit bag and what they had to eat.

Among other things, my penchant for cleanliness really got cemented thanks to my roommate Anita Sheoran. As wrestlers, tidiness isn't always at the top of the list of priorities for us. The training hall where we practise is hot and humid and usually full of sweaty people. Although the mat on which we train is usually swabbed with some sort of disinfectant before each session, the nature of our sport is such that there are always germs and bugs floating around. It's not uncommon to catch skin infections in that environment.

Women wrestlers are at least somewhat concerned about tidiness. Male wrestlers can be absolutely filthy. When I trained with them at the Chhotu Ram akhara, I found they stank really badly because they rarely washed their sweat-soaked singlets or wrestling shoes. They'd just leave them out to dry. Once I saw a wrestler shake his singlet which had been left outside in the sun, and powdered, dried salt from all his sweat just exploded off the cloth. It was absolutely disgusting.

I'm the complete opposite of that. My husband Satyawart tells me I have some sort of obsessive compulsive disorder. I don't think that's the case and I've never been clinically diagnosed, but I do seem to have many of the symptoms. I constantly wash my hands and keep pestering him to wash his too. If I need to use a plate, I have to wash it even if it has just been washed. I need to frequently change my bed sheets too. It was something that made me stand out amongst the Indian wrestlers who for the most part never demand any level of cleanliness.

If we travelled for a competition, we would usually be booked the cheapest seats, if we were lucky. Otherwise, if we were travelling on unreserved tickets, as was more often the case, we would be using the floor of the train coach to sleep on. When we arrived for a competition we would be provided only the most basic facilities. We'd have to share used mattresses or bathe where we relieved ourselves.

It was at the national camp that I learned, if only from my roommate Anita, that it was all right to be particular about one's surroundings. She had a real keeda for cleanliness in her. I was her roommate for so long that that worm infected me too and I became conditioned that way too.

Anita had very strict rules about our room. If I had visitors she'd never allow them to sit on the bed. I wouldn't sit on the bed, either. I'd either change my clothes or I'd put another bed sheet over the bed before I sat on it. I had no idea what germs my visitors might have picked up from the mat! God only knew whether they'd even washed their feet. It was a running joke in the camp that I was paranoid about cleanliness.

I'm grateful I had Anita and Poonam as my roommates because they taught me many good values. Anita, who was nine years older than me, was already a senior wrestler by the time I joined the camp. She would even win a Commonwealth Games gold in 2010. She was someone everyone trusted. She wouldn't engage in 'back-talking' or gossip. She had a keeda for honesty too, along with her keeda for cleanliness.

Anita was also one of the pioneers of women's wrestling in India. It must have been hard for girls of her generation to take up the sport since women's wrestling wasn't really a socially acceptable sport at the time. She was actually a police constable and only got interested in the sport when she began her police training at the Haryana Police Academy in Madhuban.

Camp Life

That was the story of many of the older women wrestlers at that time. They had either been introduced to the sport as part of their job in the police or had been the first to enter an akhara in their village. Some of the other girls had been boxers or judokas but had switched sports because of lack of success in their first choice.

Many of them never actually wanted to become wrestlers. They'd been forced into it by their fathers who were very passionate about the sport. That was certainly the case of Sonika Kaliraman, who was the most senior wrestler at that national camp. Her father – Master Chandgi Ram Kaliraman – was probably one of the most famous Indian wrestlers of the 1960s and 1970s. He was not only very famous as a wrestler, winning the Asian Games gold medal in 1970, but was also infamous for his colourful life, having married three times.

Master Chandgi Ram was the first to introduce women's wrestling in India in 1997, when the sport was included in the Olympics programme. He was already one of the most senior men's coaches in India at the time, and he used his position to encourage other coaches to get girls to wrestle. All the early coaches in women's wrestling in India were men whom Master Chandgi Ram had coached at his own academy in Delhi. His own daughters, Sonika and Deepika, were the first women wrestlers in India. But neither of them actually wanted to be a wrestler.

When I spoke to Sonika, she told me that her father had forced her into the sport. He kept telling her, *'Wrestling kar, wrestling kar.* [Do wrestling.]' She told me, *'Pitaji jabardasti mujhe wrestling me laye the.* [Father forced me into wrestling.]' She herself had very little interest in the sport.

The Phogat sisters' father Mahavir was another of Master Chandgi Ram's trainees, and he too had forced his daughters into wrestling. They'd have to train whether it was cold or very early in the morning, and their father would often hit them. They told me about how they were slapped when they wanted to go for a wedding because their father wanted them to train instead. They remembered how happy they were when their father fell sick one day and they didn't have to train. They later learned to appreciate what he did for them, but they had had no love for the sport at first.

But that wasn't my story. I loved training. I never had to be pushed to wrestle. In contrast to Mahavir Phogat, my family constantly asked me to attend weddings but I always found a way to get out of it. I knew that if I did, I'd miss a day of training. I did sometimes attend functions happening near our home, but I would make it very clear that I would never travel out of Rohtak to a village or to Delhi for any event, for that would cost me two days of training.

If I had a training session at 4 p.m., I'd make sure I entered the wrestling hall with five minutes to go. I have never been late for training, even by a minute, any time in my life.

My parents bought me a scooter for my travel to the stadium and back home, in place of the cycle I had been using for many years. By an oversight, I'd forgotten to sign one of the documents required for the purchase and had been called over by the scooter dealer to get my paperwork in place. I tried to refuse to go because it was close to 4 p.m., my evening training time.

My parents had to drag me to the store to fill in those forms with my signatures. And I was crying all the while because I knew I was going to be late to my training session. I was bawling and saying 'I don't want a scooty.' I insisted I'd just go on my cycle to train. I just wanted to go and start my evening training session. Eventually I did finish all the paperwork but I didn't wait to even get my scooter.

Camp Life

Instead I rushed in a rickshaw from the scooter dealer's to my akhara so I would make it in time to train.

This was one of the major differences between many of the girls at the camp and me, but there were also many things we had in common. Most of the girls at the national camp were from very modest backgrounds. The vast majority of us were from Haryana and the western regions of Uttar Pradesh, with the remainder from Punjab. Later, the camp would come to be dominated by girls from Haryana. Nearly all of them came from the villages of Haryana and none were from well-off families. If we were, it was very unlikely that our parents would have let us take up wrestling. The one exception to this was Geetika Jhakar, whose parents were both school teachers and well educated.

At that time, Geetika Jakhar and Alka Tomar were the two biggest names in women's wrestling in India. Just a couple of years before before I joined the senior camp, Geetika had become the first Indian woman to win a medal at the 2006 Asian Games. That same year, Alka had been the first Indian woman to win a medal at the World Championships – considered the most prestigious international wrestling competition outside of the Olympics.

At that point in time, winning any international medal in women's wrestling was a big deal for India. The Olympics were almost impossibly far away. While Sushil Kumar would win an Olympic bronze in 2008, it would be another four years before the first Indian woman wrestler even qualified for the Olympic Games.

I was in awe of both Geetika and Alka. I couldn't gather the courage to even speak to them at the first national camp in Hisar. I finally worked up the nerve to approach them at my second national camp in Patiala. I wanted them to know how much I admired them.

But I was certain I'd fumble with my words, so instead I just made a handmade greeting card for them.

I was fairly good at drawing and I had a bunch of art supplies from school, so I cut out a bunch of letters from newspapers and magazines and used them to paste together the names 'Alka' and 'Geetika' on thick card paper. I then used sketch pens to draw a big heart below their names. It seems very silly, but I was really desperate for them to approve of me. When I presented them a card each, they were taken aback by my offering but graciously accepted them. I think they were happy to get them, too.

Although I felt nervous and shy in front of these didis, the more I observed them I realized something that shocked me. I began to understand that I was actually out-training all of them.

No one worked as much as I did.

This would sometimes be a challenge at the Sports Authority of India centre in Hisar, because at nightfall the authorities would lock the gates of the hostel building so outsiders couldn't get in and the girls couldn't sneak out. So, even if I wanted to go for a run on the track or to the gym in the morning, I couldn't until 5.30 in the morning when the warden opened the jail-cell-like sliding gates in front of the hostel.

I didn't want to wait that long, so instead of lying in bed I'd go to a small veranda-like space in front of the gate and start doing my *utthak baithak* (free hand squats) and *dand* (what are called 'Hindu push-ups') with only the last of the moonlight for company.

It was as if there was one set of timings for every other girl at the national camp and another one just for me. I'd set my alarm clock to wake up an hour before any of the other girls in the camp did, just so I could sneak in some extra time to train. I'd wake up at the first ring of my phone alarm, climb over my roommates Anita or Poonam, who were sleeping on either side of me, and head to the veranda to start my workouts. At times some of the other girls would be motivated to join me, but they were never regular about it.

Unless I was recovering from a serious injury, I don't think I ever missed a day of training in my wrestling career. I'd even have panic attacks if I was late for a session. Many girls would skip their training sessions if they had their period. They'd tell one of the women coaches that they were suffering from abdominal pain and the coach would understand what they were saying and inform the chief coaches. Almost every girl would have one or two days in a month when she'd find it really hard to come to the wrestling mat.

Not I. I don't know if my periods were just not as heavy as theirs or if I didn't cramp as badly as the others did. If my body was really struggling, I'd hold a hot water bottle against myself after a practice session, but I'd still make it a point to go and train. Perhaps I was lucky, because there were many cases where girls struggled in a competition because it coincided with their period. That never happened to me.

The coaches at the camp too noticed how seriously I took my training. I was always the one chosen to demonstrate techniques and lead the warm-up before the training sessions. Normally, it was expected that the coaches would lead the warm-up sessions, but the average coach at the camp wasn't particularly fit, so they'd instead just chose the fittest wrestler to lead the classes. It was a reputation I enjoyed having.

The strange thing was that while I wanted the coaches to notice how good I was on the mat during the training sessions, I was always the quiet girl outside the training hall. There were girls who had a big personality – they'd say, '*Aur coach-ji*,' and comfortably interact with the coaches, asking after them and making small talk. I was the exact opposite. I used to be terrified of getting on their wrong side and generally shrank from them. If I saw them coming down a hallway I was walking up, I'd immediately turn around, hoping I hadn't caught their eye, just so I didn't have to speak to them.

I was never the most talented wrestler in India. When Vinesh Phogat joined the national camp a few years after I did, it didn't take me long to acknowledge that she was far better than me. I would marvel at the way she would just flow from one technique to another. Her mind just seemed to instinctively know what had to be done. That's something I could never work out. And she wasn't the only one who was more talented than me.

But despite that, I was still the first Indian woman to win an Olympic medal. I know that I was physically one of the strongest and most conditioned wrestlers at the camp. Because of that, I was able to power my way out of bad positions and maintain my posture and ability to attack late into the rounds. But I don't think that was the reason why I won that medal. I think it's not just about talent and hard work. It's about your heart, your discipline, and just your dedication to the sport. I don't think anyone could match me in that.

For the most part, camp life was fun. We women wrestlers spent almost as much time there as we did with our own families. Because the wrestling season starts in January and goes on almost until Diwali, we'd celebrate many birthdays and festivals together.

In my wrestling career, I've seen the atmosphere at these camps change. When I started to attend them there must have been only a couple of girls who had phones. The camps had a much more community atmosphere than they did later. There was no way to stay

Camp Life

entertained so we would make friends with the other girls. We would go to their rooms. We would chat, play cards and other games. It was a very friendly place.

As times changed, phones became a lot more common in the camps. As that happened, the girls started staying in their own personal space. The last time I was at the camp, I didn't see any girl in anyone else's room. After the entry of phones at the camp, the girls found it a lot more interesting to stay on Facebook, Instagram and WhatsApp. Many of the girls had boyfriends too. They would be stuck on the phone constantly with them. In our day, we'd rather be caught dead than openly have a boyfriend!

At least when I was a junior, camp life was fun. The established wrestlers for the most part didn't consider me a threat since I wouldn't start competing at the senior-level competitions for another couple of years. On the other hand, the fact that I was getting to train alongside them meant that it felt a lot easier to compete in the domestic competitions for one's own age group.

This meant that I was almost always a part of the Indian team that travelled for the international age-group competitions like the Asian and World cadet and junior Championships. It had taken me several years to compete at my first international tournament, but after my first Children of Asia Games, I was almost always participating in some international competition or the other.

It doesn't seem like much, but my willingness to study actually paid off now. Whenever there was some problem in filling out immigration forms, the coaches would always ask me to come and help them out. As someone who was very junior, I liked having that sense of responsibility.

A couple of weeks after I returned from the Children of Asia Games in 2008, I competed at the Asian Cadet Championships. Although I had just won a gold medal, I was beaten very comprehensively in the final by a girl from Japan.

The next year, 2009, I won another silver at the Asian Junior Championships, losing this time to a Mongolian girl, Soronsonbold Battensetseg. She would go on to compete in three different Olympics, winning a bronze medal in the 2012 Games in London.

As someone who had once dreamed of sitting in a plane, I was now constantly travelling from one international competition to another. You could say I'd made 'a rickshaw' out of the plane. But while I was regularly competing and winning medals for India as a cadet and then as a junior wrestler, things were a lot different as I approached my next goal – which was to compete at the senior level.

This was a lot harder. I wasn't just competing against girls my age but against wrestlers who had a lot more experience than I did. As I tried to build myself up to senior level, I didn't get to start by flying out and competing in overseas tournaments. I had to make use of the opportunities to wrestle wherever I could.

6

*Dangal*s

When I started my wrestling career, there were only two framed posters up on the wall at the Chhotu Ram akhara. These were portraits of wrestlers who were famous for competing in dangals. These were prize-money wrestling competitions conducted on mitti, or finely processed mud, in the villages. I never knew their names, but I knew they were champions because they carried the *gada*, or mace, usually awarded to winners at a dangal. I might have fought for medals later, but I always wanted one of those *gadas*.

Just as the akhara wasn't a woman's space, for most of history the dangal too had been a completely forbidden place for women. When I first started wrestling, I don't think women were even allowed there as spectators, let alone as competitors. I don't even recall going to watch a dangal. But dangals were a huge part of Indian wrestling.

One of the reasons why Indian men's wrestling was so competitive was that the boys would wrestle in dangals all the time. They'd win a good amount of money and became used to dealing with pre-match nerves because they took part in dozens and dozens of competitions every year. In contrast, as girls we only really got to wrestle on the synthetic mat at the district, state and national championships.

As awareness of women's wrestling began to spread, a few dangals allowed women to compete. Even though I was afraid to compete in these dangals, I didn't want my coaches to think I was scared of competing in one. I also wanted that *gada* that the winners of these tournaments would get. That was the mark of a top wrestler. And while no wrestler will admit it, I was also thinking about the money I could make.

At a dangal you could get Rs 100 for winning a bout, but you'd still be given, say, Rs 20, to keep you motivated. If you won a bigger tournament, like a Bharat Kesari, you could win tens of thousands of rupees. That was more money than I'd ever seen all at once. If you wrestled particularly well, you could make even more. There is a tradition in dangal *kushti* where a really good wrestler will walk among the crowd holding an unfurled turban, and if the spectators like his or her wrestling they put money in it. You could make many thousands of rupees more that way. I always wanted to win that kind of money to give to my parents. I wanted them to be proud of me.

There were some big dangals for women wrestlers – the biggest of which were the Manana *dangal* in Punjab and the Rajiv Gandhi Memorial dangal in Haryana. It was always hard for me to do well at these dangals because I was still very much a junior and all the senior girls would come and take part in them. With fewer dangals open to women, competition was fierce.

If I really wanted a chance to win a dangal, I had to find one which was scheduled in the middle of the international season, or which was taking place at the same time as another dangal with bigger prize money at stake, where most of the other women might be taking part.

There was one competition in Hapur in western Uttar Pradesh where exactly such a dangal was happening. It was a Bharat Kesari tournament, which was normally one of the most prestigious prize-money tournaments, but the money for this particular competition was relatively less. The winner would get Rs 21,000. In contrast, the biggest dangals offered prize money upwards of Rs 50,000, so the senior most women decided the competition in Hapur wasn't worth the effort. None of the best-known female wrestlers – Geetika, Sonika or Geeta – came to compete there. Suddenly I was the favourite to win.

Once we got to the competition itself, it was very clear what the difference between a national or state championship and a dangal was. At the nationals you usually compete inside a stadium on a platform with a wrestling mat placed on top of it. A dangal, on the other hand, would be conducted in any open area of the village organizing it. The soil would be levelled, and by way of a mat a coloured plastic sheet would be placed on top of the earth. While a mat might be springy and bouncy, this arrangement makes you slow, as when you move it is as if you are treading on sand.

There was nothing by way of facilities either. The dangal would usually be organized in a field, which was usually the only open space available in the village. If you were lucky they'd sometimes set up a tent.

There were no washroom facilities. If we had to relieve ourselves, we would have to go behind the tented area or into the fields where some of the women would stand guard while you peed in the open. While men could compete wearing a loincloth, as women wrestlers we would have to compete in our red-and-blue costumes, just like we did in regular competitions.

There was almost never a private space for changing one's clothes. We used to go to the back of the tent and get some of the other women to stand around us as some sort of shield while we changed our costumes as quickly as we could. When that wasn't possible we'd go to the fields which had tall crops, which might afford us some privacy. We'd put up towels or block the view and then change.

It was very basic, but I didn't know any better. I just knew I wanted to wrestle and I just accepted that at a dangal you couldn't really expect anything much better. That's just how it was. There were barely any rules. There was of course almost never a mat, and very often there wasn't even a timer to keep track of how long a bout had gone on. There might be a referee, but there was no expectation of fairness. If the organizers wanted to conduct your bout fairly they would, and if they didn't they could stop it whenever they wished to and help your opponent win.

I faced all this when as a sixteen-year-old I competed at a Bharat Kesari Dangal in Hapur in 2008. It wasn't easy but I won all my bouts and was thrilled when I was announced the winner. I was awarded a brass *gada*, a ceremonial sash and Rs 21,000 in cash for winning that Bharat Kesari. I was looking forward to handing my parents that money – the first time I would give them something from my wrestling career. More than that, I was excited to get a photograph taken of myself holding the *gada*, which would then be put up on the walls of the Chhotu Ram akhara.

I got back to my train with my *gada* and the Rs 21,000. Having travelled to Hapur on unreserved tickets, I used some of that money to buy a reserved seat so I could go back home in some comfort. I wrapped the rest of my money in the sash I'd been given and kept both in my bag along with my clothes. I stuffed that bag under my seat, but I was so proud of my *gada* that I held on to it all the way back to Rohtak. I held on to it even as I slept. That *gada* was special. It was the first time I'd been awarded one, and I felt I'd really made it as a wrestler.

When I reached Rohtak and opened my bag, I realized the money was missing. It was as if the ground had fallen from underneath me. It was the first significant award that I'd won, and I had had it for less than half a day. I suspected it had been stolen by a couple of the girls I had travelled with, because they'd wanted to keep their costume in my bag on the way back. I had no way to confront them, though.

I was severely depressed for a few days, before my coach finally got tired of seeing me moping around and told me to stop crying. He said I'd win much bigger competitions in the future.

I should have valued my money better. Instead of sleeping with the *gada*, I should have kept my bag with my money next to me. That *gada*, which was a symbol of wrestling, might have been special to me, but it had blinded me to everything else. When I look back, I sometimes feel that that has been the story of my career. I was so engrossed in competing and winning medals that I lost sight of what was probably more important.

I still wrestled in dangals after that incident, but I never won another. I had got lucky in Hapur, but for the most part dangal wrestling is a complete free-for-all. At one Bharat Kesari competition,

Witness

I was about to pin my opponent in the final but the referee blew the whistle signalling the end of the match a full minute before the actual end. All through that match the referee had awarded points to my opponent, even while I was sitting on top of her. That's when I finally decided I had had enough of dangals. The world of wrestling was hard enough as it was and I didn't need to venture into even murkier waters.

7

Brij Bhushan

Trouble had a way of finding me, though. And it came in the form of Brij Bhushan Sharan Singh, who was elected president of the Wrestling Federation of India in January 2012.

At that time though, I had no clue how elections to this body were conducted; nor was it something I thought too much about. The only thing I cared about then was wrestling. I knew that elections were held once every four years and someone became president. I learned only much later about who actually votes, how the state elections happen and who decides who occupies which post.

Much later I'd hear rumours that Brij Bhushan Sharan Singh became president of the WFI using his political power to call in a favour from another senior politician. I don't know to what extent that is true, but it is a fact that over the years he made sure to place his supporters and family members all across the state federations to ensure that he was always won the elections at the national federation.

His son was the head of one state association and his son-in-law headed another. Brij Bhushan wanted to control Indian wrestling entirely, and he had made all preparations to do just that. If he ever stepped down, he had enough supporters in place in the state federations to ensure his son would come in after him, and then his grandson.

Back then though, the only thing I knew about him was that he was the reason wrestling competitions were conducted in Nandini Nagar in Gonda district of Uttar Pradesh.

The standard of the domestic wrestling competitions – whether sanctioned by the federation or by *dangal* committees – was always poor. But even among the venues I've competed in, Nandini Nagar stood out for being particularly bad. I competed there for the first time in 2009 in the Junior National Championships.

It made very little sense to conduct tournaments there. Nandini Nagar is a very small village in a very backward region. If it has any real importance, it's that it's just off the highway that goes from Lucknow to Ayodhya. The nearest railway station was Gonda junction, some 40 km away.

The real reason for conducting competitions in Nandini Nagar, of course, was that Brij Bhushan Sharan Singh, who was then president of the Uttar Pradesh State Wrestling Association, had insisted on the competition being conducted there. He was already an elected member of Parliament, and Nandini Nagar was in the heart of his constituency.

Getting to Gonda was hard enough. The trains passing through that part of the country were routinely overbooked. I, of course, didn't get a confirmed seat on my first journey to Gonda and spent the overnight ride sitting on a blanket that I laid out next to the washroom. Once we arrived, there was no place to stay in the town, so I just slept on the railway platform.

It was a thirty-minute drive to reach Nandini Nagar. Brij Bhushan Sharan Singh owned several degree colleges there. The tournament was happening in the playground of one of these colleges. A shamiana tent had been erected, with three mats, for the competitions.

There were nothing by way of facilities at Nandini Nagar. There wasn't even a shop next to the ground where I could buy something to eat or drink. It was terrible.

While anyone who could afford to stayed close to Ayodhya, everyone else, including me, would be put up in one of the classrooms of the college where the competitions were held. We would move the desks and chairs to a corner and clear a space where we laid out the blankets, pillows and mattresses that we had brought from our homes. There was only one common toilet where we both washed and relieved ourselves. The door to that was broken, so we had to drape a towel across the door posts for some privacy.

Those Junior National Championships were the first time a tournament was being conducted in Nandini Nagar, but once Brij Bhushan Sharan Singh became the Wrestling Federation president, it seemed than almost every other national championship would be held there.

The competitions there weren't as much wrestling tournaments as political events. Just as local organizers would vie with each other to hold *dangal*s in Haryana, conducting wrestling national championships was a way for Brij Bhushan Sharan Singh, a many-time member of Parliament, to show his voters just how important he was. He would call people from the nearby villages to the competition and distribute ladoos and other sweets to them, as we wrestled under that shamiana tent.

When he became president of the federation a few years later and cemented his hold on wrestling in the country, he started lording over the participants at these tournaments. He'd himself be seated on a platform overlooking all the mats. He'd have a microphone in his hand and would pass comments on what was going on. He'd sometimes berate and abuse players, coaches and referees if they did something that angered him.

If there was any bout he considered important, he'd come down from his platform and stand and take pictures with the two wrestlers right there on the mat. He's stopped contests mid-bout so he can get his picture. We had to stand and wait until he came to the mat if he wished to be photographed with us. We might have just gone through a bad weight cut (more on this later) or the competition might be getting late, but we had to wait for him.

Brij Bhushan Sharan Singh was very rich, and if he wanted he could have organized competitions in a much better manner, but he never did. No one thought of complaining. At that time we thought this was just how national tournaments were usually conducted. Our job was to put our heads down, compete, win and, hopefully, move on to international competitions.

I did just that at that the Junior National Championships in Nandini Nagar. I kept my head down and won a gold. He took no notice of me at the time.

Three years later though, I wasn't this lucky. By this time he had become president of the federation, and darker stories about him had begun to spread in the camp in a way they hadn't about his predecessors. He wasn't just an ordinary politician but was what was called a *bahubali*, or strongman. Other stories too spread about him in the camps. That he'd killed someone and looted others. He had cases against him for rioting. That he was allegedly involved with the mafia. I can't say how true these stories were, although he has had many cases lodged against him. But this was his reputation among us wrestlers.

I heard but ignored these stories as best I could. My focus was always on my training. Some of the senior girls in the camp told me that he was a goonda and someone whom it was best to stay away from. I didn't need to be told twice, but even if we wanted to stay away from him, it was not his intention to allow us to. He started coming to the national camp, ostensibly to watch the selection trials for one of the international competitions for the season, but every girl figured he was someone whose interest in us wasn't just limited to wrestling.

He'd watch matches but then attempt to get overly familiar with the girls. He would get obsessed with certain girls and want to know everything about them. There were some physiotherapists at the national camp whose job it was to solely report to him on what those girls were doing. He wanted to know if they were in training, whether they would travel out of the camp, and whether they were dating anyone.

Some of the girls enjoyed the attention. They'd easily go up to him and chat with him. It was impossible to keep things hidden in the camp, and I heard about a couple of girls who either indulged him or were coerced by him into indulging him. Inevitably, these would be the girls whose names would be put up for exposure competitions and training camps abroad.

That was something that I could never do, partly given my nature and partly due to my knowledge of his background. I tried my best to avoid being noticed, but as the best wrestler in my weight class that was not possible. It was at one of the selection trials for the 2012

Junior Asian Championships, when I was nineteen years old, that his eye fell on me. After I won the trials, he came up to me and called me his bandar. Every time he saw me he'd say, 'Come here, *meri bandar*.' I resented being addressed as his monkey.

Within a few weeks I started getting the first calls from him on my phone. He started out by asking me if I needed anything. He promised me protein supplements since I was a good wrestler. When I ignored him, he told me to keep talking to him. He'd take me to incredible heights so long as I went along with him, he would say. If I stayed in his favour, he'd do all these things for me.

At first the calls were infrequent. But soon they just wouldn't stop. He'd sometimes call me on my phone and sometimes call up a physiotherapist, Dhirendra Pratap Singh Singh, who would make me speak to Brij Bhushan on his phone. I started getting calls when I returned home from the national camp, too.

He'd call on my mother's phone. He would make call after call on her phone.

The first time she got these calls on her phone, my mother physically smashed her phone, as if it would do something to us. My mother knew what was going on. She told me to keep my head down and focus on my career, and that he would eventually stop stalking me.

She'd answer the calls herself and say that I had gone out to train. She tried to be as polite as possible. She didn't want to do or say anything that would result in my career being ruined by someone who had the power to do so. There was always an underlying current of fear. He had absolute power in the federation. Every wrestler knew that. He wasn't going to go anywhere, which meant I couldn't do anything to annoy him. I had to learn to deal with him. My parents knew what a powerful *bahubali* he was. We knew how many cases he had against his name. This wasn't a secret. At the time he became the president of the federation, everyone knew that he was a gangster.

How do you fight back against someone like that? The best solution, according to my mother, was just to lay low. But try as she might, there was just no way for me to avoid him.

8

No Place to Hide

As much as I tried to avoid him, there was eventually no place to run. Unfortunately for me, that day came at the 2012 Asian Junior Championships at Almaty in Kazakhstan. What should have been amongst the highlights of my sporting career ended up being one of the most traumatic experiences of my life.

All my life I'd heard of how the Japanese and Chinese wrestlers were among the hardest to beat in women's wrestling. So far I had wrestled Japanese wrestlers three times at four separate Asian Championships at the cadet and junior levels and lost to them on two occasions. The one time I came out on top was in Almaty, when I managed to beat both a Japanese girl, Haruna Uehara, in the semi-final bout, and then a Chinese girl, Menyang Ji, in the final to win my first gold medal in the women's 63 kg category at the Asian Junior Championships.

It was easily the biggest win of my wrestling career.

As I stepped off the podium, who was there to greet me but Brij Bhushan Sharan Singh himself. He had a big smile on his face. 'I asked God to give you that gold medal,' he told me. He had been very conspicuously wearing a gold chain with a small medallion with an image of Hanuman at its tip, but he told me that it had gone missing right after I had won my match. He was saying that God had answered my prayers: 'He has taken my locket, but has given you one gold medal' – that was what he told me. Perhaps his medallion had actually gone missing. But I think it was much more likely that he was trying to trick me into thinking that he had some role to play in my winning the gold at the championships.

I didn't know what to make of this at that point. I already knew that he was trying to become too familiar with me for my comfort. He'd made all those calls to my home trying to convince me to speak to him by promising me protein supplements and other benefits. 'I'll take you to such incredible heights if you stay by my side,' he'd tell me.

I knew at that time that I was only delaying the inevitable. I knew that there was going to be a day when he would call me to his room and make a move on me. I wondered just how I would evade his advances. In the camps there were rumours that a couple of girls had been coerced by him into doing something, and I'd heard stories about how he'd call them to his room. I was terrified that this might happen with me, but had always avoided thinking too much about it.

The day I was dreading came to be at the Asian Junior Championships. After congratulating me on my win, he went back to his room while my roommate and I returned to ours. Once I was back in my room, he sent word through his physiotherapist Dhirendra Pratap Singh Singh that I should come to his room so that I could call my parents on his mobile phone and speak to them.

I started to think about what I would do if Brij Bhushan Singh did make a move on me. I told myself that if he said such and such a thing to me, then I would respond in a certain manner. If he tried to grab me, I had to push him off and kick him. I played out all these scenarios in my head.

I tried to pretend that I knew just how I was going to handle any possibility, but in truth I was terrified. Eventually though, the physio Dhirendra Pratap Singh came up to my room and accompanied me to Brij Bhushan Sharan Singh's room before leaving.

Brij Bhushan Sharan Singh connected me to my parents. It seemed harmless enough. When I spoke to them telling them about my match and my medal, I remember thinking that perhaps nothing unsavoury might happen after all. But right after I ended the call, he tried to molest me while I was seated on his bed. I pushed him off and started to cry.

He stepped back after that. I think he realized very clearly that I wasn't going to go along with what he wanted. He started saying that he had put his arms around me *'papa jaise'*, as a father would. But I knew that that was not what it was. I ran out of his room all the way back to mine, weeping all the way.

When I got back to the room I was in a state of shock. I felt physically nauseated. I didn't just feel violated, I also feared that because I had refused to give into his demands it would mean the end of my wrestling career.

I told just a few people about what happened. When I returned to India, I told my training camp roommate, Anita Sheoran. I told my mother, too. Although I didn't intend to spread the story, it did.

Everyone knew what had happened with me at Almaty. No one spoke out about it.

Neither did I.

For a long time I was both horrified and embarrassed by what had happened. I knew I had to bury this, because who would take my side against such a powerful individual? Nothing good could come out of dwelling on this.

But it was incredibly hard the first few months. A few months after the Asian Junior Championships, I took part at the 2012 Junior World Championships. I had won a bronze medal in the previous edition and was expected to do better this time. But I was just unable to focus on the competition. I felt full of fear just to get on the mat and ended up finishing seventeenth.

It would take me nearly four years to come to terms with what had happened that night in Kazakhstan. Whenever Brij Bhushan Sharan Singh came to watch a tournament or a selection trial, or if I had to compete at Nandini Nagar in front of him, I would try my best to avoid being noticed by him. That was impossible of course, because I was one of the best wrestlers in the country.

I had no option but to do well. And when I did, I had to meet him. For many years this thought was always stuck in my head – did he remember that day in his room at Almaty and what he had tried to force me into? Would he try to take revenge against me, somehow?

I tried to guard myself in every way I could. I made it a point to travel with someone from the family for the domestic competitions. I couldn't be by myself. I understood finally why the parents of so many female competitors make it a point to stay outside the national camp, somewhere close by. I'd try to pretend I was fine. But I could never chase away those feelings of fear and anxiety. It was many years later that I was finally able to interact normally with Brij Bhushan.

Although I regret not having spoken up earlier, I'm glad that I was able to at least tell many girls and my parents about what had happened. I am grateful that I didn't blame myself for what happened.

I had been molested in my childhood too, but for a long time I could not tell my family about it because I thought it was my fault. My tuition teacher from my school days used to harass me. He would call me over to his place for classes at odd times and sometimes tried to touch me. I was scared to go for my tuition classes but I could never tell my mom. This continued for a long time and I kept quiet about it.

Finally, one Sunday, he crossed all limits. I was terrified. I didn't know what to do. I thought my parents would hit me because I thought that this was somehow my fault.

When I finally told my mother, she called up one of her friends whose daughter also went to the same teacher for tuitions. This girl was older than me. My mother's friend asked her daughter if anything like this had happened with her at the teacher's and she said no. At that point my mother didn't know whether to believe me or not, so she asked if I would go for my tuition class the next day. I was in tears and said I wasn't going back to him, whatever may happen. My mother withdrew me from that class.

My mother supported completely me at the time. She told me to go for the class the next day and that she would follow me a minute later and 'show him'. She meant that she would slap him and hit him. I wasn't agreeable to that. I told her she could go his place and beat him up, but I could not face him again.

Even though I wanted nothing to do with that teacher, it was impossible to simply forget about the incident as I had to often pass by the lane where he lived. It took me many years to overcome the disgust and guilt I felt at what had happened.

This teacher always presented himself as a very decent person. His wife had passed away but he had a son and a daughter. He gave tuitions for children up to class twelve, so people felt he must be very knowledgeable. No one ever suspected him of sexually harassing school girls.

At that time I felt I was just really unlucky. I thought, 'Why me?' But I came to understand that in the 1990s, whether they were boys or girls, everyone faced this at some point in their lives. Probably 90 per cent of us from those times have faced something similar. There was just no knowledge back then that this was a very serious offence.

In the last decade, these issues have been talked about more openly. There have been TV shows on the subject. Parents too tell their children about good and bad touch. The children from the generations that came after mine are just a lot more mature that we were. They have phones, and they have a lot more understanding of the world than we did. We didn't have phones, we didn't have social media, and we didn't know how to determine whether something that made us uncomfortable was wrong or not. I was just a fifth grader who hadn't even started wrestling.

I consider myself lucky that my family and my mother were very supportive in these matters. There are many children whose parents don't even believe them when they complain. My mother supported me not just during the incident with the tuition teacher but also when Brij Bhushan started pursuing me.

I tried my best to forget about what had happened at Almaty. That's what my parents advised me to do too. They told me to focus on my training and competition. It doesn't seem like much today, but I was grateful that I was allowed to continue to train, at least. The society I come from is a conservative one. So many other parents from our community might have just taken their daughter out of training altogether in such a situation.

I still don't know why Brij Bhushan Sharan Singh chose to target me. I didn't think I was special in any way. I was a shy, quiet girl who wouldn't even try to meet anyone's gaze. I know now that it wasn't anything that I did and had nothing to do with what I was. I know now that what happened to me had happened to many other girls in the camp.

But I just kept my head down and continued to train as best I could. It was the only thing that made sense to me.

9

Making My Way Past the Seniors

Back in 2008, when I first participated in the national camp, Indian women's wrestling was nowhere near as successful as Indian men's wrestling. Indeed, right after my first national camp came the 2008 Olympics in Beijing, where Sushil Kumar won the first Olympic wrestling medal in over fifty years for India.

I didn't see the bout on TV, but I knew right away that it was a very big thing. Until then, no one really expected that Indians would do well at the world level. It was only after Sushil that many of us actually started thinking about the Olympics as a possibility. I knew what the Games were of course – the Olympic rings had been painted on the wall at the Chhotu Ram akhara, but they weren't something anyone actually considered was possible for an Indian to do well in.

I always dreamed that I would get to meet Sushil one day. I hoped I could talk with him and have pictures taken with him. I got that chance six years later, when the two of us were part of the team that competed at the 2014 Commonwealth Games.

But while Sushil's Olympic bronze was a turning point in Indian wrestling, there really wasn't an expectation that women could also win medals for wrestling in the Games. At that time, no Indian woman had ever even qualified for the Olympics, which had featured women's wrestling since 2004. Even a medal at the Asian Championships was considered a major achievement.

I was very far away from the Olympics then, though by 2008 I'd started making a name for myself. I won three cadet national titles straight and then two junior titles, too. I didn't really have a challenger at the cadet (under seventeen) or junior (under nineteen) divisions. After my first cadet nationals, I was either pinning my opponents down or beating them in technical superiority, which is when a bout is stopped after one contestant wins a 10-point lead over the other.

The other girls had an inferiority complex when it came to me. They knew I was training in the senior camp. I was already competing with the big girls. When I actually started beating the big girls, that fear got cemented. Everyone was nervous about wrestling me and I'd have almost no competitors in those trials. Most of the girls would opt to compete in a heavier or lighter weight class than mine.

By the time I competed in my first senior national championships in 2009, people had started to take notice of me. Everyone knew that there was this girl named Sakshi who was wrestling well. I went to my first senior nationals having already won the cadet and junior titles that year. I might have made history had I won the senior title too, but that was not to be. I lost in the semi-final round to Alka Tomar, who had previously won a world medal for India.

It wasn't a particularly close contest. I still had a lot to learn. But despite the loss I wasn't done with the competition. Alka reached the final, which meant I had the chance to wrestle for the bronze. This

Making My Way Past the Seniors

was possible under a rule called 'repechage'. Someone later told me it was a French word that meant 'to revive', but most of us just called it 'repcharge'! The first time most Indians, including myself, heard of this rule was when Sushil won his Olympic medal by repechage.

According to the repechage rule, if the wrestler you lose to goes on to reach the final of the competition, that gives you another chance to compete – not for a gold or silver but for a bronze medal. The wrestler who has lost to the eventual finalist in the first round wrestles the one who has lost to the eventual finalist in the second round. The winner of that match then faces the next wrestler who lost to the finalist in the quarter-finals. The winner of that match then takes on the one who lost in the semi-finals to the finalist. Repechage meant that even if you lost in an early round of a tournament you always had hope – that as long as the wrestler you lost to reached the finals, you could also return from the competition with a medal to show for it.

Having reached the semi-finals in my first nationals, I only had to wrestle in one repechage bout, which I won. Even though I did not win the gold, I was pretty happy to have won my first senior medal. I wasn't just the best junior Indian wrestler any more. I was finally making a push into the senior category.

Once it became clear that I was no longer a rookie, I noticed the attitude of the seniors towards me start to change. I was now a threat to their place in the national team. By 2009, Geeta Phogat was emerging as the best Indian woman wrestler in the 58 kg weight division. She made it clear that she wouldn't partner me even if the coach asked her to. I felt bad about it, of course, but I also understood the reasoning behind her decision.

Wrestling isn't a sport that can you can practise by yourself. If you are training technical movements you need someone to go up against. But that came with its own risk.

It's like having someone eat with you. They'll of course observe what you like to eat – roti or rice. Do you use a spoon? They'll observe how you eat and how often. It's the same thing when it comes to constantly wrestling with someone. You start to learn how they wrestle. Do they favour their right leg to attack or their left? Are they aggressive or are they counter-attackers? What would be their go-to technique under pressure? You learn to observe how they set up an attack and how to spot it early. It's true that I could also video-record an opponent's bouts and try to spot similar tells, but it's not the same. When you actually wrestle a player you can learn a lot more.

For example, when Vinesh and I were sparring together, I noticed that she was wrestling very low to the ground. I'd try to observe which direction her arm come from and which she favoured when making her attack. Vinesh was a supremely gifted wrestler, and at the start of a bout with her I'd always struggle to read what she was doing. But after a few sparring sessions I began to pick up what she was doing. My body instinctively started to react to her moves. When her arm came forward, my lead foot would automatically move back. The level of learning from this kind of practice was much higher than from any other. Vinesh and I could spar since the two of us were in very different weight classes. We knew neither of us was a threat to the other.

But that was not the same when it came to Geeta, Alka Tomar and Geetika Jhakar. Their fear was that I'd find out just how they wrestled and then use that knowledge to eventually beat them. That's how it would end up. If I practised against a lion, I might not win at first but I'd keep getting stronger. The longer I kept practising against these top wrestlers, the stronger I'd get.

Geeta's logic was that she was the number one wrestler in her

Making My Way Past the Seniors

weight category. So why should she help me get better when my goal was to replace her? Sure, I might do it anyway, but how was it in her interest to make it easier for me?

For the same reason, many of the girls would often not give their 100 per cent in the training matches the coaches would set up. I can't say that I didn't do the same thing later in my career too. When I became the best in my weight division, even I didn't like having to partner girls who I felt might become a threat to me in the future. If, for example, Geeta and I were competing together, I'd rarely spar at more than 70 per cent of my ability. I needed to keep some of my skill hidden, in case we actually fought a match which had consequences. For a long time I thought this was basic human nature. But I found out later on that this kind of insecurity was something more common in India than elsewhere.

After I lost to Alka Tomar in the semi-final of my first senior nationals, I made it to the final of the nationals in my second attempt, this time losing to Geetika Jhakhar. At this point in time, I was still competing and doing well in the junior age group, both nationally and internationally, also winning a bronze at the 2010 Junior World Championships as a seventeen-year-old.

Now I wasn't just satisfied with winning medals at the junior championships. Once I started making my place in the senior category, I started dreaming of entering the Olympics too. I wanted to fight in the Asian Games and Commonwealth Games too.

Even though it took me a few years from the time I first entered the senior category to start beating the top wrestlers of the time, I could see the gap between us narrowing. At the selection trials for the 2010 Commonwealth Games, I lost to Geeta Phogat by a very narrow 4-3 score.

I did feel bad about missing the Commonwealth Games in New Delhi that year because Geeta went on to win a gold medal there and become a household name. Her medal in Delhi resulted in Indians realizing that there was something like women's wrestling. A movie, *Dangal*, based on the Phogat sisters' achievements, was also made at the time.

After the initial disappointment wore off, though, I was filled with a sense of confidence. I was just eighteen years old. I had no business getting as close to Geeta as I did. Two years later, when she became the first Indian to qualify for the London Olympics, it really struck me how close I was to that competition myself. I felt I had almost beaten Geeta at the Commonwealth Games trials. If she could qualify for the Olympics, surely I could, too.

I finally won my first senior national title as a twenty-one-year-old in 2013, a year after Geeta competed at the Olympics. I had wrestled at the senior nationals twice before, losing to Alka Tomar in the semi-final in my debut and then losing in the final to Geetika Jhakhar in 2012.

My path to the title was anything but easy. I was once again up against Geetika Jhakhar in the final. I'd wrestled her twice before, most recently at the previous year's nationals, and had lost on both occasions. But I had been a junior then.

In 2013 though, I was ready to win. Geetika knew it too. From the time I had first arrived at the national camp, Geetika had had a bit of a reputation for being a dirty wrestler. She hadn't needed to employ her usual tactics the first couple of times we competed; that was because I really wasn't someone she needed to use them against. Now, for the first time in my career, I got to experience the range of her tactics.

Making My Way Past the Seniors

Wrestling's not an easy sport. It's a physical game and it's accepted that you have to manipulate your opponent's joints, forcing them to the ground against their will. But even in this sport there are wrestlers who stand out for being a bit free with the rules.

I later come across a few of those in the international circuit too. In India though, Geetika stood out for many years as a particularly difficult opponent.

In the final of the 2013 nationals, once she realized I was starting to take the lead, she started becoming rough. She'd scratch me with her nails. If I started going for a double-leg attack, she would grab my costume so she didn't fall over. On the ground she'd start to pull my knee joint against its normal range of motion. It served no real purpose other than to cause me an injury. I still had short hair at the time, but she would manage to grab a handful of it and yank my head back. If I put my hand out in front of me, she'd grab my fingers and twist them. When she got me in a headlock (kheme), she'd stick her thumb into my cheek, like a fish hook. At other times she'd stick a finger into my neck. I'm of course a little grateful that she didn't stick her finger in any other tender places, which was not unheard of in international wrestling.

Of course, what Geetika was doing was completely in violation of the rules. She should have been docked points for every one of these offences. But there is an art to these tactics. It's only illegal if the referee sees them. If you do it too many times, he could give you a warning or give the opponent penalty points too.

But a smart wrestler will make sure she never does anything too blatantly. There are many positions you get into in wrestling where the referee can't see what's going on. That's when you make your move. Geetika got caught smashing my fingers and pulling on my costume twice and had to concede two points as a result. But there was a whole lot of stuff she got away with.

The reason to wrestle this way is simple. You twist your opponent's fingers, bend her joints and pull her hair to get her to lose her concentration. It's in that fraction of a second that you can either attack or defend the attack on you. But Geetika's tactics didn't work.

When I was in the middle of a match, I just didn't feel anything. I might have had a terrible sense of fear in the moments before stepping on to the mat, but once on it, my mind was completely wired towards winning. The only thing I was thinking was that I had to win the match. I just wanted to make sure I applied my techniques. I didn't feel pain as much as a sense of irritation that someone was trying to break my concentration.

I was so close to winning my first national title, Geetika could have tried whatever she wanted but I wasn't going to give up. As I continued to pull ahead of her, she started to realize she wasn't going to get her way. She had tried her tricks when the score was still within her reach. Once I started leading 9-4 though, she kind of gave up. Just like that, I had my first national title.

It was only after the match was over and I had cooled down that I actually realized how tough the bout had been. My fingers were swelling and I discovered that several strands of my hair had been pulled out by their roots. The next day I noticed multiple bright-blue patches where my skin had bruised.

I'd always looked up to Geetika from the time I started to wrestle. I'd even made a card for her. But after a match like this, a distance started to form between us. It's hard to respect someone who wrestles this way. I did continue to say namaste and hello to her, but I never felt I meant it. Of course, the coaches will say this is wrestling, that all this happens. I hadn't come to play chess.

Some of them would later say I should have wrestled dirty against her too. There was no point in trying to be the good person in such a bout. But I was glad to have wrestled honestly and got to wherever that took me. All said and done, my match with her took me to my first senior national title.

10

The Fight before the Fight

It's one thing to make your way into the Indian team but quite another to compete at the international level, where the challenges only get harder. There are fewer easy matches. The opponents are less forgiving of your mistakes. You yourself have to be sharper with every attack.

I didn't last even a single round in my first senior international competition. Competing in the women's 63 kg category at the 2012 World Championships, I was pinned in the very first round by Alla Cherkasova of Ukraine. Cherkasova was a tough opponent to fight in my very first international bout. She'd go on to become a world champion and also claimed a bronze at the Tokyo Olympics. But what was really hard about that competition was that I had a massive size disadvantage.

The category in which you compete in Olympic-style wrestling is determined by your weight. If I had to compete in the women's 63 kg category, I had to show that my weight was under that limit. While the limit has been set so that wrestlers don't end up competing against opponents much bigger than them, this didn't always work out in practice.

The Fight before the Fight

From the time I started wrestling and right until 2018, when the rules changed, wrestlers had to stand on a weighing scale one day before their competition. We had to weigh in under the limit for the category in which we had entered our names. Once you had been weighed though, there was no actual limit to what your weight could be on the day of the competition.

Coaches always told us that 70 per cent of our bodies are composed of water and that so as long as you dehydrated yourself enough you could actually weigh in at a weight much lower than your normal weight.

Water weight can be regained, but it's a lot harder to compete against someone who has more muscle mass than you. If you are bigger than your opponent on the day of the competition, you have a clear advantage.

For instance, if I competed in the 58 kg category, as I would do at the Olympics, I'd normally weigh around 63 kg about a week before my weigh-in. I'd start dieting to lose that extra weight in the days leading up to my weigh-in. Once I lost the weight and got to 58 kg, I'd still have a day to recover and come back close to my normal body weight.

I'd be physically drained on the day of the weigh-in but I'd feel much stronger on the day of the competition. On the other hand, if I weighed 63 kg and competed in the 63 kg category, I'd most likely be up against women who'd normally weigh about 68 kg but would have got their weight reduced to 63 kg on the day of the weigh-in. So they would be stronger than me.

That's what happened at the 2012 Worlds. I should have competed in the 59 kg category, but at that time I really wasn't cutting a lot of weight. I was strong enough for the junior level, but among the seniors I just wasn't strong enough to wrestle someone who outweighed me by a significant margin.

It seemed obvious to me that I needed to move to a lighter weight division. What American wrestlers would call 'making weight' we called *wazan todna*, literally 'breaking weight', in India. And that was exactly what it was. It actually felt as if we were breaking our bodies each time we tried to enter at the right weight for a competition.

Losing 5 or 6 kg over a week is hard enough for a normal person. But as wrestlers we are already very lean. If you measure the fat in our bodies, it will constitute around 19–20 per cent of our body weight, which is already very low compared with the fat ratio in normal women. When you have to lose so much weight in a short period of time, you will normally losing water weight.

Losing weight is a very precise process. I'd usually have very specific targets in the weeks before a competition. I knew that after a particularly rigorous workout session I might lose perhaps 1.5 kg of water. That didn't of course mean I'd be 1.5 kg lighter the next day. I still had to eat and drink something so I could have enough energy to continue to train the next day.

Even if I ate some fruits and drank just a bare minimum amount of water, I'd still wind up recovering about 1 kg of my lost weight. So, even if I was really careful, I might lose only about 400 g of body weight each day. The next day I'd repeat the process. This would go on right until the day of my weigh-in.

Each day of the weight cut gets steadily harder than the previous one since, by the very end, your body is completely parched. There just isn't any more water to squeeze out. The last night before the weigh-in is always the hardest. We were always on the edge of dehydration by that time. That's the reason we couldn't always stay at the exact weigh-in weight over the course of the season. Weight cutting is a very unhealthy activity. As a wrestler I wanted to be in that zone of dehydration for as little time as I needed to be.

On that penultimate day before the weigh-in, I'd be constantly standing on an electronic weighing scales that the team carried along. We might forget to take our clothes with us, but we never forget those scales. Every so often, I'd hit a plateau. Everything would be going smoothly, and then I'd measure my weight and see I was stuck at 100 g short of where I needed to be. At that point I'd start to run in place, or go into the sauna and work out.

You are almost in a state of frenzy at this point, when you have brought your food and water intake to the bare minimum. This was a starvation diet, but you were constantly training through it all. For those last five days, every hour would feel as long as a day. That last day would never seem to end. You are on an empty stomach, your throat is dry and your body parched. It's impossible to sleep because you are so stressed. You keep wishing for the morning to arrive quickly, so you can have your weight taken and finally get something to drink and eat.

I'd obsess over what went into my body, almost to the gram. I'd usually have a target of a maximum of 300 g of food and drink every day the last few days leading up to the weigh-in. That meant maybe a couple of pieces of fruit and vegetables, a piece of chicken and maybe a little fruit juice. But sometimes, if you are careless or you aren't thinking clearly, you might eat an extra piece of fruit by accident. Then for the next hour I'd curse myself for how foolish I was. 'Why did you eat that extra piece? That's a hundred grams extra. How do you lose that?' I'd berate myself.

You really crave water like nothing else. I'd start fantasizing about drinking water, perhaps with glucose in it. Sometimes, if the craving became too hard, I'd take sips of water, up to 50 ml, and then curse myself as I ran to the machine to see how much damage I had done. If I saw I was a few grams heavier than target, I'd be filled with self-loathing. 'Oh shit, my weight has gone up so much, now I can't drink anything for another three hours.' Then, three hours later, I'd mount the scales once again, just to confirm that my weight had not gone up any further. I'd start praying to that machine as the digits flashed on the screen, 'Please don't go up!'

Most wrestlers have a few secrets to get to the correct weight on weigh-in day. These tips are passed on by the seniors to their juniors, should matters get desperate. Usually, the weight of a wrestling costume is about 200 g, which meant that if I was competing in the 58 kg category, I actually had to weigh 57.800 kg with nothing on. But sometimes, the machine would show 57.850 kg, so I knew that with the costume, I'd weigh over the limit. Try as I might, even after an hour of weight training and running in place, the number still wouldn't budge.

One solution was to trim the edge of the costume we wore to the weigh-in. The material of a wrestling singlet is very light, but it gets much thicker towards the bottom of the leg. There's also a ring of thick elastic there so that the costume will stick snugly against your body.

If you trimmed the bottom of your costume, you could lose another 30–40 g. And when every gram mattered, it could be critical. So instead of reading 58.040 kg as it otherwise might have, when you stepped on the scale with a trimmed costume, the weight would read exactly 58.000 kg.

The Fight before the Fight

I used this loophole in the system very frequently. My weigh-in costume would be different from the one I wore to the competition. I'd find my most worn-out and sheerest costume to wear for the weigh-ins. These would usually be costumes I'd competed in previously for many years.

Every wrestler, in India at least, kept a costume like that – the lightest one she had – specifically for weigh-ins. Even hair has some weight. But since I already had very short hair, it didn't make any difference if I shaved it. If you had very long hair, then I could see it making at least a tiny difference if you shaved it off, but that wasn't the case with me.

Cutting weight was always hard for me since my body had more muscle mass than most wrestlers. Sometimes my efforts weren't enough.

My worst weight cut happened at my first senior Asian Championships – the 2014 edition in Kazakhstan. I had a working theory that it was harder for me to lose weight in dry countries rather than in places where there was humidity. At least, that was the case with me. I've always found that where it's moist, it's a lot easier to work up a sweat.

I have no idea if there is a scientific explanation for this. It might well be just a psychological thing. But this is what I had heard and experienced. In India you have dry heat and sweaty heat, and I always found it easier to sweat when conditions were hot and humid. When you are trying to lose the last few grams of sweat, you come up with all sorts of ideas about what will do the trick. When I'd go to a country to compete, I'd scratch my forearm, and if my nail left a white mark, that meant I was going to have a difficult time. If, on the other hand, the scratch didn't leave a mark, I'd feel satisfied. '*Yaha weight todna mushkil nahi hone wala hai.*' It was going to be easy here to lose weight.

I got that tell-tale white mark when I drew my nail over my arm in Astana at the 2014 Asian Championships, where I was competing in the women's 60 kg category. I knew the weight cut here was going to be hard.

I knew from experience that I would lose my last 1.5 kg of body weight following my final training session before the weigh-in. When I stood on the scales after my workout though, I saw that I was still 700 g overweight. As I stared at the numbers, I thought there must be something wrong with the scales. They stood at an obstinate 60.70 kg. I couldn't process it.

It didn't help that I had gone three days with barely anything to eat or drink, so it was already becoming difficult to think clearly. I started looking for a sauna. Sitting in the high heat might shake off a few more obstinate drops of water. There wasn't one at the competition venue where I would train, so I went back to the team hotel.

I suddenly got this idea that if I sat upside down it might help my blood circulation or something and I might lose 200 to 300 g that way. Of course it wasn't going to work. My confusion was a bad sign that I had already dehydrated myself to a dangerous level.

I started feeling dizzy, and the next thing I remember was waking up and finding myself in the bottom of the sauna. I had blacked out, passing out on the floor. I managed to find some water and splashed it on my face. I was so delirious at the time that I thought if I sprinkled water on my face I'd absorb even more water.

Later in my career I would have a physiotherapist and a doctor with me to help me manage my weight cuts better. Even if they are not available, all experienced wrestlers cut weight with the help of a

The Fight before the Fight

partner because you will almost inevitably make stupid decisions for yourself when you are on the verge of dehydration. And sometimes, when you are on the verge of giving up too, you need someone to encourage you through the process. But during my first few international tournaments I tried to manage my weight cuts myself.

I still have no idea how I made the weight at Astana. Crazily enough, after resting about another half hour, I went back inside the sauna and once against stood upside down. I was once again close to blacking out. Although the sauna was in a hotel which was about a five-minute walk from the competition venue, I have no idea how I found my way there since it seemed like there were black curtains coming down in front of my eyes. At the competition venue I at once started working out, and after one hour of this finally shook off those final 700 g. To this day I have no idea if standing upside down in a sauna actually did something for me.

While what happened at Astana was an extreme situation, there have been many tournaments where I struggled to drop the last 200 g of body weight, panicked and began to run in place in my sauna suit inside the sauna.

It was unheard of to just give up. I knew of one instance where Vinesh wasn't able to make the weight in time for an Olympic qualification tournament and she was suspended by the federation for it. She was forced to write a very humiliating letter of apology before she was allowed to wrestle again.

Making the weight is what every wrestler considers the battle before the actual fight on the mat. At times it's even harder than the actual wrestling bout. There are some wrestlers who can cut a lot of weight and then manage their recovery faster. I wasn't one of them. After my weight cut in Astana, I was so broken physically that I was a shadow of myself on the mat and finished without a medal.

But weight cuts are a weird thing. There were some competitions, like the one at Astana, where nothing worked, and there were others where I shed weight smoothly and everything seemed to go perfectly. Not that it was easy. But at least I seemed to be getting the results I was working so hard for.

I think it's just luck that I never developed any eating disorder, messed up my periods or had any long-term health damage because of this weight cutting.

There were so many wrestlers who developed kidney problems because they dehydrated themselves to extreme levels. I know that there were other wrestlers who had it harder than me. Vinesh's weight cuts used to be extreme. I'd seen her up close at the Olympics, and the last five days before her weigh-in she was drinking just 200 ml of water a day while doing two high-intensity training sessions. She had a bottle of water where she had marked out just how much water she could drink.

I've also heard of others who would cut such extreme amounts of weight that they wouldn't be able to recover and had to hook themselves to a glucose or saline drip. I know it happens a lot more frequently in men's wrestling.

It seems insane to subject your body to all this, but I didn't think too much of it at the time. I was so laser-focused on wrestling that I'd do whatever I had to do. If *wazan todna* was what I had to do, then I'd do it. That was what I was there for. That's what I had to focus my mind on.

Certainly not on trivial things like dating and relationships.

11

Satyawart

That was what I believed, at least for much of my wrestling career – that I had no interest in boys.

My family had given me my first smartphone when I was travelling for the 2009 Junior Asian Championships in the Philippines. I very quickly learned that I could make calls over the internet and didn't need to go through the federation when I wanted to speak to my family in India.

But I also discovered that the internet was a way for me to connect with others. I created a Facebook account for myself, and very soon every other girl in the national camp was asking me to make one for them. I first made a Facebook account for my roommate Anita Sheoran, and then for Vinesh and Babita too.

We soon found out that the girls we would wrestle against in international competitions were also on Facebook. Sometimes they'd send us friend requests, and for the first time they weren't just names that we'd fight on the mat. We could now reach out and say hello to them. But it wasn't just girls from other countries who were sending us friend requests. We were getting them from some of the male wrestlers too.

One of the first friend requests I got within a few days of opening my Facebook account was from one Satyawart Kadian. I saw it and left that accept button unclicked for several months before finally responding, for no other reason than that I felt sorry for him. Later, Satyawart would tell me he thought I was very stuck up.

He sent me a 'hello' and I replied. We messaged infrequently, and then off and on, and then regularly. We mostly talked about wrestling but also got to know each other. I found out that we had attended the same school and that Satyawart was just a grade below me.

Even though Vaish School was a co-educational institute, boys and girls hardly ever spoke with each other. Even a hint of interaction would be viewed as outrageous behaviour. Although Satyawart knew that there was a girl in the same school who wrestled, he was too shy to speak to me.

I also found out that unlike me, he was from a wrestling family. His father Satyawan had even wrestled for India in the 1972 Olympics. I admit I was curious about Satyawart. He had emerged as one of India's top talents, winning a bronze medal at the 2010 Youth Olympics and in the Junior World Championships the next year.

For more than four years, our relationship – if you can actually call it that – was limited to messaging each other on our phones. Neither of us actually dared to meet the other in person.

That changed in 2014, when the two of us were picked to be in the same squad competing in the Dave Schultz Memorial competition in Colorado Springs in the USA. There, for the first time, Satyawart asked me if we could meet in person. I refused right away – just think of the outrage that we were sure to bring on ourselves. He kept at it, though. Finally, he said that if I should win a gold medal at the competition, then the least I could do was to buy him an ice cream as a treat.

I thought this was as good an opportunity as any to get him off my back as soon as possible, since no Indian had ever won a gold medal in that competition. I didn't think I was going to be the first. I was twenty-two and had never won a senior international competition, and the Dave Schultz Memorial competition was one of the most prestigious international wrestling tournaments.

Call it luck or whatever, but I managed to win that competition, beating Jennifer Page of the USA – a future Pan American champion and world medallist – in the final. Despite winning the gold medal though, I was nothing but nerves in my hotel room. I knew I now had to meet Satyawart, and that wasn't what good girls did.

I tried telling him that I wasn't serious about actually meeting him, but he said I was going back on my promise and that he would sit in protest outside my hotel door until I agreed to meet him. I was terrified a coach might actually see him waiting there, and so agreed. I told my roommate I was going out for a walk.

I warily made my way to the 7-11 outside our hotel where Satyawart said he would be waiting. I was so nervous I couldn't even bear to look at him directly. I was terrified of meeting men, especially as I knew I wasn't considered attractive.

I had my hair cut in a boy's style and I had never waxed my upper lip or shaped my eyebrows. I started doing all that when I had to go for my brother's wedding in 2015. My face was bruised from the pushing and shoving it had received in the tournament. I even had a black eye. I was as raw as I could get. I thought Satyawart was very good looking. He was tall and powerfully built, but had very gentle eyes. That made me feel even more self-conscious.

Satyawart, however, didn't seem to notice all those things I was so conscious about. Even though it was supposed to be my treat, he paid for a couple of chocolate bars, which we ate silently. In hindsight, considering that I was supposed to be in hiding, I should have chosen a less conspicuous activity. Our competition was in January and it was snowing heavily outside – hardly the right time to have an ice cream outdoors.

Once we finished our ice creams, Satyawart asked if he could hold my hand. I wasn't that bold as to allow him to. I rushed back to my room, thrilled and scandalized in equal measure.

We continued to message each other, though, and at the Asian Championships in Kazakhstan a few months later, Satyawart once again asked me to meet him. Since he was going through a weight cut, he asked me if I had any Indian food that I could share with him once he had made his weight. I justified the meeting to myself, saying this was still sports-related. I handed him some food and tiptoed back to my hotel room so that no one saw me.

I didn't do well at the Asian Championships but Satyawart won a bronze. He asked to meet me on the third floor of the hotel, where we knew no other Indians were staying. We couldn't dream of meeting where we might run into another Indian. There he handed me a rose from the bouquet that he'd been presented along with his medal.

I took it back to my room, back to India, and preserved it in resin. I still have that rose with me today!

Being in a relationship with a boy was a very big deal. There were other girls in the camp who we suspected had boyfriends, but these relationships were always kept a secret. The other girls might know about it, but you couldn't flaunt your relationship in open society.

If you were a boy, you were breaking all sorts of rules. Hanuman-ji himself never married. Wrestling boys were expected to be like him. They were supposed to be bachelors as long as they were wrestling. If you were a woman you weren't supposed to be anywhere around wrestling. It was already a very big deal that we were allowed to wrestle at all. But to be in a relationship with a boy was forbidden at a completely different level, and that had nothing to do with wrestling. That was something just not done in our society.

Some of that mindset had rubbed off on me too. My thinking in 2013 wouldn't have been very different from a woman's from twenty years before. I thought relationships with boys were a waste of time. I didn't think too highly of some of the girls in the camp who I knew had boyfriends. We had come to wrestle. We couldn't be going around with boys. I avoided even being friends with boys for a very long time.

I just couldn't put myself in a position where I felt I could be distracted from my wrestling ambitions. I wanted to go to the Olympics. I always thought a girl who talks to boys can't ever think of winning a medal at the Olympics. Even when I started talking to Satyawart, I would have doubts and wonder if I was doing the right thing. I shared these worries with Satyawart. I told him perhaps he wouldn't have a good career if he kept talking to me.

To be fair, there weren't great omens. Satyawart injured his hamstring and couldn't wrestle at the Dan Schultz tournament, while I didn't win a medal in Kazakhstan at what was my first senior Asian Championships.

But our fortunes turned. I won a silver at the 2014 Commonwealth Games after beating a very strong wrestler from Canada. Satyawart too finished with a silver there. It's only after that that I felt a little less guilty that I had developed feelings for him. He wasn't a distraction, after all.

I always consider myself lucky that Satyawart never betrayed the trust I had in him. My fears about relationships weren't just something that ingrained in me by society. I'd seen enough examples of girls whose lives were absolutely ruined by their boyfriends. The boyfriends would be possessive and controlling. They'd question what food their girlfriends ate and whom they ate with. If you looked at someone they'd be jealous.

Before I met Satyavart I had a roommate who had fallen for the worst possible man. She was one of the most talented wrestlers I knew, but she wasted the best years of her career because she was in a relationship with a man who was extremely possessive.

Once, on a Saturday, she had gone to watch a movie with some of the other girls from her hostel, when she got a call from her boyfriend. He forced her to leave the theatre and go back to the hostel. She tried to explain that she was only out with other girls, but he couldn't stand it that she'd gone out at all. Apart from the mental trauma he brought her, he'd also abuse her physically.

She ultimately left him and went on to make it to the Olympics, but she was a long way off her prime when she did do so. She was such a talented wrestler and I always felt she should have made it to the Olympics before I did. She could have been one of India's great wrestlers but she was broken by the boy she had fallen for.

If Satyawart had been that way, who is to say my career wouldn't have gone her way too.

But he's the most relaxed person imaginable. He's not from the most progressive of families, but he's never been jealous of my achievements or felt that he had something to prove.

He never tried to pressure me to meet him and he didn't even try to touch me. At one of our first meetings I told him I'd only be in a relationship with someone if I was going to marry him. I wasn't interested in a casual fling. There's nothing that could have stopped him from lying and saying he was absolutely serious about marrying me. But he didn't say 'sure' right away.

Instead, he asked me for my mother's and grandmother's maiden names. He did that because he wanted to know if they were from the same gotra or clan as his mother and grandmother. In Jat culture, if my grandmothers were from the same gotra as his, then there was no way we could get married. That would be the biggest taboo in our culture – equivalent to siblings getting married. These were very strict rules that I, despite being someone who was doing something so radically different from women of my grandmother's and mother's generations, had to accept.

My grandmother came from the Ahlawat gotra while his were from the Kadyan and Kundu gotras. Their gotras weren't the same. 'Now we don't have to worry about that,' he told me. 'I've given you my word. I will never leave you.'

I sometimes wonder just what Satyawart saw in me. He tells me he knew about me not just from school but also because some of the boys from the Chhotu Ram akhara had told him that I had trained with them and was a very quiet and disciplined girl. And he had decided that if he was ever going to be with someone, it had to be me. After we started messaging and he got to know me, he said he only had eyes for me because he felt I thought the same way as he did.

I still find that hard to believe, what with my unwaxed appearance and my eyebrows that looked like two thick caterpillars. Satyawart, though, has never had a problem with any of this. If I tell him I don't like my hair style and want to change it, he'll say it looks fine either way. He's never cared if I wax my arms and legs or not. It makes no difference to him. He loves me all the same. Even when my body hair has grown and I haven't waxed, he'll never comment on it. Most guys are not like that. They'll comment along the lines of, 'Ugh, that's disgusting.'

He doesn't expect me to wait on him, as some men do. Although I feel I depend on him immensely, our relationship is mostly one of equals. It's not the one where I'll fast and touch his feet on Karwa Chauth and then abuse him the other 364 days of the year. Satyawart always says these rituals are all a show. He's far more of a rationalist than I am. In fact, I've never ever fasted for my husband and he's never asked me to. Both of us know that cutting weight in wrestling is hard enough as it is. In a way, I have been fasting for so many years.

Although I feel I've lucked out with someone like him, I always wonder just how there's such a big difference between the thinking that prevails in India and the thinking in some other countries. Here, if a girl simply stands next to her boyfriend, all hell breaks loose. When I interacted with girls from the USA, they all seemed to have boyfriends and were happily introducing me to them. And that didn't stop them from winning Olympic medals. When I dated Satyawart, it was always this massive secret, and even after we started seeing each other, we'd never stand next to each other, for fear that someone might pick up on our relationship. We would hide and meet each other.

I finally told my family about him after about a year of meeting him. I broached the subject very gently. I told my family I was friends with this guy, and over a period of time they and Satyawart met too. My parents started to trust him, and finally they invited him to my brother's wedding in 2015. While it was hard for me to tell my family about the association, it must have been even harder for Satyawart to tell his. Their acceptance was equally significant. My father-in-law had been a wrestler. He had been raised thinking wrestling was inseparable from brahmacharya, or bachelorhood. He was an Olympian and wanted nothing more than Satyawart to follow in his footsteps.

He too came around to Satyawart and I being together. He was happy that Satyawart was still focused on training. And we weren't dating the way most other young people were. We never went out to the movies or on dates. We'd talk over the phone, but the only time we really saw each other was when we went for competitions overseas. That was probably good motivation for the two of us to work even harder. Basically, I had to become an international player to get my relationship started, and I had to stay one to keep it going.

12

Making It to the Olympics

All wrestlers have a certain level of tolerance to pain. We routinely get our hair pulled, our fingers yanked, our faces bruised and our arms and legs twisted in all directions during a match. Yet, even as I was continuing to make my mark as a wrestler, it was getting harder to ignore a persistent shriek of pain inside my left knee.

The root of the problem had nothing to do with wrestling. I had first damaged the joint at the start of 2008, at my first senior national camp. After a few weeks the pain went away and I eventually began to wrestle again. What I didn't know was that I had a far more serious underlying issue. Both my ACL (anterior cruciate ligament) and MCL (medial cruciate ligament) – the two ligaments that stabilize the knee during twisting and forward motion – had been torn.

The pain would come and go. I'd have moments when everything would be fine, then I'd land awkwardly on my knee or it would be torqued roughly during a match and the pain would start all over again. There would be a persistent feeling that my knee was going to slip. Sometimes the knee would just lock and I would have to physically pull it free. At other times there would be a burst of pain inside the joint. If the pain got too bad I'd just avoid using that leg for a few days and the pain would eventually subside.

This cycle went on for many years, until after the 2015 Asian Championships when it hit its peak. I had started being sponsored by JSW a couple of years ago and I finally decided to see just what was wrong with the knee. At that point, since I was still trying to wrestle with my injured knee, my physiotherapists tried to put me on a rehabilitation programme. They soon realized the problem was far more serious than just physiotherapy could treat.

I went to see Doctor Dinshaw Pardiwala at Mumbai's Kokilaben Hospital. Dr Pardiwala has fixed the joints of nearly every elite Indian sportsperson and is known for being something of a miracle worker. He explained the extent of my injuries with a simplicity that masked how grim my options were. Both my ACL, the ligaments in the front of the knee, which control forward movement and rotation, and my MCL, the ligament inside the knee socket that stabilizes the knee, were torn. I had to get surgery.

Because the ACL is a much larger ligament, reconstruction is a complicated process. I burst into tears when Dr Pardiwala said it would take eight months for me to recover after the surgery. Eight months away from the game meant my career over the next couple of years was as good as over. I'd miss the National Championships and the Commonwealth Games outright. I'd only be able to return to training sometime in 2015, even as qualifications for the Rio Olympics were underway. It would take me even longer to get to a position where I could actually compete seriously.

I did not want to get operated on at all. I spoke with my family and with Satyawart, who told me I could still find a way to return to training. I wasn't so sure. I had a dream, and now it seemed as if it was going to be put on hold.

Any regular doctor would have advised me to get surgery to fix my ACL. But as someone who had worked extensively with athletes, Dr Pardiwala was able to see why I was so hesitant to commit to a procedure that would cause me to miss one of the most important tournaments of my career at that point. He had another option. The surgery to repair my meniscus was unavoidable. The meniscus was in the space between my knee joints. Left untreated, it would send shards of solidified tissue travelling across my joint. It would be as if my knee was constantly grinding on glass. Those shards would damage more tissue and would get progressively harder to treat.

But I could live with and even manage to compete with a torn ACL. I'd always heard that it was impossible to play with a damaged ACL. Dr Pardiwala explained that he had seen even footballers play with partially torn ACLs. I could possibly compete for a lifetime with a partial tear to my ACL, but unless I fixed my meniscus I would eventually be back on his table. While a torn ACL would lead to a loss of stability in the knee joint and create a sense of imbalance, it wouldn't cause pain. A tear to the meniscus, though, would result in constant pain. It was also leading to my knee locking.

While an injury to the meniscus was more painful, it was also smaller than the ACL ligament injury and was easier to treat. Dr Pardiwala said I would be able to return to the mat in a little over a month and could compete at the National Championships a month and a half after that. Instead of taking eight months off for an ACL surgery, I got only my meniscus surgery done. And a month and a half later I played in the nationals and won the gold.

Over the years, I've never got surgery for my ACL injury. I never even got a test done to see just how badly that ligament was torn. I don't know if it's completely snapped or if it's a partial tear or a third

Making It to the Olympics

of the ligament is left in place. I've come to a sort of understanding with it. I accept there's going to be a problem with it every once in a while, but I've learned to deal with it.

As the doctor had promised, I was back on the mat shortly after my surgery. After winning the National Championships, I qualified for my first Commonwealth Games, where I reached the finals and won a silver. That was the biggest international medal of my career at that point.

Avoiding that knee surgery was a critical decision in my career. I know that had I undergone a major surgery, there was no guarantee that I would have been able to wrestle at the level I had done previously. Even while I managed to avoid that ACL surgery, Geeta Phogat, who was one of my biggest role models and had been the biggest star in the women's 58 kg category, wouldn't. She underwent a surgery to repair her ACL in 2014. As a consequence she missed out on the 2014 Commonwealth Games where I won a silver.

She was also no longer the same force after her return from surgery in 2015. Although she did make the team and competed at the World Championships in Las Vegas, she lost early and missed the chance to win a quota at what was the first qualification tournament for the Rio Olympics.

Later that year, we competed against each other in the first edition of the Pro Wrestling League – a professional team-style competition. There, for the first time in my career, I beat Geeta 8-8. Although the scores were tied, I won on the basis of scoring the final takedown of the match.

Despite this, my place in the Indian team wasn't a done deal. Some of the hardest competitions to prepare for aren't international tournaments but the selection trials at which you earn the right to compete at these international games. There was an air of uncertainty over international competitions. It's harder to worry about something you don't know much about. On the contrary, I knew all the girls I would have to face in the selection trials. I'd been wrestling with them for many years. Some of them were wrestlers I admired. I wanted what they had. There were others, young ones like myself, who were looking to make their own place at the top. All of us wanted the same thing.

All of us wanted to have a psychological edge over the other when we got to the trials. The best chance to do this was in the sparring matches that were conducted once or twice a week to simulate an actual competition. We would often be paired with the opponent we knew we were going to face at some point in the actual trial. I was under constant stress during these bouts. I knew I couldn't lose those matches, because that might reduce the pressure my opponents felt when they played me.

If I lost one point here and there, I'd feel sick in the stomach. I wouldn't be able to swallow my food. All I'd be thinking in the hostel cafeteria would be, 'She's scored against me. Oh no, she's countered my attack.' I'd be unable to shake off that sense of dread and worry for a few days until we had a next round of sparring matches where I could reassert myself.

Compared with the build-up to them, the competition matches themselves were easier to handle. I had had two very close matches against Geeta Phogat in the past. She'd beaten me on the basis of having scored the last point after we had been locked 8-8 at the end of our match in the selection trials for the World Championships a year before. I had beaten her by the same system, which is known as 'criteria' at the Pro Wrestling League that year.

However, in the selection trial for the Olympics, I comfortably beat Geeta for what would be the final time in her career. She would never wrestle again after that defeat and retired soon after.

I, though, had more fights waiting for me.

I wasn't able to win a quota in my first qualification tournament – the Asian Qualifiers in Kazakhstan. I got a win against China, but then was pinned even before I knew what had happened by Mongolia's Pürevdorjiin Orkhon in the Olympic qualification bout.

Instead of giving me a second chance, the federation decided to send Geeta to the next qualification tournament, the first World Qualifiers in Mongolia. Geeta once again lost early in the competition and it was decided that I would be part of the Indian squad that would take part in the final Olympic qualification round in Ankara. The Indian team which was supposed to compete in Ankara was sent to a training camp in Bulgaria along with a number of other wrestlers.

I had thought the camp was going well, and with four days left for the team to fly out for the final Olympic qualifier in Ankara, I started cutting weight in order to make the 58 kg weight limit. All my focus was on this process, and I had about 3 kg of weight still left to lose when all of a sudden I was informed by the coaches that there was to be another trial, just in my weight category.

I was the only wrestler expected to give that trial. My opponent wasn't even Geeta, whom I had beaten in the final of the selection trial, but the third-placed wrestler. She wasn't even part of the first team that was in Bulgaria, but part of a second team that been sent, supposedly to give us sparring partners. I had long felt she was being favoured by the president, but I had kept my suspicions to myself.

I called Satyawart and my family in tears and they tried to console me. Satyawart said that if it was in my destiny to qualify, then I would win those trials. I didn't want to undergo the trials because I feared I would lose. I had already beaten that same opponent in India. But cutting weight is a psychologically challenging process. Mentally I just wasn't ready for a sudden trial competition. I was only thinking about getting to Ankara and managing to make my weight.

I went to Kuldeep Malik, the chief coach with the national team. I asked him why I was the only one who had been asked to take another trial. He didn't have an answer. That was known to everyone. Brij Bhushan Sharan Singh had decided on it, and no one dared to say a thing against it. I had stood up to him. I had pushed him away when he grabbed me. Now I was going to pay for it.

I did wrestle that match. I was terrified through all of it. I wrestled as safely as I could. I was just trying my best not to put myself in a position where I could be scored on at all. I managed to eke out a 3-0 win. It was one of my poorest performances but a crucial one. It put me on the flight to Ankara.

Despite all the stress, I did manage to make my weight. That was one half of the battle won. But the other half still remained. In the line in the room where we had to show our weight, I tried to see just who my competitors might be. There were only two quotas from the competition, which meant I needed to make it to the final to qualify for the Olympics.

I singled out four competitors as the big threats to that final-place finish. There was China's Zhang Lan, a former world champion, the reigning European champion Emese Barka of Hungary, the world bronze medallist Tetiana Kit of Ukraine and the Russian Valeria Koblova, to whom I'd lost at the Junior World Championships several years before.

Making It to the Olympics

I thought to myself that this was going to be hard. '*Bhaisahab*, these four girls are going to be really tough. I need to come either first or second.' I hoped really hard that when the draw was made I would not get to face too many of them. Although we didn't have any say in the choice of our opponents, we did indirectly get to choose just what our draw would look like.

We'd go up to a computer and press a button and have a random number assigned to us. That number would determine which group we were in. We had all sorts of weird beliefs about those numbers. I'd think that if I got my lucky number I'd never lose. I was born on 3 September, so I'd hope I got the number 3 assigned to me. I'd think that that would give me a favourable draw. Other contestants would hope for a 7 or a 10. I eventually stopped believing in all this once I got a terrible draw even with my lucky number, but at Ankara at least, the number I got proved to be lucky for me.

I managed to avoid being in the same group as both Russia and Ukraine, and though I was in the same side of the draw as China and Hungary, the two were facing each other before they got to me.

I wasn't really tested in the matches I had. I beat Irene Garcia of Spain 10-0 and then beat Kateryna Zhydachevska of Romania by another 10-point margin. China's Zhang Lan beat Barka in the other side of the draw, so I knew I had that one really tough match to get through in the semi-final.

I knew it was going to be hard, but I also knew that it was going to be my last chance to make it to the Rio Olympics. I had to give my best.

I think I actually gave more than what I considered my best in that match. I was wrestling a world champion. We traded attacks all through the match. I opened with a takedown and she did the same with me. I'd go up 4-2, and before I knew it the referee had his thumb and forefinger raised in favour of her and the digital scoreboard on the side of the mat would have us level once again. I'd lead and she'd pull back. There were no slow periods where I could draw a breath. We were just constantly in range, either trying to set up our attacks or actually attacking.

Even though he was yelling from behind me, I hardly heard what coach Kuldeep Malik was saying. I didn't know if he was telling me to block or to attack, if I had to watch out for any attack or if I had to use a certain technique. It's one of the dilemmas of stress.

When I am relaxed and the match is going well, I always hear everything the coach tells me. It makes complete sense and I wonder why I don't listen to him more often. But the truth is, when you are in a really stressful situation all your focus is just on the opponent in front of you. You can't squeeze in a second thought. Even as the coach is telling me what to do, my brain shouts him down with a hundred different plans. If I am leading 8-2, I can hear him perfectly. But if it is a 5-5 match with half a minute to go, that's when feel I am alone with what feels like a traffic jam in my brain.

There are some days when I'd get stuck in that jam. Ankara wasn't one of those days. Out of instinct I landed my favourite technique – the double-leg takedown – late in the match. I threw myself at her legs, took her off the ground and landed her on her back. 10-6 to me. Four points of breathing space.

I started sneaking glances at the digital clock next to the match then, trying to see how much longer I'd have to soak in this stress. That was one of the other dilemmas in wrestling. If you are trailing, it seems the clock is running really fast. You look away for a second and it seems fifteen have passed. And on the other hand, when you are trying to defend points, like I was in Ankara, time seems to be slowing down. You can see the numbers on the watch creeping down. One minute and fifteen seconds left. Pause. One minute fourteen seconds left. You are almost praying. God, please make the time go a little faster.

It wasn't going fast enough. In my moment of distraction, Zhang made a desperate attempt, and it worked. With just seconds to go, she took me down. Just a 2-point game now. She trapped my hand and turned me on my back. Another two points gone.

The scores though, were nearly irrelevant now anyway. I was on my back, with one hand unable to move and Zhang right on top of me. It's the worst position I could have wished myself to be in. I arched my spine, and using my hips and the back of my head for leverage, pushed my shoulder blades off the mat in desperation. If they both touched the mat, the referee would slap his hand on the mat and call the pin. It was taking all my strength to simply not lose.

In my upside-down position, even as I tried as hard as I could to keep my shoulders off the mat, I could see the digital clock, upside down too. I could see the micro-seconds ticking away, but they were not counting down fast enough. I could also see the referee on his knees while looking alternately at the judges on the opposite ends of the mat. He was waiting for their approval to signal the pin.

He was going to. He had to. Any second now.

I never heard the pin.

The buzzer signalling the end of the bout sounded. But there was no slap on the mat. Still upside down, I could see some of the Indian fans in the crowd jumping up and down. It seemed bizarre that they were cheering even as I was about to lose. Then I saw the score on the scoreboard, it was still 10-10. There was a little understroke on the 10 on my side of the scoreboard. My double-leg takedown had been the biggest point-scoring move of the match.

I could see that Kuldeep coach was jumping and shouting, and I realized I had somehow managed to hold on. Maybe five seconds more and I would have been pinned. I knew that. But I also knew I'd held on. I rolled over on the mat and started to cry. I was still crying when Kuldeep coach came up to me. He didn't have to tell me what I already knew. I was going to be in the Olympics.

The match won, my body finally gave up. I'd given more of myself over the past six-and-a-half minutes than I'd ever done before in that span of time. I never felt anything during the match. My brain was just wired to have me wrestle. But now, all of a sudden, I found myself unable to breathe. All my strength seemed to have left me and I felt like dead weight as Kuldeep and another coach physically helped me off the mat and into a side room. I began to retch violently. I still couldn't stand, so coach Kuldeep held me over a dustbin so I didn't puke on the floor. He shouldn't have bothered because nothing but wet air seemed to come out of my mouth. My throat felt as if it was peeling from the inside out. As I dry-heaved into that dustbin, I was praying that I would be able to start breathing normally again.

My whole body seemed as if it was on fire. My lungs were burning. It even seemed as if there was something inside my hands too, itching violently. My fingers were no longer under the control of my brain. Every part of my body seemed to be sore all at once.

I could barely get water down my throat. Coach Kuldeep vigorously squeezed my arms trying to push out the lactic acid, but it didn't seem to do anything. I simply wanted to be able to lie down and wait for my body to recover. I had nothing more to give.

Eventually, I did recover and Vinesh came up to me to congratulate me. She'd qualified for the Olympics too, albeit with not nearly as much of a struggle. But it didn't matter. Both of us had qualified for the Olympics. Neither of us could believe it. 'Vinesh, are we seriously going to the Olympics,' I asked her. We pinched each other just to remind ourselves it was actually true. It hurt, and we knew it was.

The two of us were roommates at the 2014 Commonwealth Games, which, like the Olympics, were a multi-sport event. Vinesh had also been to the 2014 Asian Games, but the Olympics are the Olympics! Neither of us had been to one and we had no idea just what we could expect at Rio. We talked into the night about what it would be like to compete in the Olympics. We knew it was going to be the biggest competition of our career. Even though we had the pinch marks to remind ourselves that we weren't imagining any of it, it wouldn't sink in for a few days more.

I was relieved to have finally won the quota. The rules back then were clear. Anyone who won the Olympic quota would go to the Olympics. At least now I hoped I would be able to prepare for the competition instead of being subject to the whims of the president and forced to undergo trials when he felt I should.

While I was never sure if he might change his mind again, with each passing day it seemed to me that I would indeed be going to the Olympics. When I got back to India, I was included in the government's target Olympic podium (TOP) scheme, which was meant to provide funding for India's Olympic athletes. The government even gave us Rs 1.5 lakh for some shopping before we left. That's when I started to believe that yes, I was actually going to Rio.

I had three months from the day I qualified in Ankara to when I actually competed at the Rio Olympics. The national camp for

Olympics-qualified wrestlers shifted from Lucknow to Bahalgarh since the latter was closer to Delhi, where it would be easier to process our visas. Vinesh and I had qualified for the Olympics at the world qualifiers. We were later joined by Babita Phogat, who qualified after an opponent she had lost to in Ankara failed a dope test.

Each of us was permitted to take one training partner in Bahalgarh. Although she was much younger than me, I picked Sangeeta Phogat because Vinesh, who was my friend, asked me if I could bring her along. Sangeeta's brother Dushyant also joined the camp. He was of a similar weight as the two of us, but was of course stronger since he was a male, which would make him an ideal sparring partner.

Of the three women who had qualified for the Olympics, I think I was the one who was the least favoured to win a medal. Babita was a world medallist and a two-time Commonwealth Games gold medallist. Vinesh was seen as the next star in Indian wrestling and also had a Commonwealth gold. More than that, they were both from the Phogat family. The film *Dangal* had been released a couple of years before, but it was still very popular. They were the face of Indian women's wrestling.

No one seemed to have any belief in my ability to win a medal at the Games. Not even my parents, not even Satyawart. It's not that they didn't love me. But the fact was that I was a complete underdog. For most people it was already a big deal that I had even qualified for the Olympics. It wasn't just they. Even I felt I would only be ready to win a medal at the Tokyo Games in 2020.

My own mindset had really started to change in the year before the Olympics. Around the time that we first started seeing each other, Satywart had told me about a book, *The Secret*, which he said he had read. Since I did not read books, he sent me a few YouTube clips about the book. Those clips told me about the power of manifestation, according to which if I actually visualized something, I'd start working towards accomplishing it.

It sounded made-up, but Satyawart insisted I watch those clips. I started visualizing myself winning matches. I visualized that I was beating Geeta Phogat. I started thinking that there might actually be something to this concept, when I actually did beat Geeta for the first time at the Pro Wrestling League and later at the selection trials. I next started visualizing myself winning the Olympic quota, and when that happened, my belief that we could visualize things into existence only grew.

I now started visualizing myself winning an Olympic medal. I genuinely started believing it was going to happen. Geeta Phogat had been the first Indian woman to qualify for the Olympics, and I had beaten her in the selection trials. I was also at my physical peak as a wrestler.

I visualized myself winning my medal match, the Indian flag being draped on me, and then doing a lap of the mat with it over my shoulders. I had made a movie of all these moments in my head. But I was also the only one who seemed to be able to see it.

I started writing a diary six months before the Olympics. I would write down what I was doing in training each day and where I was lacking.

In that diary I'd write down how many repetitions I would do. We had a thirty-foot rope at the wrestling hall. One day I wrote I'd climbed it twenty-five times, which was a personal best. I'd note down how many free squats and *dand baithak* I did too. My record in the free squats was a consecutive 600, and I would try to break that every time I trained.

I'd record my scores in sparring matches and 'measure' just how confident I was feeling. There were many days when everything went well and I'd give myself a score of 100 out of 100. There were also days where I was tired and sore and my body wouldn't function very well. I didn't shy away from giving myself a low score on that day. I kept pushing myself to the limits every day.

I didn't just write down my dreams. I used to make drawings of myself standing on a podium with a medal around my neck and the Indian flag in my hand. Below it I would write, 'I am at the Olympics', 'I'm standing on a podium', 'I have a medal in my hands'. Each day, when I opened that diary to enter my training numbers, I'd see those pages with my drawings and I'd imagine just how special that moment would be.

Not everyone shared my belief, of course. We had a number of media persons come to the national camp to interview the three of us, and most of the questions would be directed at Vinesh and Babita. There was one reporter from The Quint who came and asked each of us in turn who we thought had the best chance to win a medal. Vinesh took Babita's name while Babita took Vinesh's. While that was happening, I was wondering why neither of them took my name.

I was working as hard as either, if not harder. I wasn't even taking any rest sessions. I felt I was more disciplined and fitter than either. So when my turn came up, I said, '*Mera hi medal ayega.*' It was the first time I'd made a public statement that I was hopeful of winning a medal. I was never one to praise myself, so when I did say this, it took not only the other girls but also me by surprise. I had said what I wanted to say. No one seemed to have faith in me so I had to stand up for myself.

As I counted down the days to the Olympics, I started preparing for what I knew awaited me. I bought a stock of ready-to-eat Indian food because I knew just how badly I'd start craving home food once I was done making my weight. A tailor was sent to the national camp to take measurements of the athletes training there for the Olympics.

The women athletes were fitted for a blazer that would be worn on top of a saree for the opening ceremony, and we got special shoes made too. When I got both, I immediately tried them on in front of a mirror. I was so excited to wear them at Rio.

Unfortunately, the federation booked our tickets for a date that saw us arrive on the day after the opening ceremony. Our events were on the last few days of the Olympics and we were being sent over two weeks before that. It wouldn't have been very difficult for the federation to book our flight just one day earlier. It was going to be our first Olympics and all three of us pleaded hard to get our tickets changed, but that never happened.

13

My Olympic Journey

It was a long flight to Rio de Janeiro. It took us fourteen hours to fly from Delhi to the USA, and then another five hours or so to Rio. Babita, Vinesh and I travelled in economy class all the way, with Vinesh and Babita in the aisle and window seats and me sitting in the middle.

Travelling economy class on such a long flight was very uncomfortable, and we were all already very tired because we had been training so hard. We'd take turns to sleep on the floor in front of the seats. So two of us would keep our legs raised for two hours while the third stretched out, across the front of the three seats. Three hours later, we'd switch places and someone else would have that space to extend their legs. Wrestlers' bodies are very tight and it's very easy for us to 'cramp up'. We would walk down the aisles every few hours to keep our circulation going.

We reached Brazil very early on the morning of 15 July. Although we knew we weren't going to make it in time for the opening ceremony of the Olympic Games, we had brought along our ceremonial dress – both the saree and the tracksuit - because we thought we could at least wear them for the closing ceremony.

We could tell the excitement around the Games at the Rio airport itself. There was no immigration line for us. We were made to follow a yellow line, which took us to a designated counter. All our procedures were done quickly because we were athletes who had come to compete at the Olympics. We got special stamps on our passports and were ushered into a bus that took us to the Games Village, to a building where the Indian contingent was staying.

At the Games Village, Vinesh and I were roommates while Babita stayed in a separate room.

Vinesh and I did not seem like we would make good roommates. As you know, I liked my room to be spick and span and for my belongings to be in place. Vinesh, on the other hand, was always leaving her things lying around and then complaining if she couldn't find something. I tried my best to adjust, but sometimes I couldn't help myself and had to pick up after her. I'd put her shoes in place. I'd fold her blanket and place it over her bed. But despite our different temperaments, we always got along well.

Being in the Games village seemed like a dream come true. There was a window in our room from where we could see the other buildings and the road that connected them all. We could also see the athletes getting on buses to go to their competitions.

Every two minutes there would be a bus arriving in front of our building. If you missed one bus, you'd be able to get on another almost immediately. These buses would run twenty-four hours. Apart from stopping at the buildings where the athletes stayed, they'd stop at the gym, the cafeteria and also the building which had a McDonald's. We'd always look longingly at that those golden arches because we knew that was forbidden for us until we made our weight for our competition.

All the athletes hung their country flags outside their rooms. You could look from the outside and say just where Brazil or Australia were staying. It's a special feeling to have all those flags outside your room.

India didn't have a very big contingent at the Rio Games Village. There were only about sixty athletes who had qualified. But of course we put up our tricolour flag outside our windows so that people could say that there were Indians in these buildings.

While I might have been amongst the best wrestlers in India, one of the best parts about being in an Olympic Village was that I was going to be surrounded by a sea of international superstars. Every day you might run into someone really famous.

The one person I really wanted to see from up close was Sania Mirza. Growing up in a small town, I felt she was everything I wanted to be. She was playing an international sport against the best athletes in the world. She looked so sophisticated and glamorous, almost like a movie star. I used to look out for pictures of her in the newspapers and my brother even had posters of her in his room. Now we were living in the same building as she was. Vinesh was an even bigger fan of hers and was completely obsessed with her.

The two of us finally ran into her when we were taking the elevator in our building. We literally cornered her in the lift but were completely tongue-tied. We did manage get a picture with her though. That was my star moment at the Games!

Apart from that moment with Sania Mirza though, we were completely focused on our matches. The three of us, Vinesh, Babita and I, along with Kuldeep coach, would go together to train in the practice hall at the Games Village. Although our physiotherapist Rucha Kashalkar had been sent with us, she wasn't able to get accommodation at the Games Village. She instead stayed in a hotel outside and came to the village every day.

I'd keep my distance from the other wrestlers at the Village. I made sure that we booked our training slots when most of them wouldn't be around. Most wrestlers try and avoid meeting their rivals before the actual tournament begins. Sometimes though, I'd find one of my opponents' coaches in the same hall as me.

They knew I was someone worth keeping an eye on. I'd already been part of a training camp in Spain just before the final Olympic qualifier and I'd started beating a lot of the women there. My opponents at Rio knew that this relatively unknown Indian wrestler was good. So they'd send their coach to my practice sessions to understand my game. They wanted to know what my strengths and favourite attacks were.

It wasn't as if I thought I was unbeatable. There had been one competition in Spain before the Olympics – a grand prix where I won silver. But I didn't have very good memories of that competition because I'd been pinned in the first round in the final. I'd also then been part of a camp in Bulgaria where there was this wrestler from Moldova who would regularly beat me in training matches. I also knew that Sweden's Sophia Mattson was in Rio, and she'd always been a tough opponent against whom I had both won and lost.

And then of course there was some really strong contestants. There was Kaori Icho of Japan who had not ever been beaten at any international competition. There was also the Russian to whom I'd lost in the finals of the Olympic qualifiers just a couple of months before and also a few years back, at the Junior World Championships. It was this recent loss that bothered me more than the others, because it was still fresh in my memory.

I would ignore these women if I ran into them, even though I knew some of them. If our training times overlapped, I'd just glare at them. We might have actually chatted at some other tournament or at the camps, but at the Olympics there was no chance I'd even say hello to them. This was of course a silly way of dealing with competition. We are only opponents on the mat. But back in Rio it was as if I was going to war.

I was focused in every possible way. Before the Olympics I had decided I liked three songs and I insisted on listening to just those numbers on my earphones when I sat in the bus to go to the training hall. I refused to listen to anything else, which I felt would be a distraction.

That was my mentality at the Village too. I never really explored the Games Village because I was training and preparing to make my weight. Vinesh and I began the usual routine we followed before every competition. We would put on our sauna suits in the mornings and evenings when we used to train. We also started reducing our food and water intake.

It was a shame that we had to, because the cafeteria at the Games Village was like nothing else we had seen. There were dozens and dozens of cuisines from around the world. It was like a global food court. Since we had arrived two weeks before the start of my competition, I could actually eat there for a couple of days before I started my weight-control routine. After that I had to avoid going there. It would just be too much of a temptation.

Even as we prepared for our event, the Olympics weren't going very well for India. As the days passed, we weren't winning anything. Every day we'd hear of someone having missed out on a medal, or of someone else coming very close to winning but falling short. It was just one piece of bad news after the other. There was a real sense of disappointment in the village when Abhinav Bindra lost. Everyone felt a little bad because he was our star athlete back then.

But rather than put me under any pressure, all this news took it off. If all these top players, Olympic champions themselves, were losing, who could criticize me if I did too? When champions are also losing on such a big platform, who would care if I lost too? No one was getting upset at them, so who would get upset at me? Even among the wrestlers I wasn't the one favoured to win. So what did I have to lose? I just had to go and give my best.

Everything seemed to be helping me do just that. Of all the competitions I've taken part in, the Olympics were undoubtedly the smoothest.

Everything went right for me. My training camp had been near perfect. The training was sharp and my diet and fitness were on point. It was held in Sonepat so I could go home every other week and recover mentally. I've never been able to recreate that feeling. The atmosphere, the preparation, the physicality that I felt at that time was like nothing else like I'd experienced before or since. I've had camps where I felt physically as strong and fast but mentally weak. For women athletes, there's always the risk that you will get your periods right before a major competition, which will make it really hard to train, but I didn't start mine until the Olympics were done.

At the Olympic Village too, nothing that could have gone wrong did. I've had competitions where I've passed out trying to make my weight, but in Rio everything went to plan. I've always felt that I could lose weight faster in humid conditions than where it's cold and dry. Rio, which is on the beach, was quite ideal from that perspective. I felt faint but I never passed out like I had previously. Every time I stood on the scale to check the progress of my weight loss, I'd see a smaller number, and that gave me the confidence to keep pushing.

It helped that my weight cut went without any complications because I had to help Vinesh a lot with hers. She always had a hard time doing this, and Rio was particularly hard for her. Our coach Kuldeep was very helpful. He'd try to motivate us, he'd press our legs and feet, but he couldn't go into the sauna room with us girls.

I knew that I was on track to make my weight cut but Vinesh wasn't, so I went with her to the sauna. I'd massage her arms and legs to get her to feel motivated. When you are that short of energy, you don't feel like doing anything. You need someone to hold your hand through the process. Vinesh always had a far harder time than I did managing her weight because she would cut so much. I'd tell her, 'It's just for a day more.'

If it was time to train and Vinesh was sleeping, I'd wake her up and tell her it was time to work out. I'd encourage her to have a little to eat so she got some energy with which she could gather the courage to lose some more weight.

The night before you actually have to show your weight is usually the hardest. In my case I had slept fairly well. It was probably my smoothest weight cut. The next day I stood on the scale and it registered 57.900.

We usually carry a few snacks to the weight room to kick-start the recovery process. You usually carry some chocolate and I opened a bar to get that immediate sugar rush. The thing I was really looking forward to having was water. You had been rationing it out for so many days that it tasted like nectar. I'm like a camel after I make weight. I could probably drink a tanker of water.

Then, in the evening, Vinesh and I opened our packets of

readymade Indian meals, which we knew from experience we had to carry with us. For all the world cuisine in the Olympic cafeteria, they would never be able serve up a proper Indian dal in Rio. So we opened up the hot water faucet in the sink in our room and heated up some dal and rajma, which we ate with bread from the cafeteria. Then, with our stomachs finally full, we went to sleep.

I slept very well. I had eaten well for the first time in a month. I'd got my first taste of carbohydrate in bread after a very long time. I had been able to drink water. My body was finally able to relax. That's changed with the new rule in wrestling. The rule now is that you have to make weight on the same day as your contest. That makes it nearly impossible to sleep. But there weren't any of those worries at Rio. Not only was my body relaxed, I also wasn't under pressure to win a medal even.

Both Vinesh and I set multiple alarms on our clocks so we didn't oversleep. Neither of us did. But even if we had forgotten to set our alarms, Coach Kuldeep would not have. We both got calls from him, '*Beta, uth jao.* [Wake up, child.]' That was always his routine. At every competition he'd note down which girl had a competition on which date, and we'd always get a knock on our door on the morning of our event.

Uth gaye, bete? [Woken up, child?]

Haan, sir. [Yes, sir.]

Aaj pura jor laga dena hai. [Try your hardest today.]

We ate, packed our bags and headed to the bus that took us to the arena. As I sat down, I played the song *'Rang teri jit ka. Rang teri prit ka'* [The colour of your victory. The colour of your love.] from the Prabhudeva and Varun Dhawan movie *Jeetna Zaroor Hai Wo* [It Must Be Won]. Over the past few months it had become a sort of anthem for me. I'd constantly listen to just that one song. It used to leave me feeling greatly motivated. As I listened to that song I started going through my process of manifestation – I imagined I was standing on the podium with a medal, the crowds around me, the feeling of satisfaction.

As I walked up to the arena I had some butterflies in my stomach, but it was nothing like the nervousness I'd felt before. I felt a sense of excitement along with some nervousness. It actually felt good that I was finally going to step on the Olympic wrestling mat. This competition was going to be televised and everyone in India was going to see me.

The stadium was full by the time I walked in through the players' entrance. I was greeted by the unmistakable, overpowering smell of menthol pain spray. That's a smell that's synonymous with wrestling. You smell it everywhere, from district-level competition venues to the brand-new Olympic stadium in Rio. The warm-up hall was full of physios and coaches getting their athletes ready for the competition. They were taping them up and emptying cans of that painkilling spray on knees and elbows.

Although there was a separate changing section for the Indian team, the warm-up mat was common to all. It was buzzing with energy. Some of the contestants were already warming up. The best of the world were there. This was Olympic level.

There were TV screens backstage from where you could see the matches going on in the main competition hall. On another screen there was the list of matches for the day.

Although I knew everyone in that Olympic field was going to be very tough, I was just hoping to avoid a scenario where the two strongest wrestlers in the tournament – Kaori Icho of Japan and the Russian Valeria Koblova – were in my bracket. There were also a few other wrestlers I hoped weren't in my half of the draw. I had competed in a training camp in Bulgaria just before the Olympics and I'd been badly beaten many times by a wrestler from Moldova. Another wrestler I was a bit wary of was Aisuluu Tynybekova of Kyrgyzstan. Although I'd never wrestled her, I knew she was very good. I'd seen her in action at the Asian Championship, where she won gold. She had also been a world medallist the previous year. I thought she was one of the favourites for the gold.

Luckily, Icho was on the other half of the bracket. But I had the Moldovan, the Kyrgyz and the Russian in my half. It wasn't the best draw, but it could have been worse.

Kuldeep coach told me my bout was the seventh of the day so I had to rush and get my now long hair braided. I used to get my hair done up in cornrows, but that wasn't possible in Rio. Usually there are girls, either from the Indian team or from one of the other countries, who will do your braids, but everyone was busy that day. It would take about fifteen minutes to do my hair, but since I didn't know anyone I could ask, I got a few hair bands and some pins from Rucha and had her do my hair.

She's not a hairstylist but she did what she could. I invented a new hairstyle, which was a combination of three different styles, for myself that day. Some of my hair was tied up in braids, Rucha had put hairbands through some other strands, and there was one bunch of hair which she just stuck in a ponytail.

I had splints put on some of my fingers so my opponents couldn't twist them. I then began my warm-up. Vinesh and I both had our opening bouts around the same time, so we started practising our techniques against each other.

Once I finished my warm-up, I went into the changing room and put on my costume. As at most competitions, I carried three with me to the Olympics. One was slightly old, which I used for weigh-ins. For the competition itself I had two brand-new ones with the sponsor's logo on them.

It's always a special feeling to snap on my costume, and that's how I felt in Rio too. My costume fitted flush against my muscles. My body felt strong and beautiful. You know how it is in the superhero movies when Superman puts on his suit? That's exactly how I felt.

I was joined by two coaches. Kuldeep Malik, who had worked with us, was joined by Kuldeep Sehrawat, who was the coach of the Indian Greco-Roman wrestling team, one of the three kinds of wrestling at the Olympic Games, the others being men's freestyle and women's freestyle wrestling. Since the Indian Greco-Roman team had lost, he'd come to help our coach. You always had two coaches come with you. That extra coach would towel you or flutter the towel at you at the end of the first period of the match to cool you down.

My first bout of the day was against Johanna Mattsson of Sweden.

Usually, before wrestlers step on the mat, they are together in a waiting room, waiting for the previous bout to end and theirs to begin. When the bout is announced you step out together. As we waited in that room, Mattsson was a bundle of energy. She shouted, jumped up and down, and slapped herself. Many wrestlers try to psych out their opponent that way.

As I walked to the mat, Kuldeep Malik started psyching me up. He said I didn't even recognize how much power I had in me. These other girls didn't have any idea who they were up against.

Despite Kuldeep coach's pep talk, I wasn't very confident ahead of that opening round against Mattsson. It wasn't because of what she did in the waiting room. She was already a world bronze medallist and a very senior wrestler. I'd wrestled against her a number of times in our practice camp in Bulgaria, and neither of us had been able to dominate the other.

Mattsson was one of those aggressive and rough wrestlers I never liked to face. She'd keep her palm out and keep jabbing with it to snap my head back. She had really heavy hands and would hit my head really hard to break my rhythm.

The match was a close one, with Mattsson leading for most of it. We exchanged 2-point takedowns in the first round before she scored another 2. I got a single point by forcing her to step off the mat, but with about twenty-two seconds to go, I was trailing by a single point. I knew I had to attack again. And just as I attacked and got my hands behind her waist and took her to the mat, time ran out, with me winning 5-4.

Next up was Mariana Cherdivara of Moldova. The Moldovan must have thought she'd beat me pretty comfortably, as she had in the past. And it looked like that at the start. Once again I was trailing in the match. I conceded a point for passivity and then, while attempting a takedown, I conceded a takedown. I was 0-3 down at the break.

Coach Kuldeep says he was trying to tell me to stay calm but I don't remember him speaking very much at all. I was down but I knew the gap wasn't so big and that I could turn the match in my favour. In the second period, it was the Moldovan who started passively and I got one point back.

She must have felt she'd done enough to take the match. But with about a minute and a half left, I ducked under her and caught her in a near-perfect double-leg takedown. I took her off her feet and on to the mat for four points. That was the only scoring move I made over the whole match. She got another takedown on me late in the bout, but I won 5-5 since I had scored a bigger throw.

I had felt good after I beat Mattsson, but it was after beating the Moldovan that I thought I might actually get the chance to make it to the medal rounds. *'Sakshi, tu sahi me kar sakti hai.'* I can really do this, I told myself.

Right after my win against the Moldovan, Vinesh got a horrific injury. She had won one match against a Romanian wrestler, and I won one against the Swedish wrestler. But in the match against China, she got caught in a very poor position and ended up ripping her ACL. I was watching the match on the TV screens in the warm-up hall and I knew something had gone catastrophically wrong right away.

I tried to keep a brave face, but when I saw coach Kuldeep with tears streaming down his face, I began to cry too. There was nothing I could do about that injury, though. Vinesh had already been taken to the medical room. It was as bad an omen as anything that could be considered one. But just because Vinesh's day had been ruined, that didn't mean my day was over too. I was very emotional for a few minutes, but then Kuldeep coach brought me out of it. He said Vinesh would be okay and that she would have many more chances in the future.

I walked into my match with the Russian Valeria Koblova feeling confident. I thought, if I can beat the Moldovan, then surely I can beat the Russian. And at the start it seemed that way.

I went to the lead at the end of the first round, so I started to think, 'Yaar, maybe today is your day. Today is when you get to beat her for the first time.' This time though, after I conceded a point for passivity, I scored a takedown early in the second round to go 2-1 up. For the first time in my career I was in the lead against her. I should have stayed focused.

Not only did Koblova take me down, she also trapped me in a cradle. She had my right arm trapped underneath my body and my leg bent at an angle and caught in the crook of her arm. It was a bad situation. I only barely escaped being pinned, but the match was all but decided by that point. I made a desperate attempt in the final few moments, but it resulted in another takedown and another near-pin before the match ended with me losing 2-9.

In almost any other sport, that was where my tournament would have ended. But in wrestling there is a rule called repechage, which I have already described. Sushil Kumar won the bronze medal in the 2008 Olympics by this rule. I too had won a bronze medal in my first nationals because of the rule. But that was the nationals. This was the Olympics.

It is an uncomfortable feeling to know that your destiny is no longer in your control. It actually feels a little dirty because you need someone else to do well. It also throws off the usual patterns of a wrestling tournament. If you enter the finals on your own strength, you get a few hours' break after your semi-final to prepare for the final.

If, instead, you lose, as I did, you first have to wait for a while to see if the wrestler you lost to makes the final and so pulls you into repechage. If you do qualify under repechage, you have to wait some more time for the first-round match of repechage to get done to find out who your opponent will be. And then, if you win that match, you have to wait for a few hours for the evening session of matches to start, where you will wrestle for the bronze medal.

I refused to watch Koblova's semi-final bout. Instead, I went to the Indian changing room and tried to get some sleep. If she won, I knew I needed to be well rested for my repechage matches. If she lost, then there was no point in exhausting myself mentally. I knew that if I was watching her match, I'd be emotionally all over the place. I'd be elated if she was doing well and I'd break down if she started to lose.

My real reason, however, was something else. I couldn't bear to watch the match because I was sure it would bring bad luck. As I closed my eyes, I pretended to sleep while praying the Russian would somehow win.

About an hour later, Kuldeep sir came to me and said what I had been hoping to hear. '*Jit gayi. Medal ka chance hai.*' She had won and I still had a chance to win a medal. All was not lost yet.

I wasn't going to get the gold or silver, but I could still win a bronze. I had to win the bronze. I'd been thrown a lifeline when I was at the brink of disaster and I wasn't going to waste it.

I was going to face Mongolia's Pürevdorjiin Orkhon, who had just pinned her first opponent. Just a few months before, she had beaten me at the Asian qualifiers. She hadn't just beaten me. I had been pinned by her in just a few seconds of the first round. That match had ended even before it started.

But I wasn't the same wrestler who Orkhon had crushed that day. My performances had definitely improved, and even if I wasn't the favourite to win, it also wasn't inevitable that I would lose. For some reason, I noticed that Orkhon didn't look nearly as confident before our match as she had the first time I wrestled her.

I think one of the reasons was that she had lost in her very first match of the main draw. Repechage wasn't what she had hoped for. On the other hand, I had beaten two wrestlers, including one I knew I was not favoured to beat.

My Olympic Journey

Indeed, when the match started I couldn't believe how easy it felt. I scored off a *dasti* – a desi *kushti* term for when you switch from an arm drag to a single-leg takedown – inside the first twelve seconds. The Mongolian managed to pull two back to level the score going into the second round.

I didn't give her a chance to come back. I attacked early with my favourite double-leg takedown to go 4-2 up. She tried her best to fight back, but I blocked everything, giving her just that one point. I sensed I'd weathered the heaviest weight of her attack, and from then on the match was mine.

I was just flowing. She would attack and I'd find a way to slip behind her and score. She tried this once more, and I once again dodged her lunge and got behind her. This time I not only got the takedown but turned her over to score another two.

With just seconds to go, she failed an arm drag and I got another takedown. I'd scored 12 points to 3. Any time you go into the double digits, it feels great. That means that you have scored on almost every attack you have made. To have done it against an opponent who was as dangerous as Orkhon was unbelievable.

This was perhaps my favourite win in the Olympics. It wasn't that my opponent was easy. But it was the closest I came come to a perfect wrestling match in Rio. In every other match there had been a sense of tension right until the final whistle. In this match, though, I was just wrestling on instinct.

I was completely in what people call the zone. I think I might have beaten anyone that day. If I had to wrestle Icho right after that match, I might even have beaten her. Both my body and mind were working well. I hardly felt tired after that match.

After the match, Orkhon was quiet. The Moldovan was absolutely silent too, while Mattson was weeping bitterly in the warm-up room, as they processed the fact that their Olympic journey was finished. Ahead of the match, both Mattson and Cherdivara had been jumping up and down and yelling in the waiting room. Once you know your loss is decisive and there's no possibility of returning, there's no more point in pretence.

While I might have wanted to wrestle right away after beating Orkhon, I had to wait. I was one bout away from the medal, but that bronze-medal match was in the evening, about three hours away. First I ate, and then I tried to sleep, right there on the mat in the training hall. Kuldeep coach was sitting next to me.

Neither of us spoke to each other, nor did we know what to say. We both knew what both of us were thinking. I was on the verge of creating history, but I just didn't want to think about it. My mind was working at 100 per cent and I was trying to slow it down. I wasn't thinking of what I had to do. Or how I was going to prepare. I wasn't listening to my music. I was just lying down and trying to keep my mind blank.

I got myself busy trying to get some sleep so I could recover a bit. I'd wrestled four matches, and all of them were hard fights that had gone the distance. Twenty-four minutes is a long time, in wrestling especially, and there hadn't been a moment where I could lose focus even the slightest bit. It was only when the adrenaline had started to wear off after my match with Orkhon that I sat down on the mat and realized that I was actually feeling tired.

Even without my telling him, Kuldeep coach was already starting to stretch my arms and massage my legs to try and relax my muscles. There was just one match to go and he was trying to get me as ready as he could.

Try as I might, I couldn't be calm. Although I'd never wrestled her before, I knew the girl I was going to wrestle for the bronze medal was very, very tough. Kyrgystan's Aisuluu Tynybekova was a top medal contender and she'd lost a close semi-final to Koblova, who had beaten me by a much larger margin. Although I'd never wrestled her before, I'd lost to the Mongolian girl in the Asian qualifier, and she had lost to Tynybekova in the next round.

That wasn't the only thing against me. At the start of the day I really had nothing to lose, but now I was very close to that medal. Just as I'd start thinking about what I was really up against, I'd remind myself that I'd beaten all these top wrestlers. What was another? Maybe I was better than I thought I was.

These thoughts kept running in a loop. Sometimes I thought the odds were in Tynybekova's favour, and at other times I backed myself to win. If the match was determined in my head, I think Tynybekova would have won. There were certainly more negative than positive thoughts in my head.

While we waited backstage, I could see could see that Tynybekova, in her blue costume, was very confident that she would beat me. Her coach was hyping her up in Kyrgyz and she was just nodding, without any worry showing on her face. Her boy-cut hairstyle reminded me of all the serious wrestlers who had dominated me in my early years. Tynybekova was infinite levels beyond them. She had been performing very well and she had the medals to show for it. In terms of results I didn't have anything to compare with hers.

The match started poorly for me. Tynybekova was the one who was setting the pace of the match. She attacked me twice and scored both times. I was trailing 5-0 in the first round. She was a seriously good wrestler. At that point I started thinking that this wasn't an opponent I could beat. She was too good for me to wrestle.

When I put my hands on her arms I could feel just how rope-like her muscles were. I always thought I was strong, but she was genuinely stronger. She was also technically sharper. When the first round ended I didn't have a lot of belief in myself.

While coach Kuldeep Sehrawat was towelling me furiously, trying to cool me down, Kuldeep Malik was doing his best to keep me in the fight. He was saying it was all right. I had to fight to the end. The gap I'd conceded was nothing. *'Do attack ka game,'* he kept yelling at me. Two successful attacks and I'd be right up at her, he was saying. I'd come back from deficits in my first couple of matches too, so this was just another match like those two.

That was exactly what happened in the second round. She'd scored five points in the first period, but at the start of the second round, I could sense that she was slowing down. I didn't allow her to score any points for the first minute of the second round. She could perhaps have just been trying to hold on to the win, but she made a mistake.

She tried to attack my right leg, but she did not commit, almost as if she was having second thoughts in the middle of her lunge. It struck me later that while she might have done a good job hiding it in the dressing room, Tynybekova was under some pressure as well. I wasn't the only one who was trying to achieve something unprecedented. There wasn't a woman, or even man, in Kyrgyzstan who had won an Olympic medal. Both of us were trying to make history that day for our countries, but only one of us could. Now that she was so close to the finish line, she just didn't want to make a mistake.

Her pause gave me enough time to sprawl and kick my legs behind me. She couldn't get a strong grip on my thigh, but because she had already attacked she couldn't recover her posture. I circled over to her left and went behind her for a takedown. In the same movement I turned her on her back for another 2 points. In just one counter attack, I'd scored 4 points. I was back in the match.

In wrestling, a 1-point gap is nothing. I was still trailing 4-5, but I had a minute and a half to work with, and an opponent who had started second-guessing herself. She started glancing at the clock, willing it to count faster. It didn't. She interlaced her fingers in mine, hoping the pain would cause me to pull back, and use up a few more seconds that way. I never felt that pain.

With about fifteen seconds to go, Tynybekova could have just run the clock down. She had me on the edge of the mat on the defensive after blocking a double-leg attack. She had sprawled out of my grasp, while her right hand was holding the back of my left knee. She could have continued to spin around to go behind me. She could also have held her sprawl and used up a few more seconds. She could have chosen either option and held on to win.

But she didn't. She just froze. She had become too defensive. That gave me the time to get my leg free and secure her right leg.

She realized her mistake too late. I spun around and exploded off the ground, pushing her out of bounds. As we went over the orange circle marking the boundary of the playing circle, she flipped me over in the air. As we landed she sat on her haunches and hopefully stuck her thumb and forefinger out, appealing for two points. Her flip was invalid. It had begun after she had already stepped off the mat.

One point to me.

Although our scores were level, I was still trailing, since Tynybekova had got her last point from a takedown while I'd got my last point from a lower-rated move (step out). There were just nine seconds remaining on the clock.

In any other match this might not be enough time. But as I saw Tynybekova labour to get off the mat and draw deep breaths to calm herself down, I knew she was done.

In a match, you can make out from an opponent's face when they are breaking down. Tynybekova had gone from leading comfortably to being one wrong decision away from losing. I might have had only nine seconds left, but I knew I was going to get another chance inside that time. That's exactly what happened. She was so mentally exhausted that it just needed a slight nudge to tip her over. She was still physically capable, but once her brain had frozen there was no way she could recover.

I shot a takedown, but my intention wasn't to score but draw a reaction from her. If I had tried this early in the match, she might have read that I was just making a feint. But, at that moment, she just fell forward, thinking I'd be underneath her, grabbing for her legs.

It worked perfectly. I wasn't where she hoped I would be. Instead I pulled back, just in time for her to overbalance as she kicked her legs back. As she tumbled on to the mat, I pounced on her right side and turned her over. The referee punched his hand with its thumb and forefinger stretched out, skyward up, for the last time in the match. Two more points to me. As soon as he had done that, the match buzzer blew, signalling the end of the match.

Although the buzzer had rung, it didn't register for a second. I only realized the match was over when I saw Kuldeep Sir starting to clap and rush on to the mat. That's when I realized that I'd won. Tynybekova's coaches challenged the last call. She was devastated and about to start crying. She started waving her finger. She didn't really have a point. But she just didn't want to deal with the fact that she had lost.

She requested a review, and as expected, there was no change made to the call. I got an extra point for the failed review too, making me an 8-5 winner.

Kuldeep Sir put me on his shoulders and did a victory lap. It was the first time he had picked me up like that. He couldn't control himself. I had always thought I'd feel just the purest of elation when I won my medal. I'd been chasing it for so long and now my dream had finally come true. But there must have been something wrong with my brain because I felt a whole wave of other emotions. I just couldn't control them. I was laughing one moment and in the next burying my face in the mat and bawling.

I still find it hard to believe that I beat Tynybekova. She was stronger than me and she had an exceptional career after Rio. But on that day her mind let her down. I've been through that too. I've found myself gaining confidence but seen it drain from me too. I've had days when I felt I could hit any attack I wanted, and there were days when it felt I was wrestling in *keechad*, or wet mud. Sometimes I've felt both in the same match. Today Tynybekova was going through all that.

I didn't have much time on the mat. Right after our match, the women's gold medal match was taking place. My event was over and the main event was up next. I was still next to the mat but I could hardly process what was happening. I was in my own world. Now everyone wanted to be part of that world all of a sudden. My phone was just blowing up. It seemed everyone in India wanted to talk to me. I just looked on as the calls came in, but for now I wanted to be by myself and did not respond.

I was remembering the time when I was twelve and had first started to learn the sport. I remembered all those intense training sessions of my early days. It seemed surreal that I was an Olympic medallist. I thought you had to be a superhero to win an Olympic medal.

I'd always placed our Indian Olympic medallists at a different level from mine. I thought they were special and I was regular. And then I realized that the very regular Sakshi Malik now had her own Olympic medal too.

Of course, later my win gave a lot of confidence to the other girls in wrestling. They started to believe they too could win medals at the Olympics.

Right after the final we had our medal ceremony, and I quickly fixed my hair as best I could. Before I climbed the podium, I finally got a chance to speak to Kaori Icho and Valeria Koblova. We'd never interacted in all the years I'd wrestled, and I'd kept to myself even at the Games Village. I told Kaori how I always admired her and how I always wanted to meet her. I told her how I had visualized I was going to be standing on the podium with her and how that had come true.

I tried my best to mix Hindi and English and sign language, but I don't think she was able to understand much. I don't think it mattered. I was just excited to be able to share a conversation with her.

I let my phone continue to ring. I finally looked at my phone after I gave my dope test sample following the medal ceremony. By then it was very late in India. I spoke to my mother and I called Satyawart. He had been up and watching the match. I told everyone to go and get some sleep and that I'd talk to them in the morning.

While I didn't reply to any of the calls, I looked at my phone to see the social media reactions. I'd not seen anything like it. There were all these celebrities sending messages and posting tweets on me. There was the regular media who wanted to talk to me, and I did interviews with them until late that night in Rio. There were people taking pictures with me. It is all a blur.

I finally got back to my room in the Games Village at 2 a.m. There Vinesh and Rucha were wide awake, with big grins on their faces. It was then that I realized I hadn't eaten anything. I was so tired and excited that I'd forgotten all about food. We got some rice and a slice of some cold pizza from the cafeteria. As I drifted off to sleep, I knew I had done something special, but it would be a few days before I realized just how everything would change for me – the way people treated me, the way the country treated me, were all going to be very different.

The next two days felt like a party. We were just roaming around in the Games Village eating what we could, making up for our fasting before the matches. Although we had a world-class cafeteria, the one place I was almost permanently camped at was the McDonald's at the Games Village. At least six of the kilos I gained at the Village must have been at that restaurant. We had been dieting for so many weeks, and suddenly we were surrounded by all that fat and salt and sugar.

It didn't hurt that the McDonald's was completely free for athletes. Since there's just that one store for the entire village, there were massive lines all the way around the block, and from morning to night.

Although there was no cutting the queue, there was a special line for athletes who had injuries and could not stand. So whenever we wanted to eat at McDonald's, Rucha, the physiotherapist, and I would pick up Vinesh, take her in a wheelchair to McDonald's and say go and get us some burgers. We'd get into the short line, and once we had made our way to the counter, we'd pile her up with burgers, fries and soft-serve ice creams and come out feeling like kings.

14

Returning Home a Champion

On my twenty-first birthday in 2013, my brother had bought a cake for me with the message, 'We want to see you as a winner in the Olympics' on the icing. At that time I was an absolute nobody. I got a total of three likes when I posted that picture on Facebook.

Now it seemed that the notifications on my Facebook page would never ever end.

Over the next couple of days at Rio, there was always someone who wanted a one-on-one interview with me. I agreed at first, after all how many could there be? But every request was followed by another. There was always someone standing outside the Games Village requesting me to come down from my room. Every Indian in Rio, it seemed, wanted to know about me.

I knew I had done something important but I didn't realize that 'I' had become important as well. My flight back to India had been booked several weeks back. I was returning in economy class, just as I had arrived. Vinesh had been upgraded to business class since she couldn't bend her knee, which was in a cast. I was just happy to be returning home, but Vinesh told me I could probably get a business-class ticket myself.

I was sure that wouldn't happen, but Vinesh insisted I speak to my sponsors. I called up Mustafa Ghouse, who was the head of JSW Sports, and asked him if I could get a business-class seat on the flight back to India. I'd never been that pushy sort of person and was really embarrassed to even make the request. But he immediately changed my ticket to business class.

Business class was like nothing I'd seen before in my travels. I'm someone who's travelled ticketless on trains, and economy class was the height of luxury for me. But I can now see why people who have that kind of money travel business class!

In business class I didn't get just a seat but one that stretched out into a bed. There was a big TV in front of my seat. I was determined to stay awake the entire sixteen hours of my flight so that I could experience everything. I wanted to eat everything they served for breakfast, lunch and dinner.

I had completely underestimated just how relaxing that bed would be, because after the first meal I drifted into a deep sleep and woke up when it was just about three hours to landing time.

I felt really bad. I had got the opportunity travel business class for the first time in my life and I'd slept through most of it. Just as I was cursing myself, the pilot made an announcement on the intercom. He said he was proud to be flying an Olympic medallist and an airhostess came out with a bottle of perfume that she said the captain wanted to gift me.

Vinesh was on the same flight as me. We chatted and took selfies. There were a few mediapersons who were travelling on the same flight and they tried to come and interview me, but Mustafa told them to leave me alone, at least for the duration of the flight.

Up to that time I would speak to whichever media person

approached me. Mustafa told me I couldn't give everyone interviews any more, and that even when I got to India, I had to be selective.

Our flight landed India at around 3 a.m.

While everyone was telling me that things would be very different for me now, it was Kuldeep coach who gave me the first practical piece of advice. Before I'd got on board, he reminded me to wear the heaviest items of clothing I could find because anything else was going to be ripped apart in all the pushing and shoving at the airport.

I wore a thick pair of jeans and a black coat on top of my T-shirt. It's a good thing I did that because Kuldeep coach had been dead right. Everyone was jostling and trying to get a picture with me. It was chaos unlike anything I'd ever experienced before.

The skywalk connecting the plane to the airport was full of security personnel. My family had been allowed to come into the airport and were waiting just outside the skywalk, and together we went to a VIP room. There was a briefing, where I was told exactly how I was to proceed. It seemed almost like a military operation.

There were people as far as I could see at the exit gate. The moment I stepped out of the exit gate, a girl from my akhara appeared out of nowhere and lifted me on to her shoulder. Even from that vantage point, the crowd seemed endless. There was barely any place to stand.

The media pushed their way forward with their cameras held in front of them. There was no avoiding them. I didn't know where one interview was ending and the other starting. I must have said the same thing to one hundred people. For the first time I started getting frustrated at all this because I was beginning to sound like a tape being played and replayed.

They all asked the same questions.

How do you feel?

How did you feel when you became a wrestler for the first time? Where did you start?

That's when I realized that being famous wasn't always going to feel special.

It was still very early in the morning when a car took me to Haryana Bhawan. I stayed there for another three hours, ate a little bit of food and then began my journey in a multi-vehicle convoy to Rohtak. It's only about 80 km to Rohtak from central Delhi, but it took the entire day to make that journey.

It wasn't hard to get to the Delhi border, but from there on we were constantly stopping at every other village. We'd travel a few kilometres when we'd be called to attend a function at a village along the way. We were welcomed in both big villages like Bahadurgarh, Sampla and Ismaila, where my mother's family was from, and in small ones like Asoda, Jasaur Khedi and Maina.

We'd stop at a village for half an hour, within which time we'd get a call from another down the road asking whether I could come just for five minutes so that they could conduct a swagat. There was a police party travelling with us. They were called protocol officers and they'd chart out my route and tell me how long I could spend at one village before our caravan had to move forward to the next expecting us.

The swagat is a tradition in Haryana in honour of someone who has achieved something significant. When you win an international medal in sports, people want to honour you. I was felicitated in my village of Mokhra when I won my first Commonwealth medal too. But that was a Commonwealth medal. Everyone wanted to give a swagat to an Olympic medallist. This is the tradition I came from so I couldn't refuse anyone. We had to accept their welcome, so we stopped and visited as many villages as we could.

Every one of the villages offered us food. I'd mostly be offered fruits and fresh milk since everyone knew that wrestlers drank milk.

That came with its own risk. I was always taught I shouldn't eat anything that I was not sure was unadulterated since the burden of proof for any failed dope test is on the athlete. At every one of those swagats though, I was eating whatever was offered to me. I never thought that the milk I was being offered might have had something added in it.

People weren't just trying to feed me, they were giving me money too. Everyone wanted to give something. Every village, it seemed, was trying to one-up the other in terms of reward money. The panchayat of Mayna village presented me with a cheque of Rs 10 lakh on stage. Others gave smaller amounts, like Rs 5 lakh, while the not-so-rich villages presented me with Rs 1 lakh each. Many placed garlands of currency notes around my beck. There was one massive garland of 500-rupee notes, which apparently totalled to Rs 5 lakh.

Although they were vying with each other to lavish money on me, the point of a swagat isn't to give money but for people to recognize an achievement in whatever way they could. There were old people who came with walking sticks, who reached into their pockets and took out Rs 500 to give me, and others who even handed me old hundred-rupee notes. That touched me a lot. They were poor people who had next to nothing, and yet they felt the need to give me what must have been a huge amount of their hard-earned money.

I felt proud but also a sense of sadness and responsibility. In their sense of duty, they had parted with what little they earned because they appreciated what I had done. This is something that you will see in Haryana. It is common for the wealthy to patronize athletes, but it's a very uniquely Haryanvi tradition for even regular people to give you what little money they have as a sign of respect.

I just wanted to soak in every moment of that day. I was a new Olympic medallist and the centre of attention everywhere I went. I must have posed for thousands of pictures and my cheeks were sore from smiling by the end of the day. I sometimes feel bad that I couldn't give everyone who came to those functions at least a good picture. There were so many people that it was just a matter of luck that I was facing in the same direction as someone else when the camera shutter snapped a picture. But I tried to give everyone at least a little time.

The first couple of months after the Olympics were crazy, in terms of travel alone. Weeks would go past before I could go home to Rohtak again. I was travelling from one hotel room to the other. I'd be in Delhi one day, in Hyderabad the next day, and I might have to catch a flight to Kerala from there, after which I'd be flying to Mumbai. I was invited by the governments of many states, including Kerala, Uttar Pradesh and Telangana. Even though I might have had no connections with many of them, a message would come from their chief minister that they wanted to felicitate me.

It was just a blur of programmes and felicitations.

There were so many programmes that JSW assigned me a personal manager. She would plan and manage my appointments, my stylists and my travel details. I just couldn't keep track of all of them myself. Everything was planned out in complete detail and my job was just to show up.

I found myself interacting with a class of people whom I could never have imagined meeting. Wrestling isn't a rich man's sport. The people I'd interacted with for most of my life were from the same background as me, sometimes from poorer backgrounds. We were the daughters of farmers or had solid working-class backgrounds. We weren't posh, sophisticated or well read.

I was invited to a programme at a five-star hotel in Mumbai organized by the owner of JSW, Parth Jindal. I'd attended many programmes, but this time I was expected to speak to a bunch of children of some of his friends. I, Sakshi Malik, the daughter of a DTC bus driver, was supposed to inspire these children who were likely the cream of Mumbai's high society.

It was a very strange feeling to do that. When I was a little girl studying at DAV School in Rohtak, I had always had this massive inferiority complex in the company of children who came from more privileged backgrounds.

I craved for their approval but never got it. They had this opinion of me that I was just this girl from a village who brought milk to school. I couldn't bring five rupees to spend at the school canteen, but now I was eating whatever I wanted. I was travelling business class. I could buy what I wanted. I finally felt I was something. I was the centre of attention for all these kids whose lifestyle I could never even have dreamed of when I was their age.

Sometimes the gap between the world I came from and the world that now wanted to know me was hard to bridge. I got to meet Sonakshi Sinha during one event on awareness about sanitary napkins. Although I loved the movies, we came from such different backgrounds that it was a little hard for me to communicate with her. I was speaking in Hindi with a Haryanvi accent, which she found hard to follow, and she was mostly speaking in English. So we mostly just exchanged pleasantries. Just things like Hi, Hello, How are you?

Things were a lot more fun around Ranbir Kapoor. It probably didn't hurt that I was a huge fan of his. Before the Olympics, one of my best friends, Shilpi, and I had been crazy about his character in the film *Rockstar*. On Sundays, on our day off from training, we'd recreate one of his scenes from the movie. Shilpi would act out a scene where Ranbir was drunkenly hitting on Nargis Fakhri. I'd play Nargis in that scene while Shilpi would play Ranbir Kapoor. I'd say 'Bugger off', like Nargis Fakhri, and Shilpi would say *'Rock kar denge'*, the way Ranbir Kapoor's character did.

Call it manifestation or whatever, but I got to meet Ranbir Kapoor as part of a TV show called *Dance Plus*. When Shilpi found out that Ranbir Kapoor was going to be there, she begged me to let her come with me.

He could sense that I was a little star-struck by him, so he told me that I'd done so much for the country and it was his honour to meet me. He did some acting with me on that show, tried to show me how to dance and even kissed my hand. It was something that might have made most boyfriends jealous, but Satyawart just found it funny. He was a lot more broad-minded than most men of his background. He'd always tell me I had to stand on my own feet and live my own life. It was great for him to see that I was enjoying myself.

Although it was fun to be on that TV show with Ranbir Kapoor, it was not something I could see myself doing regularly. I was always an outsider looking in. I had certainly never felt like a star before the Olympics. I considered myself a good international wrestler and the best in India in my weight class, but not a star. But it was nice being one. I got to meet celebrities, and people suddenly became very nice to me. At the airport I wouldn't have to wait in line and instead get priority check-in. Many restaurants refused to bill me for my meal.

The most challenging part of it all this was that I now had to look a certain way. My manager Nayantara Pani would make me wear high heels to some of the more sophisticated events. She'd tell me I needed them to stand tall and walk like a woman. She would say it in a half serious tone, but she absolutely meant what she said.

I'd never worn high heels until after I won the Olympic medal. While I learned to walk in them without falling over fairly quickly, that wasn't enough for Nayantara. I had to walk elegantly, like an actress. I could manage to walk like a human, but expecting me to catwalk was a step too far.

I hated wearing those heels. It takes time to adjust to something new, and I ended up bruising my feet in those narrow shoes. I got a few blisters too. I'd tell her, 'NTP, these heels are poking me. I'll never be able to make it through the event!'

She'd tell me to quit complaining. 'Fashion hurts,' she would say.

Dresses were another matter. As wrestlers, our concept of fashion is T-shirt and pyjamas. As an Olympic medallist, I was provided a stylist for every event. Not only would she bring me heels, she would also measure my frame and get me clothes that were made to fit. For any event I'd have five to six outfits to choose from. I had not had as many clothes changes in my whole life as I did those few months.

15

Body Talk (A Small Digression)

The one style of clothing I avoided wearing was anything that bared my arms. I was always conscious that I had very muscular, 14-inch-thick biceps. They were prominent even by wrestling standards and they looked massive in comparison to the arms of the skinny girls I'd see on film sets in Mumbai. I always felt my arms and hands looked weird. They looked like what I thought men's arms and hands did.

My stylists and Nayantara would tell me they looked amazing. My muscles were something to show off, they insisted, but I couldn't believe them.

Our wrestler bodies are built very different from most women's bodies. We develop very strong muscles in our arms and back, thanks to all the rope climbs and pull-ups, while our waist is naturally very narrow, since we have to maintain a low body-fat percentage. It's the combination of the two that gives us that characteristic V-shaped upper body, like that of boys.

While all women wrestlers have torsos with some definition, it's less prominent for some. Vinesh has more of what we consider a typically feminine body shape. Her cousins Sangeeta and Geeta

Body Talk (A Small Digression)

too don't have very prominent V-shaped torsos. They both have heavier hips and relatively leaner arms. That wasn't the case with me. Recently, Sangeeta Phogat took part in the *Jhalak Dikhlaja* dance show, for which she wore very feminine outfits. She looked so beautiful in them! If I wore the same outfits, people would think I look terrible.

I often wished I had more of what we consider a girly shape. As a teenager I'd sometimes complain to God, 'You gave me such a good body, but did you have to give me such big arms?'

It didn't help my self-image much either when other girls at the wrestling camp would comment on my arms. They'd say I had such heavy arms that I'd be able to exhaust my opponents by just hand-wrestling them (*chala chala ke behosh kar denge*). It wasn't just Indians. Once when I was overseas at a training camp, an Italian wrestler pointed to my arms and gave me a big thumbs-up, saying 'Hey big arms!'

He actually meant it as a compliment, but I felt very awkward about it. My arms were indeed perfect for wrestling, but they didn't make me feel very feminine. I didn't feel confident at all about how I looked.

That's still something I have to deal with. If I go for a function, most of the younger women are in a saree or lehenga. Some might be wearing sleeveless blouses. I always wear a western piece of clothing, like a shirt or a coat. I just feel a lot more secure in well-constructed Western clothes than in a lehenga or a Punjabi suit.

Sometimes there's no option, though. Back in 2015, for my brother's wedding, I couldn't wear Western clothes. So I told my mother I wanted to wear a lehenga with a full-sleeved top. All the other girls wore sleeveless outfits.

This is why, although I dislike the cold, I much prefer winters to summers. I always feel I have more clothes options in the winter. I can wear ruffled sleeves, or high-neck clothes, blazers and jackets. In the summer the only options I seem to have are either full-sleeved shirts or T-shirts, with my biceps out there for everyone to gawk at.

Wrestling might seem to be this tough, macho sport, and there is this perception that women wrestlers are very mean and boy-like. Off the mat though, almost every female wrestler wants to look pretty. It's just that we don't get many opportunities to dress up, and in my case it was always hard to find something to wear that I wasn't self-conscious in.

Most of us aren't from families or backgrounds with any knowledge of things like make-up or dressing up to be presentable. I knew there were other girls whose mothers would teach them to use make-up, but I had to learn all of this on my own. I wore make-up for the first time at my brother's wedding, but since I had no idea what I was doing, I didn't like it. I thought I should just stick to being a wrestler. I had no business to look good.

I did start growing my hair out just before my brother's wedding. By the time I got to Rio it was quite long. When I started using hair curlers, I realized I didn't look as bad as I imagined I did.

Nayantara taught me to use make-up and bought me my first make-up set after I started having to attend events following the Olympics. I didn't have the first clue about blushers and highlighters, and did not know what foundation was. People knew that I was a good wrestler, but there was no reason they couldn't think I was elegant too. It might seem obvious now, but it took winning an Olympic medal for me to realize I could be both.

It's just not easy to overcome a lifetime of conditioning in India.

Body Talk (A Small Digression)

The American wrestlers wear sleeveless and off-the-shoulder dresses. I don't think it suits them, but that is just my opinion. It doesn't seem to matter to them. They are happy in their skins. I wished I could just be happy without worrying about what others thought of me.

It's not that I've not made any progress on this front. I wore a sleeveless dress for the first time in my life when I came on the Kapil Sharma show a few months after the Olympics. I had no option because none of the other clothes provided for me were the right colour or fit.

Satyawart was with me backstage at the show when I nervously tried on that dress. He said I looked great, and that convinced me I could wear it. But he always says I look great. That day, though, he gave me the confidence to wear that sleeveless dress. I've had my fingers twisted, my hair pulled out by their roots and my ACL ripped. But it felt far more stressful to wear a sleeveless dress for the first time.

I'm a lot more comfortable with my body now. A few days back, I went home and modelled a dress for Satyawart before a wedding I had to attend. I tried on a wedding lehenga and another dress. I also wore a mini dress, but with full sleeves – I may have changed, but some things still remain the same!

16

Fighting for Satyawart

Even as I hopped from function to function after winning my Olympic medal, I was fighting another battle, which was completely hidden from the cameras.

Now that my professional life was at its peak, it was time to take some time out for my personal life. Over the past year, Satyawart and I had finally worked up the courage to tell our respective parents about each other. My mother had met Satyawart a few times. She liked him and told me so, too. Finally, in 2015, she had invited him to my brother's wedding. That was a very big deal for me.

I had told my mother that we wanted to get married after the Olympics. Although my parents hadn't met his family prior to the Rio Olympics, Satyawart and I had already started to think about the date for our engagement.

Soon after I returned, Satyawart's parents came to our home in Rohtak. They had brought balushahis, which were my favourite sweets, and they put a *teeka* on my forehead. In our culture, that teeka was a way of symbolizing the fact that I was going to be their daughter-in-law.

I felt very happy. We hadn't been formally engaged, but a verbal commitment had been made between him and me. Things were progressing well, I felt. My father had a big smile on his face that evening and was getting along splendidly with Satyawart's father. The two even shared a meal together.

I slept blissfully, thinking of how happy I was going to be with Satyawart.

But I woke up to a storm the next day. My mother was saying this wedding wasn't going to happen.

I was still bleary eyed, but I woke up very quickly when I heard this.

What had happened? Weren't things going well?

My mother was apparently upset that Satyawart's mother had put that teeka on my forehead. According to her, Satyawart's family was trying to trying to snatch me away from the family. 'Without asking us, how did his parents put a teeka on you?' she asked me.

She started to belittle his family. She saw them as a family that only knew how to wrestle and who weren't particularly educated. I, on the other hand, was an Olympic medallist. I was much too sophisticated to be married into a rustic family of wrestlers. She promised she'd get me married to the kind of boy I deserved. Someone rich and educated.

Huh? What was going on? Was I still dreaming?

I started to cry. I didn't know what to do. I felt trapped. I couldn't object to my parents, but I also couldn't not marry the man I loved.

I finally took a stand. That morning, for the first time for as far back as I can remember, I told my parents that come what may, I was going to marry Satyawart.

Satyawart only found out when my brother called him, asking to meet him. It was a trap my brother had planned to purposely instigate Satyawart into a fight by insulting him. Once that happened, I would have no option but to break up with a man who had fought my own brother. I found out and warned Satyawart not to go and to stay away from my family until the whole thing had blown over.

In the meantime, as a new Olympic medallist, I still had all my functions to attend. On the day of this fight in my home, I had been invited to go to Hyderabad for a function where Sachin Tendulkar was going to present me, P.V. Sindhu and Deepa Karmakar with a BMW each.

Our flight was in the evening and I had spent the whole day crying. I was crying all the way to the airport, even as the box of balushahis that Satyawart's parents had brought me lay unopened. And while I was crying, my mother kept repeating to herself, 'You are not getting married to that boy.'

Despite what I was going through, I still had to keep up appearances. I had to look like an Olympic medallist who was thrilled about collecting a BMW, which I honestly couldn't have cared less about.

This wasn't easy at all. I am a very ugly crier. My face gets hot and crimson. My eyes were swollen and red with tears. When the photographers wanted to take pictures of me at the airport, I washed my face with water and put on a big smile. All the while I was thinking, I had won an Olympic medal less than a week ago and I couldn't even enjoy it.

I stayed silent on the flight and in Hyderabad. My mother and brother thought it meant I'd finally broken. Although I'd not eaten since the previous night and was staying in a five star hotel for the first time in my life, I didn't touch the dinner that my mother and brother had ordered. I was feeling sick and heartbroken.

As my mother and brother ate, I sat on the bed and texted Satyawart from my phone. My mother caught wind of what I was doing and ordered me to put the phone away. Once again, I replied that I'd do no such thing.

My mother was shocked that I was talking back to her.

'Aren't you ashamed of yourself?'

I was of course petrified of even raising my voice against my parents until then. I'd never even questioned them or used the informal *'tu'* when speaking to them. I had no idea what had come over me.

Although I was still adamant that I would marry Satyawart, I tried to make her understand what I was going through. 'Mummy you are getting so upset with me, but shouldn't it also bother you that I haven't eaten until now?'

It didn't do any good. Neither of us was willing to back down.

After yet another fight, I went to sleep. The next day's programme was at 10 a.m. and I got up at 6.30 that morning to get my hair and make-up done. I didn't tell my mother and just quietly slipped out of the room. When my mother woke up she found the room empty. She immediately assumed I'd had left the hotel and gone away.

I'd left my phone on silent mode while I was getting my make-up done and saw dozens upon dozens of missed calls when I finally checked it. I got another one, from my father. He wasn't so invested in my not marrying Satyawart; he was just going along with what my mother was telling him.

My father said he'd agree to let me marry whoever I wanted, as long as I returned to my room. He too thought I was so upset that I had left the hotel. I wasn't actually thinking of running away, though. That was a complete taboo in our society and I'd never dream of embarrassing my family that way.

Once I returned to my room, my brother brought in a plate of breakfast as a peace offering. I ate, thinking that now that I'd taken a stand, the worst was behind me.

It wasn't.

I collected the keys of my BMW without incident and was then sent along with P.V. Sindhu and Deepa Karmakar on a chartered flight back to Delhi for the national sports awards where I was being presented with the Khel Ratna. I checked in with them into the Ashoka hotel in New Delhi, where all the athletes receiving awards were expected to stay.

After attending the dress rehearsal the following day, I was texting Satyawart and telling him about my day, when once again my mother resumed her line about not allowing me to marry him. She told me to stop texting him or she would call him and tell him to stay away from me.

All this while, Satyawart had been messaging me to be calm and that things would get better with time. He wasn't pressuring me to go against my family. But for the first time, he asked me if I wanted to take a stand. If I did, he would fight with me.

The next day I collected the Khel Ratna and smiled for the cameras as if I didn't have a care in the world. Although I pretended that everything was fine, my family was still worried. Instead of letting me speak to the media as every other athlete did, I was rushed back to my room.

Waiting for me there was my mother's elder brother. He was a government official and considered the wealthiest and, as a result of that, the most well-respected member of the family.

He asked me to stay away from Satyawart for just a couple of years and focus on my wrestling. After that, if I still wanted to marry him, he'd himself get me married to him. Of course, they were just trying to get me to leave Satyawart one way or the other.

The stress was too much. But I'd told Satyawart I was willing to take a stand, and I did just that. My brother would cry and ask why I wanted to defame the family. My mother would tell me how she'd sacrificed so much to get me to where I was.

I wasn't budging. Once again they started to think I was going to leave. When we left the hotel and headed back to Rohtak, they made me sit me in the backseat of the car with my mother and brother sitting on either side of me.

The back and forth of 'You can't marry Satyawart' from their end and 'I'm only going to marry him' from me, continued for a few days. There would be moments where they would seem to come around to agreeing to our match and, a few hours later, they'd be against it once again.

I couldn't for the life of me understand what had come over my family. Surely the incident with the teeka, or the fact that Satyawart's family wasn't very educated or their perception that he wasn't good enough for me couldn't be the cause behind all this heartache. I began to wonder if there was a financial incentive behind it.

After I'd won a medal at the Olympics and the first announcements of cash awards started to come in, my mother, who had otherwise been the most supportive person in my life, started to act in a way that was completely unlike her.

I think that, in her reasoning, if I became Satyawart's wife, then like all married women, I would become a member of his family. That meant that all the name, fame and, of course, money that I was sure to get would go to them. She felt that I'd been raised by her, and now, just when I had reached the pinnacle of my career, I was going to be a part of someone else's family. To put it crudely, it was they who had made the investment in me and it was someone else who was going to get the windfall.

It had always been the Haryana government's sports policy to award money to sportspersons for their achievements. I'd receive cash awards for winning medals at the Junior World Championships and the World Cadet Championships. I had also got close to Rs 80 lakh for winning a silver at the 2014 Commonwealth Games (CWG). The Haryana government gave me Rs 60 lakh and I received around Rs 20 lakh from the Central government, Indian Railways and other organizations.

That money might as well have been just a number to me. My focus was always wrestling, while my family handled my money for me. While I was at the national camp, I'd even signed a few blank cheques in case they needed to make big transactions. Although I had a bank account and an ATM card, both were linked to my mother's phone. I didn't really care. If I had to shop or needed to make an online payment, I'd just call my mother for the OTP. My mother never asked me what I was spending money on, and she'd always give me the code whenever I asked for it.

While I was spending money on shopping for clothes and shoes, there were other purchases and expenses too. With part of the money that I'd received for winning the Commonwealth Games, my brother opened a Subway franchise in Rohtak. Although he operated it, it was registered under the name of Sofia Foods. Sofia was my childhood name, and that was the name by which people who knew me from when I was little still called me.

I didn't question when any of these investments were made and, honestly, I didn't care either way. I was happy that my brother was doing well for himself.

All the money I'd received previously, though, had been a pittance compared to what I was going to get after winning my Olympic medal. Maybe if more of us Indian athletes had won medals at Rio, I might have had to share the rewards, but since just P.V. Sindhu and I had stood on the podium for India, it was just the two of us who were being showered with money and honours.

The Haryana government had transferred Rs 2.5 crore into my account on the very same day that I won my medal. In Telangana, I was given Rs 1 crore. Mahindra Motors presented me with a Thar and Datsun gifted me a car too. I was gifted cash prizes at every function I went to. And all that went to my account.

In all of this, no one was really thinking of what I wanted. The money wasn't even something I was thinking about. My only priority was to somehow convince my parents to let me marry Satyawart.

Thanks to all the eating I'd done at the Games Village, I'd gained 8 kg over the 58 kg I weighed at the start of my competition. Within three weeks of my return to India, I'd lost all that weight and was once again weighing 58 kg, thanks to all the stress I was under. It had always been very hard for me to lose weight, and it was a real nightmare for me to lose that last kilo I needed to shed, but I'd lost weight now without even realizing it. I guess that's a trick for weight cutting that someone should have told me about!

It finally struck me that my family wasn't going to listen to me and that I'd have to make a decision for myself. The way to do that was to make my engagement official by leaking it to the media.

I'd saved the numbers of a few journalists at the 2014 CWG and I called one of them up, asking if he wanted to publish a story. He didn't write the story but gave me the number of a Rohtak-based reporter. I told the reporter that I had a story for him, which was that I was getting engaged to a wrestler named Satyawart Kadian. He in turn gave the story to every other journalist in town. Just like that I'd fired that bullet!

My engagement made it to the front page of every newspaper in Rohtak the next day.

My parents were understandably furious. They called up the newspapers and asked them to print a correction. But of course they wouldn't do that. My family was so upset that they locked me in a room.

She said I'd scandalized the whole family and that horrible things should happen to girls like me. For all the support and freedom my family had been given me in my youth to pursue my dreams, they were in the end bound by tradition. No one in my family had ever married for love. It was unheard of.

I'd like to believe their threats were spoken out of anger, but they were certainly trying to scare me. I'd of course gone so far along in my decision that I answered back from the other side of the door that they could try to threaten me all they wanted, but I was still going to marry Satyawart.

My mother was shocked. I was always this quiet, shy girl who wouldn't raise her voice, and now I seemed a different creature.

When they finally let me out, I got into a Volkswagen Polo my family had bought for me from part of the money I had received for winning the Commonwealth Games silver. I decided that I was going to go to Satyawart's home, when my mother pulled the back

Fighting for Satyawart

door open and sat in the car. Both of us started arguing once again but I wasn't backing down.

It was only after this final showdown that my mother finally agreed to let me marry Satyawart and my engagement was announced publicly on 16 October.

By this time I'd become close to Nayantara, my personal manager. A couple of days after my family had finally come around to letting me marry Satyawart, I told her the whole story.

In turn, she told me that since I was probably going to start a new life as a married woman, it was probably time for me to start handling my own finances. Over the past several weeks, she had already been asking me to check if all my payments for the events I was attending was going into my account and I'd always put off the idea of actually looking into it. Now she insisted I at least go to the bank and see just what was happening.

This made sense to me, and I went to the State Bank of India branch near my home in Rohtak where I had my account. I went in and told the manager that I wanted to change the phone number that was linked to the bank from my mother's number to mine. I changed my signatures and asked to see my statements.

My statements showed that I had at one point had a little over Rs 4 crore in my account. But on the day I visited the bank to get the phone number changed, I only had a fraction of that amount remaining.

Over the past few days, most of my money had been transferred out of my account. I believe this happened because my family thought that if Satywart's family saw that I didn't have any money, they would themselves call off the wedding. Once I realized what had happened, I instructed the bank manager that no further bank transactions should be carried out in my account without my explicit permission.

When I returned home, my family looked at me as if I had committed a crime by taking control over my account. But I didn't think I had done anything wrong. I admit my parents had played a big role in my development as a wrestler but I had a right to know where my hard-earned money was going. I was just taking charge of it.

I did manage to see some of the prize money awarded to me after the Olympics. Some states had delayed paying me the prize money they had announced. In Uttar Pradesh, Akhilesh Yadav had announced a reward of Rs 1 crore, but that payment got delayed because of the state elections. Then, when his party lost the elections, the new government under Yogi Adityanath put a hold on all financial transactions. When the government finally released the money, I'd already got married, and so that cheque went into my account which only I had access to.

You might think I'd be furious with what had happened, but to be very honest, I didn't really think all that much about it. I wasn't worried about the money. I just wanted to get married to Satyawart. And now that my parents had finally agreed, I wasn't too concerned about anything else.

There would still be some minor hiccups until we got to that special day in April the next year, though. The tradition in the society I'm from is that when an engagement takes place, the bride's family usually gives the groom some small token – like a ring, a watch or a chain. Satyawart wasn't given anything. I can only think this was done so that he might think the relationship he was so committed to was not worth it. He never complained, though. He wanted to get married to me just as much.

What was more galling to Satyawart and me was the fact that we had to invite Brij Bhushan Sharan Singh. He would have taken it as an insult if he was not invited, and even if I was an Olympic medallist, I didn't want any trouble with him. The only concession to my pride was that I didn't give him the invitation myself; it was my parents who did that.

I might have been an Olympic medallist but I came to Satyawarts' home nearly completely empty-handed. I didn't bring most of my prize money of course but I also left behind my Nissan and the Thar. I didn't even bring that BMW car that I'd been presented in Hyderabad. Despite all of this, I didn't have many regrets. Satyawart had stood by me all this while, and the two of us were just happy that we were finally able to get engaged. We were proud that we had been able to take a stand.

Satyawart had a Swift Dzire, and while I had hoped to arrive in some style to my wedding, even that little hatchback felt like the most expensive car there was, because my life partner was sitting beside me in it.

While I was glad to be starting a new chapter in my life, I have to admit I was also experiencing the lowest point of my relationship with my parents. They had supported me so much when I was a girl, and my wrestling career wouldn't have been possible without them, but at the same time, their actions over the last few months had hurt me.

It's taken a long time to mend ties with my family. Our relationship had undoubtedly frayed. We barely spoke for a year or two and I didn't visit them for a long time. I think they too regretted what had happened because, after my marriage, they sent me my BMW, if only to pacify me a little. Then, after I won a medal at the 2018

Commonwealth Games, they reached out to congratulate me. Later, when I started the protest against Brij Bhushan Singh in January 2023, my mother came and sat with me at the protest site. She'd make a note of all the people who would come to join our protest and I am glad she was there alongside me.

I know it will be very hard to make things right as they once were between us. We don't speak over the phone anywhere as much as we used to, and I don't go home as frequently as I might have done under different circumstances, but it's better than what it used to be.

I learned a couple of things from this episode. The first was that it's important to choose a life partner well. If you are going to take a stand for someone, you'd better do it for someone who means everything to you.

The other is just the need to be aware of your own finances. This is something no one teaches Indian sportspersons, and especially Indian sportswomen. If you are a sportsperson, you are always thinking about your game. You almost never think about where your money is coming from, where it is going, where to invest it and what mistakes to avoid.

I at least had some education, so I was able to finally understand, though belatedly, when things went wrong. Most of the women who are in this sport don't even have that. I'm not the first sportswoman who has faced this and I won't be the last.

While what happened came as a shock to me, it shouldn't have. In the days after I had won my Olympic bronze, Vinesh had actually told me that I should start being a bit more careful or at least aware of my finances. At that time I thought she was being a little too cynical and told her as much. Later, when I met Vinesh at the national camp and told her what had happened, she sympathized with me but also smiled, as if to say 'I told you so!'

I now try to make other young women aware of the need to be careful with their finances. I tell them to have their focus on wrestling but also to be aware of where their money is coming from, where it's going, where their parents are investing it and what the girls are doing to secure their own future. At the 2022 Commonwealth Games, Vinesh and I sat down some of the younger girls in the team and told them the same thing – be aware of what's going on.

For some reason, this doesn't seem to happen with the male sportspersons all that much. I think it's because they are independent for the most part. Girls trust their families a lot more.

I've always believed that what happened to me after the Olympics was karma. I remembered how, when I was a seven-year-old schoolgirl, I would steal those one or two rupees from the bags of other kids. I never considered how it must have hurt them. Maybe their parents had not packed any food for them and that money was for them to buy lunch with. And now the same thing was being 'paid back' to me.

I might have earned a lot of money but I ended up having to part with it all the same.

I know people say that if you have done something wrong you come back reborn as an insect or something like that, but I don't think I have had to wait even that long. You pay for all your sins in this very life.

Although I was disappointed by what had happened, I don't dwell too much over it. I've moved on with my life. I'm lucky I have a partner whom I can trust completely. And even though Satyawart handles most of my finances now, I'm not nearly as clueless about them anymore.

   I might not be as rich as I could have been, but I'm wiser and I still have a lot to be grateful for. I've done more than I ever thought I could, and I'm lucky I've never had to worry about where my money is coming from.

17

Post-Olympic Struggles

There are plenty of perks that come from winning an Olympic medal. All of a sudden, sponsors are very willing to support you. The government approves any plans you have to train abroad. Just a few months before, I'd never be sure if there was going to be a training camp before a competition. Now that I had a bronze medal around my neck, I'd get clearance for wherever I wanted to go and train. Did I want to train in the USA? No problem. A camp in France? Of course. I was even able to get a personal physiotherapist to travel with me.

But it wasn't as if I was getting all of these privileges for nothing. Now that I had an Olympic medal, the expectations from me had grown as well. I'd always found it hard to deal with the pressure of going out on the mat. Now I had the added burden of knowing that there was all this money invested in me and that people had such high expectations from me.

At the back of my mind, I knew I didn't belong in these five-star hotel ballrooms. I just wanted to get back to the training hall. At first it was just a feeling of unease, but then it became real dread when I looked at the international wrestling calendar and started seeing the 2017 season rushing at me.

To get into some sort of competitive shape, I knew I had to train twice a day and get adequate rest too. But unfortunately, there were just two Indians with Olympic medals in 2016. All the programmes and functions across India had to be split between just the two of us. I couldn't get anything close to the kind of preparation I needed. I joined the camp late, and even while training there I had to leave it on some days to attend events because the requests had come from my sponsors. Finally, I put my foot down.

Most years, the first major competition of the season would be the Asian Championships. Usually, these competitions would be held in some obscure city in Asia. They would come and go and almost no one – unless they were associated with wrestling in some way – knew much about them. Unfortunately for me, my return to international wrestling was going to take place in Delhi.

Even with the best of preparation, the Asian Championships would have been hard. The strongest national teams didn't always send their best athletes to the Asian Championships – they'd sometimes use the tournament as a chance for their younger talents to get some international exposure ahead of the more important competitions like the World Championships. But the 2017 edition was tough. Risako Kawai, the Olympic champion, was there, as was Shoovdor Baatarjavyn, a three-time world medallist from Mongolia. Through sheer luck I found myself on the other side of the bracket from Kawai, Baatarjavyn and another strong wrestler from China. I came through a relatively weaker half to the final.

In the final though, I got a taste of reality against Kawai. Even if I had been in perfect shape I would have had to wrestle a near-perfect

Post-Olympic Struggles

match against her. That would take a miracle, what with the level of preparation I had. That miracle didn't happen. I got the silver.

Japanese wrestlers are something else. Other countries, even those with a strong wrestling background, had players of varying quality. They'd have excellent wrestlers in some years, and in other years wrestlers who were more beatable. Japan never seemed to have a bad year.

Even though we might beat wrestlers from China or Mongolia, who have very strong teams too, everyone would admit that the Japanese women operated at another level altogether.

This was especially true at the lower and middle weights. Their wrestlers in the heavier weights, like the 68 kg and 76 kg categories, didn't have that same aura, but at anything less than 65 kg you knew you were going to have a difficult day against a Japanese wrestler.

Sometimes I think was beaten in my mind even before I stepped on to the mat against a wrestler from Japan. I was conditioned to think they were better than me. Right from the time I started wrestling, I'd always hear about how good the Japanese women were. I heard it for the first time in my akhara when the senior girls would talk to us after training. They kept saying that the Japanese girls were so good, the Chinese girls were so good... We Indians were nothing compared with them.

At the national camp, the senior girls reinforced that same idea. I'd be told the reason someone didn't get a medal was because she was up against a woman from Japan. It wasn't that that aura was made out of nothing. They had so many Olympic champions. Saori Yoshida had already won two Olympic gold medals when I was at the national camp. Kaori Icho, in whose weight category I'd later wrestle, would end her career with four Olympic golds.

What stood out for me the first time I encountered the Japanese women's team at the 2008 Asian Cadet Championships, and subsequently after that too, was just how disciplined they were. They'd always come for training together. We Indians would also practise together for the most part, but might train separately if someone had a match the next day.

The Japanese girls would come as one. They'd chant hype songs together. It was almost as if they were an army. They'd come together and leave together. They'd even eat together. They were incredibly intense.

When I did wrestle with them, I didn't actually feel they were any stronger than me. But they were just so much more technical. They seemed to understand when to apply force and how to move me.

There were moments, especially in the junior age groups, when I felt I'd figured them out. I even beat one of them at the 2012 Asian Junior Championships, where I won gold. But when I met a Japanese woman at the senior level, it seemed as if she was several steps above us. I think it's because their technique has been refined thoroughly at the junior level. One of their wrestlers – Yui Susaki – became a senior world champion at nineteen. At the same age, I was still perfecting my stance and refining my technique.

They also had incredible bench strength. Risako had a younger sister Yukako, who won the gold at the Tokyo Games. And she had to beat the Rio Olympic champion to even make it to the team. They had to beat Olympic champions simply to get to the stage where they could represent Japan.

When I wrestled Risako in the final of the Asian Championships, I could immediately tell there was a gulf between us. The strange thing was that when she pushed against me, it didn't feel as if she was

Post-Olympic Struggles

much stronger than me. In fact, I think I might have been stronger than her. Risako was actually small for her weight category. She competed in the 63 kg category at the Rio Olympics and was still small enough to cut weight and make the 57 kg category in Tokyo, where she won gold.

But I never got a chance to apply my strength against her. By the time I'd set myself up she had already moved. I felt as if I was just heavier against her. She was moving so much quicker than I was. If I started to make an attack, she seemed to read it before I'd even made my move. The only way I can describe her wrestling style is with the word 'contactless'.

I wasn't ready to face someone of her calibre. I knew that very early into our match. I didn't just lose that match, she crushed me to win by superiority in the first round itself.

Although I have beaten one Japanese girl as a junior, I've never beaten a wrestler from Japan in the senior category. The closest I got to understanding their style was when, for the first time, I wrestled Risako's younger sister Yukako Kawai at the 2018 World Championships. I knew that she was Risako's sister and, of course, since she was from Japan, she was surely good. But she was in her first year on the international circuit. She had also not wrestled me previously, so I didn't really fear facing her. Moreover, I'd beaten a Russian wrestler in the previous round and was feeling good.

I actually got a takedown against her early in the match, and although she won a step-out point against me, I had defended well. If I had just been a little careful I might have won that bout. But I got greedy. I tried to make an attack without really waiting for the right opportunity and left myself open to a counter-attack. I got caught in a wrestling technique known as leg lace. That's next to the worst grip you could find yourself in. Once you get tied in one, it's next to impossible to get out because your legs, which are your base, are interlaced with each other and completely in your opponent's control. It was doubly hard for me because I had had my knee operated on. By the time I faced her again at the 2019 Asian Championships, she'd improved exponentially and pinned me quickly.

That loss to Yukako at the 2018 World Championships sometimes pricks me because I was in fairly good form in that competition. I still had a chance to win a medal through repechage, but I narrowly lost a bout to a local contestant from Hungary. Despite this, I don't have a lot of regret that I never did win a world championship medal. It's not that it wouldn't have been nice – if I had to rate international competitions in terms of difficulty, only the Olympics are a harder competition to medal in, but the fact is that the World Championships took place every year and you didn't really have to qualify to take part in one. The Olympics, on the other hand, took place only once every four years and you had to earn the right to even compete in one.

More significantly, unlike the World Championships, the Olympics were a multi-sport games. The medal you won there counted towards the Indian team's total. You weren't just competing as an individual wrestler but also for your country.

That's why I'll always feel that the one competition I really regret not winning a medal in was the 2018 Asian Games.

I think I've done fairly well in my career. I have three medals from the Commonwealth Games, which just one other Indian woman wrestler has. I'll always be the first Indian woman to have won an Olympic medal, and I also have many medals from the Asian Championships. But I'll always feel bad that I missed the gold at the Jakarta Asian Games by the barest of margins.

Post-Olympic Struggles

I was coming to that tournament with a point to prove, because I'd just won a bronze medal at the Commonwealth Games in Glasgow earlier that year. I had really struggled in that tournament because one of the bone fragments from my knee surgery had come loose. I was in excruciating pain every time I bent my knee, Naturally, I lost to both Nigeria and Canada and very nearly lost to a relatively unknown wrestler from New Zealand before managing a bronze.

Just like that, the pain went away right after the competition, and my luck only seemed to get better at the Asian Games in Jakarta, where I got a very favourable draw. The World Champion Purevdorjiin Orkhon of Mongolia was on the other side of the draw, as was Risako Kawai.

I beat Ayaulym Kassymova, an Asian championships bronze medallist in the second round, to set up a bout against Aisuluu Tynybekova in the semi-final. After she'd lost to me in the final seconds of the Rio Olympics, she'd gone on to win a bronze at the 2017 World Championships, but I still carried the confidence of having beaten her when it mattered at the Olympics.

I started the bout well. I made two takedowns to go 4-0, but Tynybekova scored six to make it 6-4. In the second round, I again took her down and then scored off a step-out to make it 7-6. It was close, but I was almost through to the final.

At this point it was my turn to make the same mistake in Jakarta as Tynybekova had made against me at Rio. I was looking at the clock, so I knew I had just ten seconds left. I was just running the clock down. As I paused, she attacked. She tripped me and secured a last-second takedown to win the match.

I lost 9-7, and that was that. I still had a chance in the repechage, but there was no happy ending like in Rio. I was so mentally broken at losing a match that I should have won that I was beaten very quickly, 12-2, by a North Korean wrestler.

I've played that moment multiple times in my head since. If I had just faked a move, if I had just defended a little better, I would have had an assured silver. Eventually, although Tynybekova lost to Orkhon in the final, she was upgraded to gold because the Mongolian would later fail a dope test. That meant that if I had held on against Tynybekova for just a second longer, I would have won a gold and become an Asian Games champion. I don't have many regrets about anything in my career, but this is the one result that troubles me.

I think her last-second win against me at the Asian Games turned Tynybekova's life around. After she won gold at the Asian Games, she went on to win gold at the 2019 World Championships, and she won that Olympic medal she always wanted in Tokyo.

I was happy for Tynybekova when she won her Olympic silver. While we were opponents I always respected her on the mat. She was a thoroughly fair wrestler. I've later travelled with her to Kyrgyzstan for a tournament and training camp. She's a bit of a star in her country because she was its first world medallist in wrestling. She was a very generous host. She fed me and treated me as a friend. She's by nature one of the kindest persons I've met.

While my poor performance at the Commonwealth Games and defeats at the Asian Games and the World Championships that year were disappointing, I still hoped to turn things around at the 2020 Olympics. After my bronze in Rio, I was India's undisputed number one in the 62 kg category. I'd not been beaten in India since 2015, when Geeta Phogat beat me in the selection trial for the World Championships.

Post-Olympic Struggles

Even if I wasn't the very best outside India, I was still competitive. I might not be in that absolute elite group, as my results had shown, but if I prepared better I knew I could get there. I was so focused on the international scene that I didn't even notice that I had started getting challengers in India itself.

I found that out the hard way when I lost to Sonam Malik in 2020 during a selection trial for the Rome Ranking series wrestling competition. I had only the slightest idea who she was. I knew she was talented – she had two gold medals at the World Cadet Championships already and regularly beat Japanese girls, something I hadn't done. She was only seventeen years old back then and had taken special permission to be allowed to compete in the senior category.

But for all her potential, I didn't see her as a real threat. I started the match really well, taking her down multiple times to lead 6-0. She scored 2, and then again to make it 6-4. She'd taken me down twice in a row, but she was racing against the clock. She was fighting hard, but I scored another two takedowns to one of hers to lead 10-6.

With perhaps a second left, I relaxed for just a bit and she found the opening she was looking for. In the very last move of the match, she caught me in a move called *dhaak* and threw me over her shoulder for four points. The scores were tied 10-10, but because Sonam had made the biggest move of the match she was declared the winner. Just like that, my unbeaten streak in India was over.

With that her confidence bloomed even as mine sank. Not only did my confidence sink but I was also seized by a fear, which didn't leave for the next two years. I still don't know why that happened. I was training at the same level and intensity as I had before the Rio Olympics. And when I had practice bouts and sparring matches inside the camp, I was still winning. But when it came to the actual matches that mattered, I wasn't able to come through.

A month after I lost for the first time domestically, to Sonam, I lost again in another trial, this time for the Asian qualification tournament for the Tokyo Olympic Games a month later. Knowing I had been careless in the first match, I was completely defensive the second time around. I tried my best to not give her a single opening, but with just over a minute to go, she turned me over her shoulder, threw me on the mat and pinned me.

That loss really shook me. A single defeat could be explained away by a momentary lapse of concentration. But I had been so careful in this second match. And yet I couldn't have lost it in a more comprehensive manner.

Even as I was coming to terms with what had happened, the COVID-19 pandemic struck and we went into lockdown. The Olympic qualifiers were cancelled and the Games were postponed. It might have been a terrible time for the country, but I was sure this was the universe looking out for me. Because the Olympics were postponed, there would have to be another set of trials again. This time I vowed I would win.

I did everything I thought I needed to. Now that I had at least another year to prepare, I underwent another surgery on my knee. I trained as hard as I ever had. At the National Championships in Agra in February 2021, I was as well prepared as I'd ever been. And when I came up against Sonam in the final, was sure I was going to beat her.

That didn't happen. The result was a close one – 8-7 to Sonam – but it was a defeat, nonetheless.

If I had first thought that my defeats could be explained by a few moments of carelessness on my part, by third and fourth defeats I

Post-Olympic Struggles

began to accept the problem was far deeper. I started wondering if there was something wrong with me. It wasn't that I didn't respect Sonam. I knew she had a very impressive resume, and while she was still breaking out of the juniors when we first met, she was now slowly reaching her physical peak and getting ever stronger. Like it or not, I had to accept that by losing to her again and again, I'd built up her confidence. She had acquired that self-belief, now that she had beaten an Olympic bronze medallist. When I beat Geeta Phogat for the first time at the Pro Wrestling League in 2015, I got that same shot of self-belief. At that time Geeta was the first Indian to have qualified for the Olympics, and after I beat her I too started believing I would go to the Olympics myself.

For all my dominance in the years gone by, I knew it was inevitable that someone would come along at the right time to beat me. And I saw a lot of myself in Sonam, too. I remember the first time she came to the national camp, I'd sometimes look up from my training routine and catch her staring at me. At first I wondered if she was trying to intimidate me. Or if was she trying to see what I was doing so that she could copy me. It took me some time to realize I'd behaved exactly the way Sonam did now, when I was new to the camp. I'd constantly stare at Geeta Phogat during my early years in the national camp. I would always want to see how she was training. I was obsessed with Geeta.

It was the same with Sonam. She idolized me just the way I had idolized Geeta.

But that was then, and this was now. When I was facing Sonam, I was in reality facing just a younger, stronger version of myself with as much to prove as I once had.

It was just my bad luck that she was reaching her full potential as an athlete just as my mental weakness was making things even harder for me. But at that time I was struggling to process all of it. I just couldn't understand why I couldn't beat this girl.

It was almost a relief when Sonam won the Olympic qualification tournament and earned the right to compete at Tokyo. During the pandemic, when I was at home, I'd made a drawing of the Tokyo Olympic logo. I kept repeating to myself that I would certainly go. I was the one who would go. Even when I lost twice more to Sonam and I battled self-doubt, I was sure that there would be a miracle and I'd ultimately go to the Olympics. All that hoping against hope was now over. I felt a sense of finality; that the pressure on me was finally over.

I took my failure to qualify for the Olympics better than I had expected. Although I wasn't going to the Olympics, I didn't have a problem watching the competition on TV. I followed Vinesh and Sonam's bouts. I watched the women's hockey matches too. When I watched the tournament I felt a little nostalgic. I missed that feeling of being there myself. As an athlete who has been there once before, you can watch the Games as a fan, but it's impossible not to see yourself on that platform.

18

My Struggles Continue

Failing to make it to the Indian team that would try to qualify for the Olympics was one of the lowest points in my career. But I had further to fall still.

Just a few weeks after the Olympics concluded in August, I took part in the selection trials for the 2021 World Championships. With Sonam not competing, I expected this to be a relatively easy tune-up for the World Championships. It was anything but, as I lost my first-round match to another relatively new wrestler, Manisha Bhanwala. I started the match well enough, going into the break with a 3-0 lead. From there on, she took control of the match, scoring 5 unanswered points to win 5-3.

And just as it was against Sonam, once I lost that first match, I went on a downward slide, which I just had no idea how to turn around. Two months after losing to Manisha for the first time, I lost to her once again, in the quarter final of the 2021 National Championships in Gonda. In all my previous matches against both Sonam and Manisha, I could have argued that I had my moments. I had lead in all of them before things went wrong. But I was almost never in contention at Gonda. Manisha attacked from the start right until the end, winning 7-1.

Every loss is painful, but the defeat in Gonda was particularly bad. It was one thing to lose to Sonam – I could console myself saying that at least I had lost to an Olympian. And honestly, I saw a lot of myself in her. She had the same passion and dedication to the game as I did.

Manisha, who was four years younger than me, didn't have a record nearly as good as Sonam's. In fact, much of what motivated her was a deep grudge she held against me. In the past, Manisha had been in a relationship with Satyawart's younger brother Sombir. They were talking of marriage, but her mother belonged to the same clan as Sombir's father. Since this was a big Jat taboo, the entire family was opposed to the wedding.

Manisha had always hoped that I would speak out in her favour. I found out later that she believed that I had not only not helped her but had also refused to give my consent to the match. The truth was that although I didn't take her side, I hadn't spoken against her either.

This wasn't my decision to make at all. This was a choice to be made by Sombir, his parents and hers. At the end of the day, this was a union between two families. Regardless of how open-minded Satyawart and I are, we can't take that decision for someone else. It will be different when it comes to my children. I'll stand by whatever choice they make, but I can't do the same for someone else. Sombir went by his father's choice in the matter. I couldn't intervene there.

But that didn't matter to Manisha. She always held me responsible for what happened and she always fought me with even more intensity than she might have otherwise.

That day I walked off the mat dazed, almost sleepwalking. There were people who still wanted to get clicked with me because I was

My Struggles Continue

an Olympic medallist, but I don't remember smiling in any of the pictures. There I was, a former Olympic medallist who didn't even know whether she would win a medal at the National Championships.

I wouldn't.

After I lost to Manisha, my only chance for a medal was if she made the final and pulled me into repechage. The way she was wrestling, it should have been easy for her. But instead, Manisha forfeited her next match against Sangeeta Phogat. As a result, I didn't even have the chance to win a bronze medal. Despite forfeiting that one match, Manisha came out and wrestled for the bronze herself.

The nationals were won by Sangeeta. Later, when I would wrestle her in practice matches at the national camp, Sangeeta would barely be able to score points against me. There was no way that she would have been able to beat Manisha at the nationals.

Manisha had conceded her match against Sangeeta simply so that I would return empty-handed. Indeed, I returned medal-less at what I didn't know then was to be my last National Championships.

I'd already found a way to rationalize my previous defeats. But there was no explaining away this one. My first couple of losses to Sonam were because of a few seconds of carelessness. Then I felt that maybe I was struggling against her specific technique, and that even if I was, it was against a very worthy opponent. But now, when I had lost two matches against yet another wrestler, it really made me question myself.

Anyone can have a bad day. But when I lost again and again, that made me think there was something very wrong with me. I've never felt as much self-doubt as I did then. It's one thing when people start counting you out. It's another when you start telling yourself that maybe you aren't good enough.

As I sat and watched the other girls wrestle in Gonda, I grappled with dark thoughts. I kept thinking, 'I can't be this bad. This can't be the end.' The next day, as Satyawart and I drove back from Gonda, he reinforced that belief. He said that this wasn't the way my career would end. Something better had been written for me.

There's a piece of dialogue in the film *Band Baaja Baaraat*, saying that sometimes when things go so badly, the only way forward is up. The hero has to start winning eventually. But it had been two years since I'd won anything. I just couldn't place my finger on just why I was doing badly. To this day I don't know just what happened to me. I'm not at all superstitious, but if someone says that I had a hex cast on me during that phase, I might actually think there is something to it.

That's actually what my in-laws thought had happened. They were convinced that Manisha had performed black magic on me! She had always competed in the lighter weight categories because she wasn't very tall, but had moved up to my weight class just for that national championship. Of course I didn't believe any of that, but that's what my in-laws at least thought.

Unknown to me, Satyawart's parents went to a jyotish. My in-laws could see just how low I was and maybe they just wanted some reassurance that things would be all right. The jyotish told them just that. He said that although I had had a bad year, 2022 would be the year my luck changed.

He even told me that I should wear a certain gemstone to bring me luck. My mother-in-law did buy me a white stone to wear around my neck, and I did put it on just to make her feel better. But I didn't really have any faith in it.

Against my better judgement, I also went to a numerologist. He told me to change the spelling of my name from Sakshi Malik to

Sakshee Malikkh. I changed the name of my Twitter handle to the new spelling in the start of 2022. I was thinking of changing the name of my other social media accounts but then I decided against it.

Changing my fate was in my hands, not in the stars, planets or coloured stones or strangely spelt names. Indeed, when I went back to the national camp in Lucknow in the 2022 season, I lost to Manisha once again in a selection trials match for the 2022 Asian Championships, and I stopped wearing that stone not long after that.

Even though I'd lost for the third straight time to Manisha, I started to regain some of my confidence at the start of the national camp. One of my first sparring sessions was with Sangeeta, and just like before, I didn't concede a single point to her. That gave me some confidence – that I still had something left to give. I was at least capable of beating the national champion, if not Sonam or Manisha.

Despite my struggles, I never thought I'd deteriorated physically, or that perhaps I wasn't as strong and fast as I was in 2016. At the national camp, I could compare what I did with what the others were doing. I was always the best in the camp. If it was something they could measure – physical fitness, sprints or power training – every girl there knew that Sakshi Malik was the benchmark to beat. That's one of the reasons why my performance on the mat those two years confused me. I'd always been the strongest girl in the camp. We had an American coach, Andrew Cook, who told me he hadn't seen anyone as strong as me. He said I was as strong as a horse.

I might have had a reputation for intensity in the national camps, but I exceeded my own level in 2022. The Commonwealth Games were in six months' time. I had already started preparing, right after losing at the National Championships. But I knew that my struggles over the past couple of years weren't so much physical in nature as they were psychological.

I had developed a genuine mental weakness, but I was also too hesitant to seek help for it. I had had sessions with a psychologist before the Rio Olympics, but I'd only gone for them because my sponsors had insisted. There hadn't been too many athletes who had worked with psychologists at that point, and I wasn't interested in being one of them. I used to talk freely to the psychologist, but I used to wonder just how talking about my feelings was going to change my thoughts.

I didn't mind talking to one, because at least the psychologists were encouraging, but I also didn't think it was of any use. And then, because I had won an Olympic medal, I just took it for granted that whatever issues I had – and I knew I had them – I would be able to deal with them once I got on to the mat.

It took me two years of losing in India to finally admit that I might want to rethink my beliefs. I was still not sure how therapy worked, but I was desperate.

I didn't go looking for a therapist. One day I got a call from a man called Anirudh Shah. He had been a wrestler in India before becoming a referee and emigrating to Australia. He had been a fan of my wrestling, even before Rio, and he couldn't understand why my form had dipped so precipitously.

He insisted that I speak to his wife, who was a psychologist in Australia. His wife was an Australian who could barely speak any Hindi. But Anirudh-ji made sure to sit in on every call and translate between his wife and me. For four months before the Commonwealth Games, we'd get on regular calls. Anirudh-ji would listen to what I said in Hindi and translate it into English for his wife. Then he'd listen to what she said and translate it into Hindi for me.

One of her suggestions was that I get my mental well-being

My Struggles Continue

measured. I'd kept a journal during my preparations for the Rio Olympics, where I wrote down how I was doing physically. But for the first time I kept a journal charting my emotional and mental health. I'd have to answer questions on how optimistic I was feeling, whether I was in control of my emotions, what my concentration levels were . . . I was also given a list of twelve questions that I had to send more detailed answers to. Anirudh-ji would translate my answers for his wife, who would send another set of questions to me.

Anirudh-ji and his wife must have spent dozens of hours over those four months helping me, and neither charged me a single rupee. They did what they did solely to help me. I will never be able to thank them enough.

My sessions with Anirudh-ji and his wife helped me to process my emotions better. What also helped me overcome my fears was simply just the passage of time.

In the past I'd kept away from practising with my rivals, just like every other Indian wrestler. In the national camp for the Commonwealth Games, I finally started sparring with Sonam in the practice matches. She wasn't able to attack me anywhere as well as she did in the matches in which I had lost to her. In all our bouts, I had wrestled thinking I had to stop her from beating me. I was wrestling out of fear of losing, and when that happened I started to think before every move. My body wasn't working as smoothly or as fast as it would have if I was wrestling out of instinct. I was responding to her rather than initiating action against her.

I'd always had that fear of losing. That was the reason I took so long to win at the start of my career. In the past couple of years, that fear had spiked to levels I'd never known, but at its core it was the same fear I'd always had.

I began to spar not from the position of being an Olympic medallist with something to defend but as a wrestler trying to perform as best she could. Sonam was good but not unbeatable. She was too obvious and didn't disguise her shots. She wasn't the monster I'd made her out to be.

Despite that mental breakthrough, despite all the help I got from Anirudh-ji and his wife, and despite how well I felt my training was going, the build-up to the selection trials was easily the most stressful time of my sports career. Even my stress at the Olympics in Rio couldn't compare with the pressure of those few months in the start of 2022.

I retreated into myself for the most part. I wouldn't talk to my roommate. I might talk to Satyawart, but I wouldn't say much.

The only time I stepped out of that funk, temporarily at least, was when I was training. In the middle of a practice session, everything would seem to be all right once again. I'd have a good training session, I might hit a new personal best in the rope climbs or sprints and I'd feel elated once again. And then that feeling would wear off and I would realize that I had two opponents whom I had never beaten in the past couple of years, and that would send me spiralling into despair once again. Before some sparring sessions, I'd be visibly shivering on the mat. My heart would be pounding in my ribcage, loud enough so my opponent could hear it, I felt. I'd feel as if I had insects crawling on my skin.

There were good days, but there were mostly bad days. There were days when I would just go to the washroom and cry. There were days when I didn't even make it to the washroom but my eyes would well up with tears, out of emotional exhaustion, while I was on the mat

My Struggles Continue

itself. Some of my coaches would try and support me. They'd say, 'You can do it.' They'd say, 'You still have that ability in you.'

I knew it wasn't that easy. I knew that if I didn't win those trials, I might not have the courage and determination to continue to wrestle. This felt like my one last shot. If I didn't win, I knew I would have to pack my things and go home. For the first time in my life I was starting to contemplate what life after wrestling would look like. Just the thought of that made me feel sick.

There was no guarantee I would win. I wasn't the favourite at the trials. There were younger girls who had already started to make a name for themselves. I was thirty-one already – much closer to the end of my career than to the start. I hadn't even won a medal at the nationals. But I also knew that I had to win. I couldn't let my career in a sport to which I'd dedicated my life, end in such a sorry manner. If I couldn't even win a selection trial, it would be a disgrace. It would also justify what many people had been saying about me for a long time

Right after I became an Olympic medallist, I started hearing people belittle my achievement. They'd point out how I didn't have a world medal or an Asian medal or a Commonwealth Games gold. They'd say that my Olympic medal was a *tukka*, a fluke. No one would say this to my face, of course. But you would hear people whispering about it. At the camp, wrestlers can be great gossips, and I'd always hear of someone who was saying this about me.

After the Olympics, it was almost as if there was a vigil to see where I would fail next. There was this pleasure people got from seeing me fail just so they could say, 'Yeah, I told you so. She's not nearly as good as people think she is.'

Over the past few years, the whispers had grown steadily louder.

'Oh look, Sakshi just lost to a junior girl.' 'Oh, she's lost to another girl. Sakshi is finished.' 'She's losing to these new girls now.' And I didn't have anything to counter them with. And now, if I lost in the trials and left the sport after that, they'd say what they were saying openly. They wouldn't say that everyone has high points and low points in their career and that the best of us can lose. What they really wanted to say was that my Olympic medal was a fluke. A *tukka*. What else could it be if I couldn't win even in India?

Even though my belief in manifestation had taken a hit after I hadn't qualified for the Tokyo Olympics, I once again started my practice of visualization before the Commonwealth Games selection trials. Every time I entered the wrestling hall where the trials were to take place, I'd close my eyes and imagine myself participating and winning there.

It helped that the competition hall the trials were to be held in was one I had never competed in before. I remember that when I entered the wrestling hall on the day of the trials on 16 May 2022, I was just thinking that I was going to win that day. No matter what happened I was going to win. I was going to make positive memories in this hall.

I had started the day in control of my emotions, but I was also aware that it wouldn't be too hard for me to swing into despondency if things started going poorly. For the duration of the camp, I'd been swinging between those extremes.

I didn't have too long to worry about that. I won my first bout quickly and then was up against Sonam. Although I felt my nerves were spiking, I wasn't wrestling fearfully. I made the first takedown, then another. Before I knew it, I was up 5–0. As I relaxed, my movements became smoother.

My Struggles Continue

She wasn't the same wrestler who had beaten me the first time, and I too wasn't the same one who had lost to her four times straight. It wasn't as if she was wrestling poorly, but as the gap between us increased, she was being forced to rush her attacks, and as she did so she made mistakes that I scored on.

Even as the lead increased I wasn't getting over-confident. I had led 8-0 in our first match as well and 4-0 at the Agra nationals before losing. I was far more focused this time. I didn't want to make a single mistake that would allow her to come back. Although I was defensive, I wasn't being passive. I knew that Sonam had to do all the attacking, and that meant I'd always have opportunities to score. That's exactly what happened. As I scored, my confidence grew.

There's nothing that compares to wrestling with confidence. My attacks became sharper because I wasn't second-guessing myself. My mind wasn't confused. My nerves, body and brain were all working in sync. The success rate of a technique, which might have been 50 per cent just a few minutes ago, now became 100 per cent.

As the match was turning in my favour, I could see one of the coaches in Sonam's corner trying to motivate her. It was the father of Anshu Malik, Sonam's friend. I had noticed him yelling in support of her the first time the two of us had wrestled. He would hoot, '*Thak gai, thak gai. Kuch na hai tere saman.*' He was telling her I was tired out and nothing in front of her.

I remember feeling irritated at the time. He could, of course, cheer for a friend of his daughter's. But nonetheless, it rubbed me the wrong way. At the CWG trials, as Sonam tried to come back against me, I could hear him yell, '*Kuch na hai beta, kuch na hai,*' again saying I was nothing. It still irritated me, but this time I knew that he was only doing this to convince Sonam that she was still in the fight. That got me even more confident.

With an 8-1 score line, I finally got my first win against Sonam. I felt that maybe today was the day my luck had turned. It's not every day that you beat someone who has had such a stranglehold over you.

Manisha had made it to the final after beating Sangeeta. I knew what to expect from her. Manisha was at the best of times a rough wrestler. In all our bouts, she would yank my hair, scratch me, stick her finger into my flesh and pull my costume. With a place in the Commonwealth Games at stake, I knew this bout would go the same way.

She came out fighting not so much as a wrestler but as a bull. She was grabbing, pulling, scratching, twisting my fingers. She was doing everything but wrestle. At another time it might have thrown me off, but with my confidence back after beating Sonam, I was able to divert her attacks. I conceded the first point for passivity because I was just trying to block her while she was just pushing and shoving. If she had been more focused, she might have scored more points, but she was just rushing at me.

Eventually I sidestepped one of her attacks and got a takedown for 2 points. I was just letting her momentum carry her forward, stepping off to make way and going behind her. Once I got her to the ground, I scored twice more using a *bharandaaz* (gut wrench). I was 6-1 up. We traded step-out points, and then I scored once more to make it 8-2. That's how the score stayed when the referee blew his whistle for the final time.

I can barely describe exactly how I felt after that match. It was as if I had finally woken up from a nightmare that had lasted nearly two years. I didn't feel the kind of elation in Rio after I'd won the Olympic medal as I felt in that wrestling hall in Lucknow that day.

My Struggles Continue

If I could have had a coach carry me on his shoulder and then run around the hall with an India flag, I would have liked that!

I'd finally made my comeback.

Unlike how it was at Rio though, I didn't get to celebrate much.

After winning the trials in Lucknow I wanted to rush back to Delhi to be with Satyawart. He had his own trial in the men's category in Delhi the next day and I wanted to surprise him after his competition. I travelled back to Rohtak that evening, and the next day I drove to Delhi and booked a hotel room so we could celebrate together.

I had no doubt Satyawart would win his trials. The two hardest years of my wrestling career had coincided with two of Satyawart's best. While I was losing, it was Satyawart who was out representing India. He competed at the World Championships, the Asian Championships and the Ranking series. Throughout all this, he was constantly supporting me. There were days when I was packing his suitcase for the World Championships, feeling really low since I wasn't going to be part of that team. And then he'd tell me that I would soon join him and we would wrestle as a couple in a competition soon.

I was sure that this would be at the Commonwealth Games. We had gone together to the 2014 Commonwealth Games where we both won silver. But at that time we were still hiding our relationship. This time we would go as a married couple.

So, to celebrate, I booked a hotel room in Delhi. I planned to wait until the evening, when I would get the news that Satyawart had won his trials, before I'd surprise him.

I'd just checked into the room when I got a call I hardly expected. Satyawart had lost.

He was completely gutted. I felt terrible for him. He had supported me during one of the lowest periods of my life, and then as soon as that phase ended for me it began for him.

Satyawart had many Asian Championships medals, but he always had the worst luck when it came to events like the Commonwealth Games, Asian Games and the Olympics. In 2016, he lost the bout that would have secured him his Olympic qualification when he stepped out of bounds in the final seconds of the match. Then, in his qualification bout for the Tokyo Olympics, he was leading 4-0 before he lost 4-4 with his opponent scoring the final points of the match. Just a month and a half before the Commonwealth Games trials, he'd beaten by an 8-0 score the same opponent to whom he'd now lost in New Delhi. But when it came to the Games, he just had bad luck.

Satyawart is by nature very stoic and hates showing any emotion. He's the rock of my life. I'd never seen him even cry. But I saw him tear up for the first time in the days after this loss. He's the strongest man I know, but for the next fifteen days I was the one who had to support him. For those few weeks I couldn't celebrate one of the most important wins of my career because I was also grieving one of the hardest losses for the person I was closest to. I wondered why God could not give me unqualified happiness just once! Try as much as I want, I'll never get all I want in life.

Compared with the selection trials for the Commonwealth Games, the Games themselves, which happened two months later in Birmingham, were hardly a test. As usual, the National Federation was incompetent. As part of our Commonwealth Games build-up, we were sent for a Ranking series competition in Tunisia. For some reason, our flight to Tunisia was only booked for the day before the competition. Once we reached that country, a seven-hour delay in getting our visas followed. We finally only checked into our hotel on the morning of the competition. I was cutting my weight in the hotel gallery, and although I just about managed to make my weight, I was in no real condition to wrestle for a medal. I had barely had any sleep and hadn't recovered at all. I wrestled two matches, losing both.

Although the results were disappointing, I was much more confident that I would do better in Birmingham a couple of weeks later.

19

The Final Hurrah

Of the many international competitions, the Commonwealth Games were always special. They are what we consider 'Games', just like the Asian Games and the Olympic Games. It's not just a two- or three-day event, like most wrestling competitions. It has its own opening and closing ceremonies. We aren't just going as wrestlers but as part of a much larger Indian contingent. The medals we win aren't just for ourselves but also go into the medal total for India.

Although Indian men had won medals at the Asian Games and the Olympics before, I always felt that one of the biggest moments in Indian women's wrestling was when Geeta, Babita and Anita won gold at the 2010 Commonwealth Games. It raised the profile of the sport and got so many young girls interested in the sport.

But it is also true that the Commonwealth Games aren't the hardest competition for wrestlers. The pool of talent isn't particularly deep at the Commonwealth Games. In the women's weight divisions, you knew that outside of Canada and Nigeria, there wasn't going to be any real threat. At the lighter weights there wasn't a strong

The Final Hurrah

challenge from even these countries, but it was different in the higher weight classes.

But while the Commonwealth Games were easier to medal in, it wasn't a competition where you could just show up and win gold. I had first-hand experience of this. I'd already wrestled in two Commonwealth Games. I'd run into Nigeria's Aminat Adeniyi in the final of the first one, and in 2018 I had lost against both Adeniyi as well as the 2017 World bronze medallist Michelle Fazzari of Canada.

While I was confident about medalling in Birmingham, the challenge for me was to win gold. I knew that both my opponents from Nigeria and Canada were very talented but relatively inexperienced. The Nigerian, Esther Kolawole, was a two-time African champion, but only twenty. The Canadian, Ana Godinez, was someone I saw as the bigger threat. She was a Pan American champion, and at twenty-two had won the U-23 World Championships the previous year.

The competition couldn't have gone any smoother. The 2022 Commonwealth Games were conducted on a far less grand scale than any of the multi-sport games I'd previously competed in, but they had their own charm. While all the athletes at the Olympics and the 2018 Commonwealth and Asian Games had stayed in the common Games Village, this time around we were hosted at a university campus. Instead of sharing rooms, we got one each to ourselves, and we felt as if we were living in an old-fashioned town rather than in a concrete tower. That calm and relaxed vibe carried over to the tournament too. My weight cut, usually the hardest part of any competition, was effortless.

The draw favoured me, with both the Nigerian and Canadian wrestlers in the opposite bracket. I had two bouts – first against a contestant from England and then against a wrestler from Cameroon – before the final. They were essentially warm-up bouts for me, and I won both with a 10-0 score line. That Commonwealth Games was the first tournament I remember actually enjoying. I went into each match laughing and joking.

When you have wrestled for as long as I have in international wrestling, you get to know where you need to conserve your strength and where you are going to be in for a fight. I knew that my real fight was going to be in the final only. Between the semi-final and final there was a five-hour gap. In that time, Anshu, Vinesh and I got some lunch. We talked about how our matches had gone. It was the sort of relaxed atmosphere that I'd never experienced before.

By the time I was done with my semi-final, I knew that my opponent for the final was going to be the Canadian, and I was prepared for it. I'd been following her ever since I had first qualified for the Commonwealth Games. I knew she was a U-23 world champion and the 2022 Pan American champion. She'd later managed to qualify for the Olympics too. She was a solid wrestler. Technically sharp and very fast.

In the waiting room, I could see that she was confident – at least that was she was trying to portray confidence. I've been in this long enough to know that's what she was trying to do, and it made me smile.

Even though she was warming up on other side of the mat from where I was, I could see she was jumping around and bouncing all over the place. It was as if she was trying to tell me, 'Look how high I can jump. That's how much stronger I am than you.'

Whether or not Godinez was trying to psych me, the fact was, she was naturally quick. When the bout started, her movements were

The Final Hurrah

surprisingly fast. She made the first attack, and although I tried to counter her, she won the scramble and scored the first 2 points. Late in the first round, she shot for my ankle and went behind me for another two points.

Even though I was down 0-4, I didn't think I was finished. I've won matches from 0-5 down and I've lost them from 8-0 up. I've both won and lost in the final seconds of a bout. Wrestling is unpredictable that way. I knew that I had enough time on my hands, and that if I just kept my mind strong I'd always have a chance in the match.

I had to keep my mind in the fight. I couldn't think that the match was done. Only if that happened would my body give up too. That's what I told myself: This is nothing. There's lots of time.

What stood out for me was just how fast she moved, especially when she attacked. If I tried to match her for pace, she would just beat me to the strike. Instead, I needed to break her flow and hold her.

That had always been my style of wrestling. I wasn't the fastest or the flashiest. My game was about slowing down my opponents and breaking their flow. If they are moving too fast, I have to check their attacks. The reason your opponents have a high pace is to confuse you with their movements. The more you try to match their speed, the more areas and angles you leave open for them to attack.

So I grabbed her wrist with one hand, and with the other hand I secured a grasp on the back of her neck. You can be as fast as you want, but if you are caught like that your energy drains very quickly. I held her like that for five to ten seconds. That slowed her down.

At the break, I was running the plays in my head. I knew she was slowing down and I was going to get an opportunity to attack.

That's exactly what happened. I blocked her and saw an opening. It was a very small window. As a wrestler you understand when your opponent is standing still for a fraction of a second too long. You notice when her arm is not going down fast enough to block your attack. It's just something that you observe instinctively. It's like when you are driving down a busy road and you know exactly when and how much to turn the steering wheel when you see a gap in the traffic.

She didn't make any obvious mistake. It was just that I had grabbed her left hand with my right, and in doing so controlled her movement. In desi kushti, we call that a *dasti*. And because she was slowing down, she didn't get her right hand down in time to defend. Her left foot stayed in place for just that little while longer than it should have. And I used that moment to do a single-leg takedown.

It was one of the first techniques I'd learned in my akhara in Rohtak, and I'd been practising it nearly every day for nearly two decades. Shoot low, get your hand to the back of your opponent's knee and pull up while pushing your head into her chest.

As she collapsed underneath me, my hand went from the back of her leg to trap her right arm behind her. I knew I couldn't let her escape. I knew that if she somehow got out of this position, there was no guarantee I'd be able to catch her a second time. But there was no way she could have. I had all my weight on her and with her right arm trapped, she had just the one free arm with which to push me off. It was an impossible situation.

I'd been in similar situations before, so I knew what she was going through. There's a moment of shock when you know you have been caught in a bad position. You try to fight it but you know very quickly that you aren't going to be able too. And then your muscles relax, as

The Final Hurrah

I felt hers did, just that fraction of a second, telling me that she had given up, just before the referee slapped the mat to let everyone else know that I had secured the pin.

That was it. I had won the one medal that I wanted.

I called my family. Satyawart had been watching the match in his akhara in Rohtak, and when I was 0-4 down he had walked away from the TV because he couldn't bear to see me lose. He had only come in a couple of minutes later, after the shouts and cheers from inside the akhara told him how the match had concluded.

As we talked on the phone, both of us were thinking ahead.

I was thinking I was back in the game, and planning ahead for the Asian Games. If I did well there, I would be able to go to the Olympics and maybe even hope for a medal there. Little did I know that I'd just wrestled for the last time in my career.

20

How the Protest Started

The 2022 Commonwealth Games were one of the highlights of my career, but one facet of it kept that experience from being perfect. After we won gold, some of us wrestlers got a message from the physiotherapist Dhirendra Pratap Singh.

He told us to make sure we praised the federation and the president when we were being interviewed. I did just that, as there wasn't any questioning of orders when they had come from the president. I said Indian wrestling was doing very well because of the president, and that was the reason I had won a gold medal.

It wasn't as if trying to stay on Brij Bhushan Sharan Singh's right side did me much good. Two weeks after the Commonwealth Games, trials were held for the 2022 World Championships. The male wrestlers who won gold at Birmingham were exempted by the Federation from those trials. Neither Vinesh nor I were given the same privilege. It was obviously unfair, but I didn't argue with the decision. Because of my history with the president, I knew I had to pick my fights with the federation carefully.

Just a few days after the Commonwealth Games, we had started hearing complaints from the wrestlers who were competing at the Junior World Championships. They told me how Brij Bhushan Sharan Singh had booked a room for himself on the same floor as the female wrestlers and would leave his door open. The girls were troubled by his behaviour and would only leave their rooms in groups. But as always, I heard these stories and chose not to act on them. Over the years I'd learned to keep my mouth shut and focus on wrestling. It's not something I was proud of, but I didn't feel I had any other option.

I focused, as I always did, on my wrestling. I decided to give the World Championships a miss. I had to attend a number of felicitations and ceremonies, and I knew I wasn't going to be able to prepare to the extent required for the tournament. Both Bajrang and Vinesh took part, and the two won bronze.

At that time I was just looking at qualifying for the next Asian Games, doing well there and then going to the Olympics. I was very positive about the future at that time. It all seemed very doable. I had emerged from the worst slump of my career – where I was almost tagged as a wrestler who wasn't good enough to even make it to the Indian team. I had reasserted myself as the best in the country, had won the Commonwealth gold, and now I was going to win a medal I hadn't so far – from the Asian Games.

Things were progressing well at my job with the Railways too. I had joined the Indian Railways in 2014 after the Glasgow Commonwealth Games where I had won a silver. Although my job allowed me to train for much of the year at my akhara, I still had to work out of the New Delhi office for a few weeks every year. When I was staying in Rohtak, that meant I had to make the five-hour round trip every working day.

After my gold in 2018, though, I got a promotion, and with it a flat at the Railway quarters near Connaught Place in New Delhi. Although it would take me away from my father-in-law's akhara, I found the location very convenient. The flat was within walking distance from the Railways' Karnail Stadium, and I wouldn't have too much trouble arranging training partners there whenever I wished to train in Delhi. Satyavart and I moved into our apartment in the first week of January 2023. I wouldn't know it then, but that flat would prove to be very convenient, but not for the reasons I first imagined.

I reckoned the next few months of the year would follow a simple timetable. I'd work out of Delhi and train at Karnail Stadium over the week, and on the weekend I'd go back to Rohtak to train at my father-in-law's akhara.

But the plan remained just a plan. A day after we moved into our flat, I got a call from Babita Phogat. She said she wanted me and Satyawart to attend a meeting. Although she couldn't tell me what it was about, she reassured me that all of India's top wrestlers would be there.

We drove down to a dhaba near Sonepat called Choki Dhani. The owner of the dhaba was from a wrestling family himself and was friends with most of India's elite wrestlers. He was someone who could be trusted to keep a secret.

I knew everyone in the restaurant. Apart from Satyawart and me, there was Babita, Bajrang, Vinesh and her husband Somvir, and Sumit Malik, who wrestled in the heavyweight division. Although they weren't there in person, the Tokyo Olympics silver medallist Ravi Dahiya and the World silver medallist Deepak Punia joined us on a phone call.

Babita told us why she had called us. We were going to force Brij

How the Protest Started

Bhushan Sharan Singh to resign from the Wrestling Federation of India. We were going to clean everything up. I didn't know it at the time, but the plans for protesting for Brij Bhushan's removal had already been well underway by the time Babita called me in January.

At the meeting Babita convinced all of us that now was when we had to take a stand. It was true that the mess in the federation and Brij Bhushan's own actions had been going on for many years. But his term as president of the federation was ending the next year. According to government rules, he could not stand in the elections for another term. But what was likely to happen was that his son Karan Bhushan Singh, already the vice-president, was going to succeed him as the president of the federation.

If that happened, none of Brij Bhushan Sharan Singh's crimes would see the light of day and the federation would continue to run as it always had. Babita had convinced us that she was very close to Home Minister Amit Shah. She could call him any time, and if she called him once we had started our protest, he would very likely listen to our demands. I had no reason to doubt her. Babita was a member of the BJP and had stood for elections in Haryana too. She was always getting pictures taken with the senior leaders of the party. I thought it was safe to assume that the government was also with us. Why else would she, a party member, have called me to be part of such a protest?

After all those years of being quiet, I was happy to finally be in a position to participate in a movement asking for action against Brij Bhushan Singh. I knew that if I had raised my voice after my encounter with Brij Bhushan Singh, I wouldn't have become the Olympic medallist I was now. But now I saw that there were many wrestlers who were willing to speak up against him. We had united, and that gave me confidence. I was finally going to get some sort of justice. Although so many women, including myself, had been victimized, I knew we could put an end to his reign.

In my eagerness to make Brij Bhushan pay for what he had done to me, I made many assumptions about what everyone else's motivations were. The meeting to which I was called was just another step in a bigger plan of which I had no inkling.

Although I didn't know it then, both Vinesh and Bajrang had already met Amit Shah earlier that year after they returned from the World Championships. They had told him all about Brij Bhushan Singh's actions and how badly the Wrestling Federation of India was being run. Amit Shah had promised them that he would look into the matter but had asked them to wait until the end of the Gujarat elections so that it wouldn't become a political issue. It was after the elections, when it didn't seem like any action was being taken, that Babita – who was Vinesh's cousin and Bajrang's sister-in-law – decided it was time to call the other wrestlers and pitch the idea of a protest to them.

If I had given more careful thought to what was going on, I might have been a little more cautious, or at least better prepared for what was to come in the months ahead. Although most of India's top wrestlers had come to that restaurant, two of India's Olympic medallists hadn't. Two-time Olympic medallist Sushil Kumar obviously couldn't, since he was in prison on a murder charge. But Yogeshwar Dutt, who had medalled at the 2012 Games and who, like Babita, had stood for elections as a BJP candidate, was also absent.

In hindsight, while I know that ending Brij Bhushan Sharan Singh's reign was the primary goal for Vinesh and Bajrang, I made the mistake of thinking that that was Babita's sole intention too.

How the Protest Started

I didn't think too deeply about what should have been an obvious point of caution, because I too was very blinded by the prospect of getting rid of Brij Bhushan Sharan Singh. And I was relieved that I was no longer by myself in my wish to see him go.

Our first protest began on the morning of 18 January in 2023. We had hardly planned anything. My only knowledge of protests had come from the movies, where people sat on the ground holding placards and shouting slogans. We hadn't got any of those made.

Satyawart and I drove from our apartment, and we met up with Vinesh, Somvir, Bajrang and his wife Sangeeta, as well as Babita and her husband. We were also joined by the fathers of Sonam and Anshu – Sonam Malik, who had beaten me all those times before the Tokyo Olympics and Anshu Malik, who had won a silver at the 2021 World Championships – and another of my former rivals, Sarita Malik, and her husband Rahul Mann. Bajrang's friend Jitender, a former national champion in the 74 kg category, and Sumit Malik, who had competed at the Tokyo Olympics in the heavyweight category, were there too. There were also a few of Bajrang's supporters and friends.

From there we headed to Jantar Mantar. When I was a little girl, my father had taken me to Jantar Mantar on one of our trips to Delhi, and I knew it was a monument built many hundred years ago. I thought we would be sitting on the steps of one of the buildings and raising slogans from there. As we drove past that monument, I finally saw where we were going to protest.

The protest site is actually in a cordoned-off lane to one side of the monument. I found out later that it had been demarcated as a protest site by the Supreme Court. Funnily enough, that same road leads to the Wrestling Federation of India office.

To get into the lane, we had to go past a police checkpoint and barricades. There was a public toilet at the start of the lane and a tea shop on the other side. For company we had some policemen who were always deployed there and a few stray dogs that lived on that street. There were another couple of protests going on simultaneously, one of which was by some nurses who hadn't been paid for their work during the COVID-19 pandemic.

They'd already taken up the spots below the trees in the area, so we had to start our protest on the section of the pavement next to the public toilet. It didn't look anything like I'd envisioned. Although it hadn't struck either Satyawart or me, we needed some place to sit. Luckily, some of the other protesters had brought mattresses, which we laid out on the pavement. And then, finally, five minutes before we sat down, we all posted a common message on our social media handles.

'Although wrestlers are working hard to win medals for the country, the wrestling federation is doing nothing other than trying to humiliate them. Players are being harassed by imposing arbitrary rules and regulations. #BoycottWFIPresident #BoycottWrestlingPresident.'

We also tagged the home minister and the prime minister in these messages.

Within a few minutes the first media person had showed up at the protest site. He asked what our protest was about, but we had made it clear that we were not going to say anything until our press conference at 4 p.m. We wanted as many media people as possible to listen to what we had to say.

We didn't have to wait that long. Within a couple of hours the area was crowded with media persons.

There were a couple of other reasons for delaying our press conference until the evening. Although we had no shortage of

How the Protest Started

complaints against the federation and the president, we hadn't, until the morning of the protest, actually noted down what they were. Now we decided to get our complaints in order. We were very conscious of the fact that we had no experience in raising protests and we felt that if our complaints were presented in an organized way, we might be taken more seriously.

There was another reason. None of the girls really wanted to make the incidents of harassment publicly known. Almost every woman wrestler was from a small town or village. We didn't want to have to publicly discuss the subject. We thought that perhaps the prime minister or the home minister might feel the pressure to dismiss the president, with so many Olympic and world medallists protesting against him without mentioning sexual harassment.

News of our protest reached Brij Bhushan Sharan Singh. Within an hour he had Vinod Tomar, the secretary of the federation, come to the protest site. *'Kya hua, pehelwanon?'* He wanted to know what had happened that we wrestlers should be protesting.

Vinesh's husband Somvir Rathee told Tomar he very well knew what the protest was about. He'd been in the federation before Brij Bhushan Sharan Singh had been elected president and knew all the ins and out of how it functioned. Somvir (Vinesh's husband) told Tomar that in case he didn't know all this, he could find out with the media at 4 p.m.

I wasn't at the protest site when this exchange took place. Along with Bajrang, Babita and Vinesh, I was sitting in Babita's car, which was parked near the federation office, trying to put together a list of the points we were going to present at the press conference.

Although we had just come to her car to get our points in order, Babita had been absent from the protest site from the very start.

This was odd, and Satyawart had been the first to notice it. When the rest of us had laid down the mattresses and had sat down, she was nowhere to be seen, and Satyawart had wondered aloud where she had gone.

Before a protest can take place at Jantar Mantar, you need to take permission from the police, and the permission slip for our first protest carried the names of Babita and a man named Teerath Rana. Both were members of the BJP and had contested elections for the party. But neither was with us at the protest. We later found Babita cowering in the back seat of her car, as if trying to avoid being seen by anyone.

At that time Babita explained her absence to me by saying that while she was with us, as a member of the BJP she couldn't be seen as part of our protest against a member of Parliament from her own party. She said she was communicating behind the scenes with the home minister to ensure our demands were fulfilled.

I had my doubts, but I went along with her explanation.

It took me a long time to figure out that the truth was something else. Although all of us wanted to see the end of Brij Bhushan Sharan Singh at the federation, that wasn't the only thing that Babita wanted.

I think that Babita knew that any protest by India's top wrestlers on the streets of New Delhi would be embarrassing to the government. The government would want to get us out of Jantar Mantar as quickly as possible, and Babita acting as an intermediary would convince us to pack up. That way she'd be able to solve the government's headache and tell Amit Shah that she had got the wrestlers out of Jantar Mantar. And if she got us off the protest site, what could be a suitable reward for her? She didn't just want to just get rid of Brij Bhushan Sharan Singh – she wanted to replace him.

How the Protest Started

That's also the reason I think Babita didn't call Yogeshwar to the meeting where we first decided we were going to protest. He was in the BJP too, like her. She feared that if Yogeshwar was able to get us to talk to the government, then she wouldn't have any card to play. She didn't want that competition. There was no other reason to exclude him.

Even as all these machinations were going on, as 4 p.m. approached the protest site was packed. There were video cameras all around us. The last time I'd seen as many was when I came out of the exit gates of New Delhi international airport after arriving from Rio.

At the time we were discussing what to say at the protest, we had wondered if we should first talk about the harassment that the women faced at the hands of Brij Bhushan. It was the biggest issue for all the women who were protesting. One of the reasons we chose not to was that if we mentioned the harassment issue up front, we knew that the media wouldn't pay attention to any other point we were making. Why would they?

While this was something that had caused us trauma, we felt that for the media it would just be something to sensationalize. It would be treated as 'masala'. The other problems, which affected all young athletes, male and female, would be ignored. We wanted people to know how money that should have gone to the junior athletes was being misused, how sponsors were being driven away and how good coaches and physiotherapists were being discouraged.

Bajrang spoke about how the federation was trying to control athletes' funding by sponsors. Many young wrestlers were being sponsored by foundations like Olympic Gold Quest and JSW, who were providing top-quality physiotherapists and nutritionists to them. The federation had felt they were losing control over athletes.

Brij Bhushan Sharan Singh had told the sports bodies that they couldn't approach players directly. He'd make it impossible for physiotherapists or even personal coaches to come to the national camps. Everything and everyone had to go directly through him.

I spoke about the financial irregularities happening with athletes' contracts. After the Rio Olympics, the federation got Tata Motors as a new sponsor. In 2018, the federation announced that with the sponsorship money coming in, they would sign Indian wrestlers on year-long contracts. This was a great idea, since apart from our government jobs, there was no real money in wrestling. I was an Olympic medallist and they announced that my contract was going to be Rs 20 lakh a year.

I remember I got two cheques, each of Rs 4.5 lakh. And after that I didn't get a single paisa. This wasn't just my story. Every wrestler who was signed on a contract with the federation either got a couple of cheques for part of the amounts promised or nothing at all. When I'd ask Tomar what happened to the rest of the money, he'd say that Tata Motors had stopped processing the payments. But later, when I was in a programme with Tata Motors and asked them directly if this was the case, they insisted that they had been paying the federation the sponsorship money every year.

Tomar would never give a clear answer as to where our money was going. He would just say there was some issue with the money transfer, or that they were talking to Tata Motors to solve the problem. There was always some paperwork that was taking place, and when that was finished we'd see the money in our accounts. It was always work in progress. The money was always just around the corner. He was just dragging us around in the dark.

There's one thing the federation could be guaranteed to do, and that was to make things difficult for us – even things as simple as our travel arrangements would be bungled. It was so common for us to reach competitions with just hours to go for the competitions to start. It had happened just a few months earlier, when I arrived at my hotel in Tunisia on the morning of my bout. And this wasn't just my case. At the Olympic qualification tournament a year before, both Anshu and Sonam reached their hotel two hours before their weigh-in. They had to wear sauna suits and cut weight at the airport layover. Every wrestler had faced these problems.

We had gone through all the points we had written down. So far, most of the media seemed disinterested. We could hear people talking in the back. There was just one thing left to say. But it seemed as if none of us wanted to be the one to say it out aloud.

It was finally Vinesh who showed the courage to and said it out aloud:

'Brij Bhushan exploits girls.'

All the chatter in the back of the crowd stopped. Suddenly there was absolute silence.

'What do you mean?' someone asked. 'Do you mean *yaun shoshan* (sexual exploitation)?'

Vinesh gathered herself and repeated herself again.

Brij Bhushan sexually exploited female wrestlers.

Suddenly we heard all the media squawking. 'What? What? What?'

No one could believe what she had said.

Vinesh said it for a third time. She said it was true. That many girls had faced this.

After that we answered the media's questions, and they had many. They asked us what we wanted. We said we wanted Brij Bhushan

Sharan Singh to be removed, and in his place we wanted some decent person brought to the federation. But before that we needed Brij Bhushan Sharan Singh removed. That was our constant demand.

When Vinesh finally spoke of how Brij Bhushan had harassed young female wrestlers, I was both relieved and scared. The truth was finally out. I was sure the protest was going to be a one-day matter. I thought we would sit down at 11 a.m. and someone from the government would come up to us and tell us they'd agreed to our demands.

But that didn't happen. No one reached out to us. We didn't get any call from the government. Right after our press conference though, we started getting calls from our families, friends and sponsors. They had seen us on TV.

Almost everyone was supportive. No one said that we had done something wrong. At that time everyone was swept away by the scale of the protest and the magnitude of our allegations. There had been nothing like this in India against such a high-profile politician.

But while everyone would tell me that there was nothing wrong with what we were doing, I soon realized that I could count on their support only when it was clear that there was no one else was around.

I was able to speak with Parth Jindal, the son of the owner of JSW who had sponsored me for nearly a decade. He was very supportive but he couldn't say anything publicly. He had a business to run and everyone was scared of the government. They'd shut his company down if they wanted.

After we concluded our press conference, we spoke to every media person we could. On that first day we were giving media bytes until late in the evening. We gave interviews in groups and individually. We spoke non-stop from five in the evening to nine at night. We finally stopped to get something to eat at 9 p.m. and then left, thinking we would we would go back home and return the next day at 11 a.m. to resume our protest.

Brij Bhushan, in the meantime, rushed to Delhi and held a press conference, where he accused us of lying. He insisted he wasn't going to step down.

That night as I went to sleep, I thought, 'The government didn't listen to us today but they have to listen to us tomorrow.' I had been incredibly nervous about sitting down in protest on that first day – it was completely in contrast to my nature. I was someone quiet and shy – but the fact that I was part of a larger group, all fighting for the same cause, had emboldened me.

We went back to the protest site, tired from the previous day but still confident we would get what we were fighting for. That day, even more people joined us. There had been only twelve of us on the first day. Now we had wrestlers coming in from the villages around Delhi. Most of Chhatrasal Stadium – which is considered the best wrestling akhara in India – showed up. Ravi and Deepak had missed the first day because they were in Mumbai, but they came and sat with us. We finally wrote down a list of our demands, and had them signed by everyone.

The numbers that had joined our side gave us confidence. We felt we were part of something bigger than all of us. We had gathered to fight for the same cause.

It wasn't just wrestlers who came out to support us. The first few politicians to support us had started to come too. Vijender Singh, the Olympic bronze medallist in boxing, came out to our protest. There were some representatives from women's organizations – Brinda Karat of the Communist Party and someone from Aam Aadmi Party.

We didn't know who they were, but we knew they were in opposition to the BJP. They wanted to use the platform to raise slogans against the government.

At that time we were worried about going against the government since we still thought Babita was communicating with the home minister, who in turn was going to get rid of Brij Bhushan Sharan Singh. We decided we couldn't allow these politicians to sit alongside us. Instead, we laid out carpets on the road just below a section of the pavement at Jantar Mantar and asked them to sit there.

They could support us but they couldn't use our platform to make political statements against the government. We said the protest was only for sportspersons, not politicians. If someone wanted to say something, we wouldn't even give them a microphone if we felt they were from a political party.

While the rest of us sat in protest at Jantar Mantar, Babita, who had brought us together in the first place, continued to play her double game. She told us that she was in touch with the government and that it was only a matter of time before they listened to us. Though she didn't sit with us, she came up to the protest site on the second day and made a public statement that she was going to take our voice to the home minister.

The protest became even more intense on the third day. So many had come to support us that there were people on the pavement on the other side of the road too. We had to use ropes to keep them from rushing on to the mattresses on which we were sitting. The media was there too.

We heard that there were wrestlers from Maharashtra and other states too who were getting on trains to come and join us. We also started getting calls from young female sportspersons who said they too had faced harassment and wanted to join us.

How the Protest Started

Finally, towards the afternoon, we met with a lady from the Sports Authority of India. She told us she would find a solution to our problem, but before that we had to end our protest. For all her assertions that she would help us, out we realized soon afterwards that she had no real authority to make the decisions we wanted. Then Bajrang got a message. The sports minister Anurag Thakur wanted to meet us. We were asked to go over to his house in the evening.

All of us who were protesting went to Anurag Thakur's house at 7 p.m. Apart from those who had first made the decision to protest at Jantar Mantar on 18 January, we were joined by some other female wrestlers who too had faced sexual harassment. Just like me, they had stayed silent until now.

While many of the men waited in the lawn outside the minster's house, the minister called Bajrang and the girls into a room. There he sat down on a chair and asked us to explain what had happened.

I felt a sense of relief. Although we had hoped to speak to the home minister or the prime minister, I still felt it was a breakthrough to be able to speak with Anurag Thakur. He was a senior government minister, and finally we were able to put forth our problems directly to someone who we felt had at least some say in the matter.

Bajrang once again listed out the problems that we had been facing at the hands of the federation and Brij Bhushan Sharan Singh. He then asked the minister to hear directly from the girls in the room about just how we had been harassed.

A woman coach, Sudesh, spoke of the harassment she had faced at the national camp. Sarita Malik spoke next. I told the minister what had happened to me at the Junior Asian Championships at the hands of Brij Bhushan.

Although I had known Sudesh for a long time and knew that

she wasn't always treated fairly, this was the first time I had learnt what she had to face. She told her whole story in front of the sports minister. She told him about how a coach had told her that if she needed to get something done, she needed to do something for the wrestling president.

Anurag Thakur sat there, listening quietly. There was no emotion on his face. If he was shocked by anything he heard, he didn't show it. His reaction was in complete contrast to everyone else's. As each of us told our stories, the atmosphere in the room became steadily more emotional. Some of the younger girls were already breaking down in tears. But Thakur could have been listening to someone talking about the weather. It was as if he was bored and just wanted our meeting to be over. He came across as a very harsh individual. I was unsure of just what we had achieved, if we had indeed achieved anything at all.

Shortly after we had told our stories to Thakur and he had left the room, Bajrang got a call. On the other end of the line was Amit Shah. Bajrang said he was told that it was time to end the protest. Amit Shah told Bajrang to trust him and that he would make things right. Bajrang felt that since he had been clearly promised that things would be made right by Amit Shah himself, perhaps we ought to listen to him.

Babita had come with us to Anurag Thakur's house as someone who was supposedly acting as the interlocutor between us and the party. She told Bajrang that Amit Shah was just like her father. And that if he said something he wouldn't backtrack from it. His word was all the guarantee we needed.

Not all of us who had come to Anurag Thakur's house believed this. If one group wanted to take Amit Shah at his word and end the

How the Protest Started

protest, the other was adamant that we were not going to end the protest until Brij Bhushan Sharan Singh had actually stepped down as the president of the federation or until Amit Shah gave us his word in writing. Until that happened, it made no sense to end our protest. It was clear to me that not only had we not really accomplished anything yet but also that Babita was ensuring that nothing would get done. By now it was evident that she was trying her best to get us to end the protest.

I was part of the group that wanted to stay on at Jantar Mantar. Satyawart, Deepak Punia, Ravi Dahiya, Amit Dankhar – a former Asian Championship gold medallist – and Sumit Malik were also with me on this. Of them, Ravi and Deepak were willing to continue even if the original group split. At that point, I was the only female wrestler who wanted to continue the protest.

Babita had already managed to convince Bajrang and Vinesh to trust Amit Shah. She was Bajrang's sister-in-law and Vinesh's cousin, after all. She also managed to convince the female wrestlers. It didn't take too long for them to change their minds. Initially emboldened, they were starting to come to terms with the magnitude of what had been unleashed.

Most of us who wanted to continue the protest had already wrestled for many years. We already had made a name in the sport. Many of the girls who had spoken about being harassed were just beginning their career.

As we differed on what to do, the atmosphere in Anurag Thakur's house grew heated. Eventually discussions broke down. Bajrang asked me if I was going to continue to protest, and would I be willing to file a case against Brij Bhushan Sharan Singh too? That was the logical next step if I wasn't going to trust Amit Shah at his word. He told me that since I wasn't willing to listen to him or Amit Shah, then I would have to go and file a case against the president.

The idea of going to court scared me. I hadn't realized that I might actually have to do that. It was already well past midnight. All of us were tired and mentally exhausted. We had started fighting among ourselves. That was it; I had no choice but to go along with the decision to call off the protest.

Anurag Thakur told us Brij Bhushan Sharan Singh would be made to withdraw from the day-to-day functioning of the federation and that an oversight committee would be formed to oversee the running of the federation and prepare a report on all that had happened. We were asked to give the names of two people we wanted on the committee. We proposed the names of Radhika Sreeman, an official with the Sports Authority of India, and Babita. I also suggested the name of Mary Kom, because I felt she was a fearless sportsperson. I didn't really know her, but had sat on a panel with her after the Olympics.

We had a press conference at close to 1 a.m., where Anurag Thakur paraded us in front of the media and said everything had been sorted out. He announced that an oversight committee would be formed, but he danced around the specifics of it.

Even as he spoke, I knew we had been gamed. We didn't answer any questions from the media and left quietly for our cars.

It wasn't just I who felt that way. Amit Dhankar, who was in the same car as us, said, '*Bada khel ho gaya. Naash ho gaya.*' He was not wrong. A great game had indeed been played and we were ruined.

I broke down. I had done everything with absolute sincerity, and despite that, I'd been tricked. It felt as if the wind had been kicked out of my stomach.

How the Protest Started

As we went home, Satyawart and I were worried. We tried to convince ourselves that maybe our gut instinct was wrong and that maybe the ad hoc committee would actually listen to us. Maybe everything would be all right, after all.

21

The Committee Fails Us

It was to the oversight and fact-finding committee appointed by the Wrestling Federation of India that I first openly spoke in detail on what had happened to me at the Junior Asian Championships. It wasn't that people hadn't heard the story before, but it was mostly through hearsay. I had told only a very small number of people the entire truth – my roommate at the competition of course knew, my roommate at the national camp, my mother and Satyawart.

But it's only when I realized that I would have to testify in front of the oversight committee that I finally put it down in writing for the first time.

Bajrang had arranged a lawyer, whom we met at the Lalit Hotel near my house. Bajrang, Vinesh, I and all the other girls who were willing to testify met at that hotel, where we narrated what we had faced even as our lawyer noted it all down. I told the lawyer about the harassment I had faced. But I also told him about the financial issues and my contract money, which was never paid to me. The other girls did the same. The process lasted all day and concluded at two in the night. Then, the next day, the lawyer printed out my statement and I signed at the bottom of the paper.

The Committee Fails Us

Each of the girls presented her affidavit and then testified to the sports ministry's committee individually. Our testimonies were recorded too, although some girls complained that the recorder stopped working midway through their session.

I wasn't nervous at the time. Although this was a written account, I didn't think I was filing a case, which was what always worried me. I also thought I had no option but to do what I did. I had to tell the committee everything. If we did, maybe they would be willing to remove Brij Bhushan Sharan Singh from the federation.

It might have been naive on my part, but I felt a little hopeful about the process, in view of the composition of the committee. Mary Kom had a reputation for being a no-nonsense person and someone who would always wave her flag of honesty regardless of the consequences. She had spoken about how she had been harassed when she came to the national camp from the Northeast. It was a huge thing for any woman athlete to speak about. She was one of the few sportspersons I really admired.

Radhika Sreeman, the official with the Sports Authority of India, was a very sweet lady who had even got a wrestling hall named after me at the Sports Authority of India Centre in Sonepat. She was very helpful to the wrestlers. None of the men who had participated in camps there had a single bad thing to say about her. She'd solve whatever issue they had promptly.

The sports ministry's committee wasn't the only one we testified in front of. The Indian Olympic Association also formed a seven-member committee, which also had Mary Kom and a few other women members on it. But on that committee, there was at least one member who was hostile to our cause.

Yogeshwar Dutt hadn't been called to the meeting where we first decided to protest. Unlike other wrestlers who joined us later, he started speaking out openly against us. I knew that he knew what had happened to me. One of my roommates, whom I had confided my story to, had been his girlfriend at one point. I knew that she had told others, and she would have told Yogeshwar as well.

Our testimonies to the sports ministry committee were a mixed bag. I had reason to believe my account had made an impact. When I finished Mary Kom said, 'It's the same as my story. It's the same way I was harassed.' I felt a sense of relief hearing her words. At least one person here knew what I'd gone through. Finally, someone believed us.

Some of the younger girls, however, found the process of testifying in front of a group of people on video camera overwhelming. I wish we had been able to support them during what must have been a hard time for them.

We tried to do better when we testified in front of the IOA committee. That time, instead of going one by one, all the girls who had come forward to testify went in together so that everyone knew they were being morally supported.

All of us thirteen female wrestlers sat in the same room and told our stories, one after the other. It was difficult for the younger ones, but they knew that their seniors were standing right alongside them. One of the girls telling her story was very young. She said that under the pretence of getting a picture taken with her, Brij Bhushan Sharan Singh would put his arm around her waist and pull her close. After she had won a medal at one tournament, she realized what was going to happen and so tried to move away from him.

Brij Bhushan Sharan Singh had said, '*Pakad ke leke ao*'. He was actually asking for her to be caught and brought over to him! He

The Committee Fails Us

asked her if she was trying to be 'too clever' in trying to avoid getting a picture taken with him. He'd take care of her for trying that. And he did just that. At the next nationals, her name was removed from the entry list of participants.

She started to cry as she recalled this, and the other young girls started to cry too. Once they began to weep, I couldn't control myself. I started tearing up, and then Vinesh did too. The women members of the committee who were listening to us, and finally the woman lawyer, who were in the same room, started to cry too. They started to hug the girls who were testifying. They said 'Please don't cry, we will get you justice. Don't worry.'

Although Yogeshwar was silent, Mary Kom too said she would get us justice. It was a very emotional moment for all of us, but it was cathartic too. Finally, everyone had to started to understand what we were dealing with. Their tears told us they believed us. Now they would go to the IOA and the government and tell them just how rotten the state of Indian wrestling was.

But nothing happened. One day passed. Then a week went by. We were constantly sending emails or calling up members of the committee and asking if there was any update. I was thinking maybe that a week was too soon. Maybe things would get done the next week. Then it became the week after. And then the week after that.

As if to show that they were still working on the matter, they'd keep us updated on irrelevant things. They sent us a mail saying they had called in Brij Bhushan for questioning, where of course he would deny everything. They sent another mail listing out the payments made for recording our statements. They would write at the bottom of the mail that all this was confidential. But there was no point in those mails. Even if they was confidential, they were pointless. But they never sent an email telling us what we wanted to hear – the dismissal of Brij Bhushan from the federation.

I started getting angrier and angrier. We began to realize that this man was far more powerful than anyone of us had fathomed. The government was protecting him completely.

We had done everything we could. There were young girls who had stepped up with so much courage. We had submitted evidence in the form of flight tickets to prove we were where we were when these incidents of harassment had occurred. Despite that, nothing happened.

The number of girls protesting against Brij Bhushan kept falling. At the start fourteen girls had testified before the oversight committee. By the time the committee produced their report, there were just six who were still part of the protest.

Finally, the committee sent us an email with their resolution. We couldn't see the report since it wasn't made public. Even Babita, who was part of the committee and thought she might get a role in the federation for playing her part in getting us to withdraw our protest, found she had outlived her usefulness. The report was meant to be read and signed by every member of the committee, but Babita said she was only given a few hours to read her copy. She wrote on the report that she was signing with objections, but that didn't make any difference.

There was no admission of any guilt on Brij Bhushan Sharan Singh's part. The committee only reported that the federation should have had a woman on its sexual harassment committee and that the federation should have had better communication with the wrestlers.

The Committee Fails Us

Even though I had realized what was going to happen, this outcome still made me feel sick. Were the committee members' jobs and positions so important to them that they couldn't even stand up for what was right? That they couldn't admit that women wrestlers in the country were facing sexual harassment?

But every time I got angry with them, I realized that I too had been quiet for so long myself. I had held my tongue because I too was thinking about my career. The Indian system is such that no one is able to speak out against injustice. Not a lot of people have the courage to speak up against the government.

It wasn't just Mary Kom whom I considered an idol and role model. I used to admire Yogeshwar Dutt too. It was such a big thing for me to go with him to the 2014 Commonwealth Games. I was so excited to be in the same team as an Olympic medallist. I was getting pictures clicked with him at Glasgow. But he didn't support us at all. Some of the girls who testified before the sports ministry's committee had come with their fathers. We found out from some of the girls that Yogeshwar told their fathers that nothing good would come out of testifying and protesting, and that it was best for their daughters to go back and train. We later also found out from within the wrestling community that Yogeshwar was also leaking to the media and others who weren't supportive of our protest just what was going on inside the committee room.

So many of my idols turned out to be only too human. They were as selfish as anyone. I admired two of them for their Olympic medals, but what good were they? I used to think I was special for having one of my own too. But I know now that that medal isn't anything special. It's not that I don't care about my medal. It's very close to my heart. It's given me a life I couldn't have imagined. But it's not everything.

The Olympic medal gave me a name and some respect, but it doesn't guarantee that they will endure. If you win a medal, people might remember it for a few days, or maybe a few years if you are lucky. But if I am a good person, people will always remember that. It's more important to be a good human being. Medals lose their shine eventually. After you, someone else will win one. There is no respect for Yogeshwar in Haryana now, because everyone knows that he was on Brij Bhushan Sharan Singh's side.

I was completely disillusioned after the report was released. I didn't want to have anything to do with protesting for some time. If we had stayed at Jantar Mantar for one more day, the government would have been very vulnerable. But we'd been taken in by words and had been persuaded by Babita to abandon our protest. We gave up the advantage we had, and over two months gave our opponents enough time to fight back.

It was Bajrang and Vinesh who reached out to me once again. They had by now realized that they'd been taken for a ride by their own family member. They decided they needed to protest once again. They came to me with folded hands.

Everything had been ruined, they said. The federation was starting to return to Brij Bhushan Sharan Singh's hands – although the oversight committee was officially running the federation, all the work was continuing to happen from the old office at Brij Bhushan Sharan Singh's official MP's quarters. They told me we had to protest once again and begged me to join. But we couldn't just protest this time, we would have to register an FIR against Brij Bhushan Sharan Singh.

The Committee Fails Us

Initially, I refused to take part in a second protest. I said no to Vinesh and Bajrang again and again. They knew that if they wanted to start a second protest, I had to be part of it.

I was still not convinced. If I did come forward this time, what was the guarantee that they'd not listen to Babita once again. We might put everything we had on the line, but would she do that? Would Vinesh's own sister and Bajrang's own sister-in-law join us?

The two accepted that I had been right about everything that I had said at the sports minister's home. I was right about what I had said about Babita. They admitted that they had been played. Vinesh said Babita had ruined our careers and that she'd kill her if she got the chance. She said Babita had now stopped responding to calls.

They had put their weight behind the decision to call off the first protest, not just because they had been convinced by Babita but because they too had hoped to restart their wrestling careers, which had been interrupted by the protest. But they now knew that there was no way that things could go back to normal.

They told me that their own careers had been wrecked. Both Bajrang and Vinesh knew they weren't going to be able to wrestle if Brij Bhushan Sharan Singh remained in control of the federation.

Even after Bajrang and Vinesh had requested me to join their protest, I was not convinced. The previous episode had left me with such a bad taste in my mouth that I wanted nothing to do with any protest.

But, for all my hesitancy, I also felt a sense of urgency. In the time that it had taken the committee to produce their report, it would have been easy for Brij Bhushan Sharan Singh to identify all the girls who had come with us to the sports minister's house and to the committee. It wasn't something that could be hidden any more.

We couldn't stop other people from getting in touch with them. In the weeks that had passed, a number of girls who had initially testified had already begun to waver. The longer we took to protest again, the greater the number that would falter.

A number of coaches also pleaded with me to join the protest for a second time and be part of the legal battle. On the second day of our protest, we had promised that we would go to the courts if the government didn't listen to our demands. We had to do that now.

Despite the emotional pressure being heaped on me, I was still uncertain. By going to the courts, I knew I was in for a lengthy fight. Finally it was Satyawart who convinced me. Despite all that had happened, despite all the mistakes that had been made, this was still my fight to fight. I couldn't leave it in the middle. Even though it wasn't what I wanted to do, a week after Bajrang and Vinesh first approached me, I finally decided I would register an FIR.

Bajrang chose a lawyer – Narendra Hooda – who was willing to take our case, and we started filing our complaints.

The wrestling community in India isn't a very big one. I knew most of the girls who were filing their complaints from even before our protests. Some of them were juniors whom I'd often seen in Lucknow. I'd seen others at the nationals. Apart from a couple – Anshu and Sarita – who were in the same camp as me, I didn't know the others very well, though.

As we sat in that lawyer's office and filed our complaints, I got to know them better. They were young girls, just as I had been, with the same hopes and dreams as I had. I admired their bravery in stepping forward. I was a senior wrestler and had achieved a lot already. I had a job and I was married to a man who supported me absolutely. Those young girls had none of that to fall back on.

The Committee Fails Us

I felt sorry for them too, but I also felt a sense of motivation by being around them. Here I was so afraid of filing a case despite having such a strong safety net, and these girls, despite their entire future being in doubt, were willing to step forward and take on Brij Bhushan Sharan Singh. These girls were neither married nor had a job. I knew I had to fight with them and stand by them, because if we lost they would be ruined completely. Their careers would be finished. Brij Bhushan Sharan Singh would destroy them.

The youngest of the girls who was willing to register an FIR was a minor. The fact that she was a minor accusing Brij Bhushan Sharan Singh of sexual harassment meant that the POCSO (Protection of Children against Sexual Offences) Act would be applicable in her case. Our lawyer told us that when an FIR is registered under the POCSO Act, the accused has to be arrested immediately.

I felt we were finally getting somewhere. We weren't just sitting and hoping the government would help us. Once a POCSO case was registered against him, Brij Bhushan Sharan Singh would have to be arrested by the police. When that happened, there was no choice but for the federation to be taken away from his grasp.

Unlike the single day it took to draft our affidavits for the oversight committee, it took three days for the completion of the recording of our statements for our police complaint. It took multiple hours to record and write down our statements. If our affidavits gave only a general idea of what Brij Bhushan Sharan Singh had done to whom, our lawyers tried to extract as much detail from us as possible for the police complaint.

We had finished drafting our complaint on 20 April and went the following day to register our FIR. We went about our day as usual. Some of us had to train, others like me had to do that as well as my job in the Railways. In the evening we headed together to the Hanuman Mandir police station at Connaught Place.

The station officer at the police station understood who we were. But he didn't want to register the FIR even as our lawyers went inside the station with him to try and get him to register it. For the next couple of hours, the station officer kept coming out to see if we were still waiting for our copy of the FIR. When he saw we were, he'd go back inside.

He was asking his superiors whether he should register the FIR or not. He was clearly told not to. The longer it took, the more I started to understand that our fight this time around wasn't going to be a whole lot easier than the first time we protested.

Finally, as it was getting late, our lawyers suggested that we go home and that he and some others would wait at the station until the FIR was registered and a copy given to them. Our lawyers waited until 2 a.m. in the night but the police never registered the FIR. They did finally make a note of it in the complaints register, but it wasn't a formal FIR.

We waited for one day for the police to register an FIR. When they didn't, we decided to return to Jantar Mantar. Unlike our first protest, we didn't have a permission slip this time. The rules of public protest at that site said that we had to take permission to protest, but we decided there was no way they would give it to us if we asked politely. So we decided to just show up and protest. It was against the rules, but we decided to brazen it out.

We'd travelled by train without a railway confirmation ticket so many times before that it wasn't a shock for us to sit somewhere we didn't have official authorization to. We weren't going to get up willingly. But because we were well-known faces who had represented

The Committee Fails Us

the country so many times, the police were also not going to beat us with their lathis to get us out, as they might have with others.

Just like the first time, we reached Jantar Mantar at 11 a.m. We spread out mattresses and sat down once again.

22

Second Protest

In January of 2023, we had mistaken our gathering courage to step onto the mat against Brij Bhushan Sharan Singh with actually winning. This time we knew that there was no guarantee of success. We were gambling with everything we had. It wasn't that we could not lose. We must not lose.

This time we weren't going to be deceived by anyone. We were not going to get up, no matter what, until our work was done. I was mentally better prepared this time around. We would stay at the protest site all day, every day, until we got what we wanted.

We had informed many of the people who had joined us in our first protest that we were going back to Jantar Mantar. Several of them joined us once again. Whenever we needed something, there was always someone to arrange it for us. Vinesh's husband Somvir Rathee was very resourceful. He was a man of few words, but if there was a shortage of something he would sort it out. He got mattresses on the first day, and a week later found a way to arrange for coolers and fans, and even a tent. He made the protest site habitable to a great extent. Everyone had their role to play. But the one thing

Second Protest

everyone agreed on was that the three of us – Bajrang, Vinesh and I – had to be the face of the protest. I had been happy not to be front and centre of the first protest – that was just who I was. But I started finding my own voice in the second protest. I was part of a larger group in the first protest. This one felt a lot more personal to me. I had been one of the women who had testified against Brij Bhushan. Now I was defending my own honour.

Although we were better prepared, there were things we hadn't counted on. We had first laid out our mattresses near Jantar Mantar in the third week of January, just as spring began. We returned just as north India's brutal summer was about to hit Delhi. Our protest site, which was nice and cool the first time around, was baking hot now. After the first day, we shifted our protest site, from the side of the road where the public toilet was, to the other side of the road under a large neem tree, which at least brought us some shade

We also hadn't counted on another natural phenomenon. Summer brought with it insects. We had been speaking to the media all through the evening and night, and finally, at 12 a.m., we decided to sleep. We had already decided we were going to stay the night on the pavement and had brought blankets and bed sheets along.

Although the police didn't try to force us off, the mosquitoes definitely did. If we lay still for even a moment, a buzzing cloud would gather above our heads. Every time we dozed off, they bit us wherever they could. Anti-mosquito sprays did little to discourage them. After a few minutes of this, we covered ourselves from head to toe under blankets. We looked like a row of dead bodies covered in shrouds. Those mosquitos kept up a persistent attack on us from 12 a.m. to 6 a.m., when we'd get up.

Despite the mosquitoes having a free run over us, we slept well that first night. We had been exhausted the previous day. We were talking to every media person we could and were physically and mentally worn out. Eventually, that won out over the insect bites. We'd be woken by a particularly bad bite, but then we'd go back to sleep right afterwards.

Since we were all government employees, we had all taken leave in advance, before starting our protest, to ensure that we couldn't be accused of breaking our service rules. It wasn't that they didn't try to accuse us of this, though.

The government soon sent a vigilance team to investigate me. The one thing that I could guarantee about my career as a wrestler and afterwards was that I'd never cheated anyone. They might have wanted to transfer me out of Delhi to get me away from the protest, but they couldn't accuse me of any wrongdoing. That was the one tactic I was least worried they would use against me.

What I was more frustrated about was the police not registering the FIR against Brij Bhushan Sharan Singh. We had to approach the Supreme Court, simply to get the FIR registered. We weren't getting a hearing at the court at first. It was Kapil Sibal who approached our lawyer and was able to get the case heard in the Supreme Court, which finally forced the police to register a case and start investigations.

Even after the FIR was registered, Brij Bhushan Sharan Singh was not arrested.

Although a POCSO case had clearly been made out, the police still had to investigate the charge and file a charge sheet. It took them nearly two months to do that. They were in no hurry to proceed with the investigation.

Our protest continued at Jantar Mantar. Unlike at the first protest,

Second Protest

we were a lot more humble about our limitations. We had been kids playing at revolution the first time around. The moment things went in an unexpected direction, we had listened to whoever promised us they'd make things all right. We fell for every trick there was.

This time we understood we needed to take help from those who were more experienced than us. We decided to involve our elders and the leaders of our khaps (clans). There were those who later said this made it seem our protest was only the work of our Jat community. It was indeed a matter of honour for them, and we needed someone whose support we could count on unconditionally. Many of our community leaders had been part of the farmers' protest the previous year, and they knew how to stand strong against tactics we might not have known how to deal with.

One of the men who helped us a lot in the second protest was Mandeep Punia, a man from Bajrang's village of Khudan, near Jhajjhar in Haryana. Although Khudan is a village mostly famous for wrestling – they say that there is a langot outside every door – Mandeep was someone who had cultivated his mind. Even though he was younger than all of us, he was a very well-read and educated person and had studied at Jawaharlal Nehru University. He had been a part of the farmers' protest a few months before, during which he had been detained by the government. He was someone who was still connected to the farmers' protest and seemed to know exactly what we should do and at what time.

As the days passed, our protest grew much larger than we might have been able to deal with by ourselves. Our camp site grew too. To our bare mattresses, we steadily made additions. Mosquito tents came in, followed by a generator to power loudspeakers. Our protest site started resembling a small village at one point. There were people coming from all over the country.

Our day would start early, by about 5.30 a.m. We never had to set an alarm clock. Either our eyes would open by themselves under the first rays of the sun or the street dogs would start barking around us. Some of our elders who had come to our protest site might be lying on mattresses we had placed around the campsite. They'd wake us up as if we were kids once again.

'*Uth jao balakon. Kaam karna hai.* [Wake up, children. We have work to do.]'

We would be busy the entire day. There would always be people coming to meet us or some media person there to conduct an interview. There would be fans of our sporting achievements who wanted to take pictures with us, and parents who would bring their children to see us. In the afternoons we would hold press conferences, where we would update our supporters on the status of our protest and try to encourage them to stay strong.

It wasn't easy. At the start of our protest, the government thought that if they made it simply too uncomfortable for us to stay in the heat and grime, troubled by insects, we might just give up and go back. A few days after we started our protest they instructed the police not to let us spread our camp any further. They were to stop us from bringing anything to the site that would make it a little easier for us to camp on that pavement.

I don't hold any grudge against the average policeman. He or she had a government job, just like I had with the Railways. They were following the government's orders, just like I did at my job. They too had to run their households on their government salaries. Their wives and children were waiting for food too. How could one tell them they needed to stand against the government?

Many policemen and women admitted they were actually on our

Second Protest

side. A large number of them hailed from Haryana and felt a sort of kinship towards us. When we were about to sleep at night, many of the policemen patrolling the campsite would ask, 'Is everything okay, beta?' And we would reply, 'Yes, Uncle, we are fine.' They were very sweet older men, not unlike the coaches and uncles many of us had grown up with. We would often sit and talk with them.

But in the morning when we restarted our protest, we would return to our roles in opposition to each other. There was one day when things got really bad. There was a single washroom at that protest site, which was used by everyone who visited. By the end of the day it was absolutely filthy. Water had been cut off so there was no way for us to clean it, either. The police also unplugged a couple of generators that we had brought in to provide us electricity. They erected police barricades around the campsite and began to stop us from bringing food and drinking water from our homes.

One evening we had heavy, unseasonal showers that soaked our mattresses all the way through. As we tried to bring in some foldable cots to the protest site, the police refused to let us bring them past their barricades. They tried to push them out, while we tried to pull them in. We tried arguing with them – what was the harm in letting us bring in a bed to sleep on? That seemed to be the last straw for us. They'd already cut our electricity supply, made it hard to bring in food, and now even a folding cot seemed to be forbidden.

They were just trying to squeeze us out. They were trying to leave us with the least amount of facilities possible. But we weren't going to give up without a fight. In our pushing and pulling, a scuffle broke out. One of the policemen appeared to be drunk, and he hit Vinesh's brother Dushyant with some sort of a baton, leaving him with a deep gash on the back of his head.

I broke down in tears, as did many of the others at the protest. Had we fought so hard for the country, carried our flag high on foreign soil, just so we could be beaten up, simply for asking for our rights? Still crying, we broadcast what was happening to us on our Instagram accounts. Some of the media, too, was witness to our assault.

It was only then that the police backed off a little. We were able to get our cots inside and our electricity supply was resumed. While the police gave us a little breathing space at the campsite, there were other hazards we hadn't expected. A few days after the fight, we were hit by another rain storm at night. Any storm would be followed right after by a swarm of mosquitoes, so we retreated under some mosquito nets that we had hung up.

I don't think I've slept as deeply either before or after that protest. I had no dreams at all those nights I slept on the pavement at Jantar Mantar. It was the kind of deep sleep you'd only get when you'd worked hard the whole day on something that was very important.

On the day of the storm, I woke up in the middle of the night because of the noise of the storm, and I'm lucky I did. As I opened my eyes, I saw that the heavy winds had all but pushed over two of the heavy iron barricades the police had placed around our campsite against the thin mosquito tents. They would have fallen right on top of Sangeeta or Satyawart, who were sleeping closest to them. Somehow, Bajrang had woken up too. He sprang up and caught the two barricades with his hands.

We all woke up after that. The storm was intense. The electricity went out and it started raining heavily. The wires that we had used to connect our fans to the generators were about to start short-circuiting. We ripped them from their sockets in the nick of time.

Second Protest

The police had also started making it hard for people to come in to support us. They blocked off the road that lead from our protest site to Janpath Metro station, the nearest stop on the metro. Despite that, people still managed to come and meet us.

Although I appreciated people's support, I had to overcome a lot of my own conditioning. It's not easy to stay in a space close to other people. I've always been obsessive about cleanliness. I learned very quickly that it was impossible to be clean when you are sharing a 100-square-foot protest site with dozens of people.

There would be people climbing all over the mattresses on which we were sitting. At the start, I'd try to tell everyone to take off their shoes when they came up, since we had to sleep on those same mattresses later in the night. Sometimes they'd forget and just step on it with their shoes on. I'd cringe every time I saw that happen, or when I saw footprints on the mattress just as I was about to sleep. But I had to get used to all this.

The only concession I made for myself was in the morning, when I would go to my Railways flat to use the washroom and take a shower. It was just a few minutes away from the protest site and I'd be back right after.

Our supporters might not have left our protest site clean, but they more than made up for it. They'd tell us their stories and motivate us. Some of them would thank us for raising our voice against our oppressors. Because of us, they said, other girls could now gather the courage to speak out against the abuse they had faced, too. They saw in us their own struggles. We had initially begun our fight specifically to get rid of Brij Bhushan Sharan Singh, but at the second protest we realized we had become a symbol of something far bigger.

At times we felt small, because people who had far greater battles than we did saw themselves in us.

We met many women who had faced horrific harassment and abuse. Many had been the victims of rape. They didn't have lawyers who fought for them, like we had for us. And unlike us, who could at least find strength from belonging in a group, almost all these women were fighting by themselves. Despite the odds they faced, they were absolutely fearless. They were fighting as hard as they could.

There was one woman who came up to us. She was in a simple salwar suit and could be any woman on the street. She told us how, after she had been raped, her husband threw her out of their home. She was fighting her case entirely by herself. She'd go to the police station where she would be made to wait the entire day and night to get an update on her case.

When we listened to their problems, we felt ours were so insignificant. Many of them would come up to us, sit next to us and talk to us. When we showed interest, they'd tell us their whole story. Sometimes they would start to cry, and we would start to cry too. They just wanted to tell us their stories. They wanted to believe they were not alone.

While we were still at the protest, the police had begun their investigations in our case. I recorded my statement once before them and was then asked to give my statement in front of a magistrate.

During the protest, every woman whose name was in the FIR, all six of us, went one by one to have her witness statement recorded at the Rouse Avenue courts.

Someone remarked to me how strange it was that I, Sakshi, was going to be an actual witness, just like my name signified. I suppose that was my destiny, in a way. Who would have thought that when Sofia became Sakshi how exactly my life would turn out?

To my surprise, I was not at all nervous in testifying before the

Second Protest

judicial magistrate. Over the past few months I'd told my story so many times ... It had been written down on paper and I had repeated it to lawyers, committees and the police. I had met officials from the Women's Commission and I'd told my story to them too.

I had wondered what the point of their asking me all these questions all over again was, since I had made a written affidavit too. I had made a very detailed statement to my lawyers too, which had my signature at the end of it. Yet, this statement to the court was the most important one. A written statement could be made and signed under duress. When you make a statement to the court, the judge is right in front of you and can determine if you are being pressured in any way, if you have been coached to say what you are saying or speaking of your own free will. This was the statement that would be admissible in court in the case we were making a case against Brij Bhushan Sharan Singh.

My lawyer told me to make sure I told the exact same story, or else the defence lawyers would try and find inconsistencies in my statement. I wasn't worried about that. I was not lying. The words might come out in a different order, but my story would be the same. My story was true. I didn't have to struggle to remember it.

I'd imagined giving the witness statement just like in the movies. I'd imagined there would be a black-robed judge behind a wooden podium and I'd have to stand in a box and give my statement.

They do have rooms like that, but I simply went behind the courtroom into a smaller cabin, which looked just like a normal office, about the size of a large washroom. There was a lady judge sitting across a desk. She was wearing a salwar suit and did not have black robes on, but I presumed she was the judge since she had a black coat hanging off the side of her chair.

Although I thought I'd said everything I knew, I was aware that the judge was going to probe even further to get more details of what had happened. The judge asked if Brij Bhushan was sitting to my right or to my left during our encounter. She wanted to know what he had attempted to do physically. She asked me if there was anyone else in the room. I answered to the best of my ability.

While I had to admit that my roommate had been sleeping in our own room during the time of episode, I had told what had happened to some others too. I'd told my mother and Anita Sheoran, my roommate in the national camp. Anita backed me unhesitatingly. She said, 'Yes, Sakshi did tell me this the moment she came back to the camp.' She told them just how nervous and scared I was as I recounted the incident to them.

My mother too affirmed what I had told the judge in my statement.

I was in the magistrate's room for several hours. I was offered a glass of water because I had been speaking for so long. Finally, I was asked to sign a document to certify that I was not speaking under any pressure and that I was in control of my senses.

If earlier the police had been instructed to make things hard for us, at times I wasn't entirely sure if the media was on our side either. Early on, one journalist asked why it had taken so long for us to speak out. He couldn't understand just how hard it was, considering our background, to even acknowledge that something of this nature had happened.

I found out much later about a severe case of exploitation in the USA Olympic gymnastics team. It had taken the gymnasts, many of whom had won multiple Olympic medals, years to speak out on what had happened to them. And they were born and raised in the USA, where girls are so confident, educated and bold. And our media

Second Protest

here was asking why girls who came from poor families with little education, and whose livelihood depended entirely on their career in wrestling, would not want to speak out against the man who controlled their federation.

At the protest, of course, everyone seemed to be on our side, and that might have given us a wrong understanding of the extent of support we had. So I'd sometimes speak to some of my family and friends who hadn't come to the protest, simply to try and understand just what the perception of the protest was back home.

They told me that after the first few days, the mainstream media was no longer covering our protest very extensively. The IPL cricket tournament had started, and many channels started covering that instead.

But if a twenty-four-hour news channel couldn't find time to cover the story of Olympic medallists protesting harassment by a politician, then I'm not sure what they use their time for. At that point, we understood that the media too had been pressured into not giving us the kind of coverage our protest needed so the issue didn't become bigger than it was.

Some of the media began to do critical stories about us. There were others who started Twitter hashtags saying that we had taken so much money from the government and that we should return it since we were protesting against them. It was a bizarre accusation to make – as if the government was doing us a favour. I was willing to return all the money they gave me. But could they return my struggle and sacrifices over eighteen years? I had trained every day in the morning while everyone else was sleeping. I've stayed hungry and thirsty just to get a chance to fight. I gave up my family. If they paid me back my sweat and blood I'd happily give them back what they had rewarded me with. And did the prize money we were given justify our sexual harassment?

We fought in whatever way we could. We tried to get our point of view out through our social media presence. We streamed all our press conferences to the public. We would post all our appeals on the same platforms. They might not reach everyone, but they'd reach at least someone.

But if we were trying to get our voices heard, we sometimes felt we were being drowned out by other voices. Slowly but surely, many accusations began to be made against us. If you throw enough dirt at someone, something is bound to stick. A huge percentage of the population, especially in the villages and small towns, sits in front of the TV at dinner time and watches the news. So, when the mainstream media stopped covering our protests, that space was filled by rumours doing the rounds on WhatsApp and other social media.

I started seeing some of these messages myself. According to them, we were protesting for selfish reasons, like not wanting to compete with younger athletes. We wanted to run the federation. We were over-the-hill athletes looking to wheedle out a last round of favours for ourselves. A lot of people started to doubt our intentions. We were now anti-national.

If our protest and struggle been shown fairly, I don't believe anyone would have thought that we had compromised our careers and slept on the footpath of a road out of greed. All of us were well-known, accomplished wrestlers. Had we reduced ourselves to camping on the side of the road because we wanted to run the federation?

But we couldn't change that mindset among the people. It was especially disappointing that those who did have that kind of reach

Second Protest

to communicate the truth to the world did nothing to help us. I had so many sporting heroes growing up... I was a huge fan of Virender Sehwag. I had been a fan of Mary Kom, too. When it came to fighting for a cause though, all these social media heroes stayed quiet. Many of the wrestlers who had come to the first protest too were silent this time around. Standing with us meant standing against the government, and no one wanted to take that risk of offending them. Everyone just pretended there was nothing of note happening at Jantar Mantar.

A few did speak out in support of us on social media, and I'm grateful to them. Aisuluu Tynybekova, who once lost an Olympic medal because of me, posted her support for me on Instagram, as did some of the Japanese wrestlers and a couple of Americans I had once wrestled with.

We knew that we were going to be painted as anti-government protesters, and for as long as we could, we tried to avoid getting branded as anti-government. We tried to make it very clear that we wanted members from the BJP to join us too. Our protest was against Brij Bhushan Sharan Singh, not against his party. We even wrote an open letter to the women MPs from the BJP, inviting them to come and stand with us.

Those politicians who did come to meet us were from the Opposition. I met Priyanka Gandhi and Sachin Pilot for the first time at our protest. I'd met Arvind Kejriwal and Deepender Hooda at the protest previously, but I met them once again this time. I also met Satyapal Malik, the former governor of Jammu and Kashmir.

The backbone of our support, though, came from people whom we recognized from our roots.

Some of the first people to come to our protest site were farmers, who saw our fight as an extension of their own against the farm laws the previous year. I had sympathized with them at that time because my own grandfather had been a farmer. My oldest memories were of spending my days going to the fields with him.

I was reminded of another old memory – of stopping at the villages of Haryana post-Rio on my way home – when, a few days into the protest, an elderly gentleman tried to give us a few five-hundred rupee notes. He wouldn't be the only one. We tried to refuse the money at first, but then we realized we could do more for the protest with the money they gave. There were so many people coming from so far away. Many of them had no place to stay and had made no arrangements for food but had come just to show they supported us. We had started getting them packed lunch and arranging a supply of water and refreshments because it was so hot at the time. We would ensure that everyone who came to our protest had lunch and dinner.

We were paying for this out of our own pockets at first, but as the number of people who were joining us increased, we started accepting donations to pay for these things. Although we weren't fighting on the mat, we were fighting for a righteous cause and people had noticed it. They were giving us whatever they could, as if to say 'well done'.

Someone gave us Rs 10,000, some gave us Rs 50,000. When Satyapal Malik Sir came, he donated Rs 1,100 to those of us who were at the protest site. It was a token amount, but as a gesture it was important. He is a Malik, like me. He donated the money not to me; not as he would to Sakshi the wrestler but as if I was his daughter. Others gave what must have meant a lot to them. There was one farmer – who looked exactly like my grandfather – who pressed a hundred-rupee note into my hand.

Second Protest

None of this money went into our pockets. We put it straight into a donation box. Every single paisa went into supporting the protest. We designated one of our supporters to collect the money, note down the name, address and phone numbers of the donors and the amounts they were donating.

For all their support, there were days when I felt uncertain as to where our protest was headed. I was getting up every day to the sound of barking dogs. I was having my breakfast at the protest site, and living and working there. This had become my lifestyle. Negative thoughts would creep in. Why was I fighting for such a thing? Were we doing something so wrong that very few wanted to help us? From the time I'd started my wrestling journey, I could never bear to be away from the training hall. Now I had spent weeks on the road. It put me on edge, and sometimes I'd find my mind wandering and thinking about being back in the hall performing a double-leg takedown.

Then I'd snap out of my daydreaming and realize I was sitting on a mattress placed on the pavement of a street in Delhi. I'd often wonder how many more days I would have to sleep on the pavement. How many more days would I have to be away from the training hall? Would I be at Jantar Mantar for another six months, or even a year, like the farmers who protested?

Invariably, someone else would read my mind. Either Bajrang or Vinesh would remind me that we were not going to leave, no matter what. For every moment I felt tired, there were many when I felt excited by our actions. We had heard stories about Bhagat Singh. If he too had thought, like many others, that there was no chance of India being able to get freedom and that it was time to sit at home, then nothing would have happened. The revolutionaries weren't sitting at home. They fought, and they paid the price for it. Some got hanged, some went to jail. We hadn't paid anywhere close to that cost. The media would ask us this too, as to how long we would protest. We had only one answer – even if it is going to be a year, we are not going to leave until we get proper justice.

If we weren't budging, then neither was the government. They didn't block our electricity any more but they slowly kept squeezing the support we had away from the protest site. The media had become slowly more apathetic.

We would try and find creative ways to keep our protest relevant. A few days in, we started training in the morning next to the protest site, as if to let the government know that we weren't planning on moving out any time soon. We held candle marches. When Delhi hosted an IPL match, we tried to go into the stadium but were prevented from entering it. We planned and then discarded the idea of a hunger strike. There were some wild suggestions from Vinesh too. She said we should write the letters in our own blood and send it to the BJP members of Parliament, but we decided that wasn't going to work.

Finally, a little over a month after we returned to Jantar Mantar, we decided we would do one more march. The prime minister had announced that India's new Parliament building was going to be inaugurated on the 28 May. Brij Bhushan Sharan Singh was also going to be part of the function. We announced we would go to where our leaders were honouring themselves and conduct our own Parliament – a 'Mahila Samman Mahapanchayat'.

The moment we announced that we would be holding a panchayat, the police intensified the barricading around our protest site so that none of our supporters could come to join us on the march to the new

Second Protest

Parliament building. That morning, they blocked many of Delhi's border roads so that many of the farm leaders who had wanted to support us couldn't come. They also enforced Section 144 in New Delhi, so people couldn't gather for any protest.

Although all these restrictions meant that there would be very few marchers with us when we set off, we weren't very worried the night before. We felt we were reasonably experienced protesters at this point. We cracked a few jokes and planned what would happen the next day. Mandeep told us, speaking from experience, that although the police were unlikely to let us get to the Parliament building, we had to get as close to the new building as possible. If we were stopped we had to make sure we sat right where they stopped us and hold our protest there itself. If were denied the right to sit there, we would return to Jantar Mantar and resume our protest.

That night was the last I spent at Jantar Mantar.

As the events of the next few days, both in Delhi and then at Haridwar, showed, we gravely underestimated what we were up against. Not only did the police detain us, they made sure all of us were detained long enough for the protest site to be uprooted.

23

Aftermath

A week after we went to Haridwar to immerse our medals in the Ganga, the father of the minor girl had withdrawn her complaint. It had not been easy to break them. They had stood firm through our protest, but once it was broken, he lost hope too.

We hadn't tried to control any of our witnesses. We didn't, for example, convince them to stay with us even after we heard that Brij Bhushan Sharan Singh was sending representatives to talk to their families.

We also worried that we might be secretly recorded while trying to convince girls to stand with us. We could very well find ourselves the target of a viral audio where we were begging girls to join us so that we had a case.

I broke this rule only once with the minor and her father, when they were being subjected to immense pressure. Her father said that there were some cars being driven up and down in front of their house and his daughter's school. Someone even threatened to kill him. We tried convincing him that we were there to stand by his family and there was nothing to worry about.

Aftermath

But then he stopped taking our calls, and I knew what had happened.

It was only after the minor's complaint was withdrawn that the police finally filed their charge sheet. The withdrawal of the minor's complaint meant that the POCSO Act was no longer applicable when it came to Brij Bhushan. That was what they wanted.

Around this time, we finally decided to drop our lawyer. Although we had got our case registered while we were working with him, we began having doubts as to whether he was as invested in the case as we were. We started doubting whether he had our best interests at heart when, at the start of our protest, the police refused to register an FIR. It was a very senior lawyer named Kapil Sibal who finally got our case listed in the Supreme Court, which forced the police to register the FIR.

Sibal wanted to work with us and was even willing to partner with Hooda on this case. But Hooda worked with him just once, then refused to work with him after that and started sidelining him. At that time I was not aware of how reputed Sibal was as a senior lawyer. We had no idea about the legal system in general. When I did find out, I was very puzzled. Why would we not want to work with someone who had such a strong name in the legal field? This was someone who charged many many *lakhs* of rupees to represent people, and he was willing to work for us for free.

While we were stepping into this legal world for the first time, we were also smart enough not to trust anyone absolutely. While working with Hooda, we were simultaneously seeking opinions from other legal experts too. They were surprised that someone as senior as Hooda was making very basic errors.

It was at this point that we were told to meet Rebecca John.

We were told that she had won a case for a woman who had been harassed by her employer. None of us had a clue as to who she was. After some online search, we found out that the lady she had successfully defended was Priya Ramani who had been sued for defamation by a member of the government whom she had accused of sexual harassment. We found out that she works on many women's cases. And when we asked people we trusted, we found that she had a reputation for incorruptibility.

Rebecca John told us what she expected from us. She said that we would have to meet her from time to time, and if we couldn't do that we would have calls on Zoom. She had a way of speaking that made me trust her right away. She didn't tell us what we wanted to hear but told us what we could realistically expect.

She already knew our stories and she had read our affidavits. My biggest worry was that I might have to stand in front of Brij Bhushan Sharan Singh in the court and testify against him, and she said that was possible.

24

Cracks Start to Appear

After our fiasco on the ghats at Haridwar, the government tried to make a deal with us. If we promised we wouldn't return to protest, they promised they would take back all the cases that had been slapped on us after we broke Section 144 by attempting to march to Parliament. They also promised that the police would complete and file a charge sheet against Brij Bhushan Sharan Singh. Although they did file a charge sheet, it was a watered-down version since the strong POCSO charges were no longer applicable.

However, they did withdraw the cases that had been filed against us, which meant that we could return to wrestling. After a month and a half on the streets, all of us wanted to return to the one thing we did understand. I still held out hopes that I would be able to qualify for the Asian Games. After so many weeks on the streets, unable to eat or train, I was out of shape and I knew my chances were going to be slim at the trials which were to be conducted in the last week of July, a little less than two months away.

The ad hoc committee that was still governing the sport held out a sweetener, though. They promised us that although trials for most weight categories would be held as scheduled, the ones for our weight divisions would be held at a later date. When we then requested the government to allow us to train abroad in privacy, they agreed to that too.

Bajrang and Vinesh were in the government's Target Olympic Podium Scheme, or TOPS. Bajrang quickly left for Kyrgyzstan while Vinesh went to train in Hungary. Satyawart and I left for the USA, since we had long-term visas to that country.

We should have known why this arrangement suited the government perfectly too. We wanted to go, the government wanted us gone, and when both our interests met, the government expedited everything. Within a week all our travel, hotels and tickets had been booked for us.

This was an obvious mistake on our part. There was no need to rush back to the Asian Games, a challenging competition at the best of times. Instead of running back to train, we should have put in our best effort to get the federation formed with a decent set of people in charge. Once we had solved the biggest issue facing us, we would have had enough time and more to prepare for the next set of trials, whenever they were held.

But we were not mature enough to anticipate all this. If you have wrestled all your life, you can't bear to think of what life will be like if you can't compete. Wrestling has been the central pillar of your life. Without it your life feels meaningless. If you are an elite athlete, you always want to believe you have one more tournament in you. The Asian Games are held once in four years and they were the only Games in which I hadn't won a medal. Like a falling man grabbing at the thinnest of ropes, I was snatching at what I thought was my only chance of competing once again.

Cracks Start to Appear

We first met up with Andrew Cook, one of the foreign coaches who had worked with me at the national camp in Lucknow. He would conduct a general fitness camp for us at his home in Oregon, after which he arranged a training camp for us at the University of Iowa.

The first fifteen days in the training camp in Oregon were excellent. At the start, my sparring partners were just throwing me around the mat, but within a couple of weeks I was returning the favour to my opponents, one of whom was an under-23 medallist in the US.

Andrew was optimistic, too. Returning to the sport is like riding a bicycle, he kept telling me. I'd been wrestling for nearly twenty years. That was a lifetime of knowledge that didn't just disappear overnight. I just needed to pedal a bit faster and I'd be right back where I had left off.

I was recovering mentally as well. Andrew's home is beautiful and right next to the Pacific Ocean. I'd train on the beach and also teach some kids who had come to train. It was cool, uncrowded, calm and relaxed – the complete opposite of everything I'd left in India. Yet I couldn't wait to get back to the blistering July heat of north India. I wanted to get as physically ready as possible and then compete in the trials to try and earn my place in the Indian team.

Not everyone was thinking the way I was, though.

While in the USA, I found out that the ad hoc committee had decided that they were not going to conduct separate trials after all, for my weight category. I also learnt that both Bajrang and Vinesh would be exempted from giving trials. The ad hoc committee said the two of them had been given exemption from the trials and I could also ask for it.

None of this made sense to me. The government had promised us they would conduct trials for all seven of us who were part of the protest. They had given it to us in writing. The ad hoc committee had told us to go and train since they would conduct our trials around 10 August, when we got back to India. Now they were conducting it for everyone except Bajrang and Vinesh while I was outside the country.

The three of us would regularly get on conference calls with the members of the ad hoc committee. On one call, Bajrang and Vinesh told the government representative that they should probably give me an exemption too from the trials. The committee member said I should send him an email requesting an exemption and they would consider it favourably.

When I got to know what was going on, I asked Satyawart to broach the topic with Bajrang and Vinesh. He told them this was the time we had to stand firm. If we were able to stay united, then the government would have no option but to hold trials for all of us, together.

He said this in as respectful a manner as he could. This was a very awkward situation for him too. Even though he knew what was happening was wrong, he didn't want Bajrang and Vinesh to feel that he was only complaining because they had got an exemption and I hadn't. But neither Bajrang nor Vinesh was willing to budge.

Satyawart told them this was going to be a big mistake, since they were only going to prove the point Brij Bhushan Sharan Singh had made – that we were trying to protest so we could wrangle an exemption from the trial for ourselves and thereby deny younger wrestlers their chance.

I even told Bajrang and Vinesh that if they needed time to train, they could take the exemption for the Asian Games trials and then compete in the trials for the World Championships. And they could say that if they lost there, they would withdraw from the Asian Games team too. But they didn't take that advice.

I can't say that I wasn't tempted to ask for an exemption from the trials. I thought about it more than once. The chance to compete in the Asian Games was certainly enticing. Furthermore, if Bajrang and Vinesh had accepted the offer, why shouldn't I?

But I chose not to because it was wrong. I felt we were being led into a trap. If I sent a letter asking for a special favour for myself, what would stop the government from holding that against me if I was to protest again? I refused to send any email asking for anything. So I wrote to them saying very clearly that I did not want any exemption. I always wanted trials so that I could be assessed on my skills.

It was terrible decision on Bajrang and Vinesh's part. Whether we wanted to or not, we had become part of a movement that was bigger than us. We couldn't think just for our own benefit.

When we first started the protest and thought that Brij Bhushan Sharan Singh was going to be deposed, there was a proposal made to make me the secretary of the new federation. Vinesh had disagreed. had said that none of us could be part of the federation, or else it would appear that our protest was only a ruse to grab power for ourselves. That was the correct way of thinking. I withdrew my name from that proposal, agreeing that it gave a wrong impression about the cause we were protesting for.

Perhaps if the three of us had been in India, it might have been easier to convince Bajrang and Vinesh against their decision. But we were all in different parts of the world – Bajrang in Kyrgyzstan, Vinesh in Hungary and Satyawart and I in the USA. Very often, their phones were out of reach. Instead of just leaning over and being able to ask them what was on their mind, a communication gap developed.

We had been thinking selflessly and as one at Jantar Mantar. The old way of thinking selfishly was taking over once again. The people close to Bajrang and Vinesh had started filling their minds with greed. Now they were talking about this exemption from trials for the Games.

Once it became clear that Bajrang and Vinesh were being directly picked for the team, rumours started to spread that I too had asked for and got exemption from those trials. If I had stayed silent this perception would have grown. I posted a video on my social media account emphasizing that I had never wanted to avoid a selection trial. I said that I was in the USA because the government had told us they would conduct trials after we came back. I was clear that I was not in favour of direct entry into the Indian team. I wanted the best to go.

Nothing good came of Bajrang and Vinesh's decision to take the exemption. Bajrang went to the Asian Games, where he didn't win any medal, and Vinesh had to withdraw from the tournament because she suffered a knee injury and had to get surgery. But beyond that, their decision badly hurt the image of our protest. It put us in a situation where many supporters started to think that we were actually in the protest for selfish reasons.

What happened undeniably caused a rift between the three of us at the time. But at the same time we know that whatever bitterness might exist between us, there is a bigger cause to fight for. So when we go to the government we go as one. After Bajrang lost at the Asian Games, I still posted a video in support of him. After Vinesh was disqualified from the Paris Olympics, I still tweeted in support of her. The battle the three of us were fighting was bigger than the misgivings that existed between us.

25

Dabdaba Tha, Dabdaba Rahega

There have been ups and downs in our fight for justice.

Perhaps the hardest day was 22 December 2023, when fresh elections were to be held to the Wrestling Federation of India. I was optimistic at the start of the day. For one, Brij Bhushan Sharan Singh's name was not going to be on the ballot. The federation had been suspended at the end of the first protest and Brij Bhushan's term ended shortly after. And, as per the Indian Sports Code, he was not eligible to stand for another term.

Following the incident at Haridwar, we had been called for a meeting by Amit Shah. We met him and the sports minister at his office. He gave us a commitment that we would have a candidate of our choice as president – and he was smart to have had us leave our phones and any recording device outside. If we could promise that we weren't going to protest on the streets once again, then he would give his word that the new federation would have representatives that we had chosen. He asked us who we wanted as president, and we were clear that we wanted a woman president. He accepted this, and based on his promise we gave our word that we were withdrawing our protest. Several months passed and we kept our side of the deal. Our legal case continued against Brij Bhushan Sharan Singh, but we stayed away from the streets.

When it was time to submit our names for nominees for the post of president at the federation, we unanimously chose Anita Sheoran. She had just retired from the sport, but at thirty-nine she was senior enough to hold such a post. As a Commonwealth Games champion and multiple-time Asian Championships medallist, she was an athlete who would bring prestige to the post. She was an innately trustworthy person.

Along with her name for president, we also pitched a few other names for office bearer positions. One was Prem Lochab. He was the secretary of the Railway Sports Promotion Board and also the man who had acted as an intermediary between the home minister and the protesting wrestlers.

Even the day before the voting was to take place, we were fairly certain that even though Brij Bhushan Sharan Singh had put up rival candidates – including one of his business partners, Sanjay Singh – for the posts, it was Anita who would be the next president since the home minister had given us his word that we would have our choice. We had also spoken to the sports minister a few days before and reminded him that we had lived up to our side of our deal. He assured us he would speak to the state bodies, who were the ones casting the vote.

We continued to believe this even when, on the eve of the elections, Sanjay Singh publicly announced that he had the support of the majority. Even Brij Bhushan Sharan Singh was giving bombastic interviews to the media where he kept saying that it was Sanjay Singh who would indeed become the new president.

That commitment from the government to us wasn't fulfilled. Sanjay Singh won comfortably. Of the fifteen posts being contested, thirteen were won by Brij Bhushan Sharan Singh's associates. Our intermediary Prem Lochab won too, but the main post in the federation was going right back into Brij Bhushan Sharan Singh's hands. We should have known better. After all, it wasn't the first time that the government had promised us one thing and done another.

The betrayal was bad enough, but what was worse were the celebrations that took place outside Brij Bhushan Sharan Singh house that day. There wasn't even a pretence being made to show that Sanjay Singh was not a lackey of Brij Bhushan Sharan Singh's. They were both hoisted on the shoulders of their supporters. But while Sanjay Singh was the new president, it was Brij Bhushan Sharan Singh who was garlanded with thick chains of flowers. The media cameras focused on him and not Sanjay Singh because everyone knew that this victory was his.

Brij Bhushan Sharan Singh had a giant grin on his face and he was shouting '*Dabdaba tha, dabdaba rahega*.' He had control, and he would continue to control.

At that time Bajrang, Vinesh and I were in a hotel, waiting for the results of the elections. We had planned to hold a press conference thanking the government for their support. We had prepared a statement appreciating them for standing with us in the fight for all our sisters and daughters. We were ready to put aside any ego we might have had in the matter and express our gratitude to the government. Instead of that we were watching video clips of Brij Bhushan Sharan Singh, laughing and grinning. We were all in a state of shock. Both Bajrang and Satyawart were tearing up.

I just couldn't fathom what had happened. I turned away from the TV but I couldn't turn off that image of Brij Bhushan's grinning face. He had won everything.

His words struck me particularly hard because they were true. He had always had control.

I remember when I had won the selection trials to take part in the final Olympic qualifiers in 2016 and was then suddenly told that only I had to give another, for no other reason other than that Brij Bhushan Sharan Singh wanted someone else to go. I'd gone up to Kuldeep Malik, who was the chief coach of the Indian team at the time, to ask why I was being targeted. He didn't have an answer. But the reason was that Brij Bhushan Sharan Singh wanted it that way. He had the power to decide.

No one dared speak in front of him. There's a saying in Hindi – *Mera wazan hi mera shasan* (my dominance is what gives me the right to rule). He did what he did because he could. There was no arguing with him. He did what he wanted to, and everyone else's job was to suffer what they had to.

Even if we had managed to shake that power with our protest, we had not been able to break it. As the days passed and the people saw that nothing seemed to be dislodging him, everyone started feeling that *dabdaba* once again. That fear got into the wrestlers – that there was nothing that could dislodge Brij Bhushan.

Even after all of us had protested, he was still in control.

It made complete sense why so many of those wrestlers who had once stood with us had now chosen to take a step back.

Think of how young Anshu Malik stood up so boldly in that first protest. She had taken the microphone and shouted to everyone who could hear just how Brij Bhushan Sharan Singh had behaved around young women at an international tournament. She hadn't been prompted by anyone. She took the microphone and spoke from her heart for fifteen minutes straight. She showed so much courage and strength to say what she did. She spoke about how she would keep fighting. But she did not come for the second protest. I wasn't able to speak with her, but I tried to call her father and ask him to tell Anshu that we needed her. I pleaded with him. 'Uncle, we need all the support we can get.' He kept saying she'd come the next day or the day after. But she never did. He didn't want to say no to us, because he knew we were fighting for a right cause. But he also couldn't send Anshu. She is just twenty-two. She had her whole career in front of her. Why should I have expected her to give all that up and come and join us? She had understood by then that the president wasn't going anywhere. He was being supported by the government. His *dabdaba* was as strong as ever.

It wasn't just Anshu. There were so many girls who were with us at the start of the protest who had stepped away later. There was a girl from Uttar Pradesh who sent me a message saying she had faced something similar to what we were complaining about. I was receiving so many messages of that nature that I didn't respond that day to her message. By the time I began to tap out my reply the next day, she had deleted her message. I called her up to ask what she had wanted to tell me. But she cut my call and never communicated after that.

There were many girls who lost or were made to lose their nerve. When we first spoke to the oversight committee and to the sports minister, there were fourteen girls who testified. There are just six who continue to stand firm now. Even the minor girl's will was broken. Her family could see that Brij Bhushan Sharan Singh wasn't going anywhere and it was best to come to terms with what had happened.

The father of that minor girl told us that he feared for his life, what with those unknown cars constantly driving past his home and his daughter's school. He said it was out of fear that he withdrew the case. People sometimes ask how so many wrestlers can tolerate so much pain and show so much bravery on the mat but not in real life. But that's because of the way our society works. You know that on the mat there are still some rules and order. Where's that in society? Where do you get justice that easily?

Against someone who has the ability to change the rules as it suits him, why would you want to jeopardize that small chance of success in your own career for some sense of justice? How could I say anything against these wrestlers for not standing together with us when I couldn't even stand up for my own self when I was harassed the first time? I didn't put my own career on the line at the time. I was just nineteen and had my whole career in front of me. I didn't speak at that time myself. I just kept my mouth shut and focused on my career.

Within a few hours of Sanjay Singh becoming the president, he put out a letter to say the WFI was going to be hosting a competition for under-15 and under-17 boys and girls in Nandini Nagar. One of the main reasons we had fought so hard was for competitions to not be held in Brij Bhushan's home turf and for the national camp, where girls were being routinely exploited, to not be held in Lucknow. Now they were rubbing our noses in our defeat. This is all I had achieved.

As news of the results spread, I started getting calls from some of the girls I was training at Satyawart's father's academy in Rohtak.

'Didi, they are going to make us go back to Nandini Nagar? Is the camp going to be held in Lucknow again?'

Once again I was reminded of the extent to which I had failed. I was reminded of Nandini Nagar and Lucknow. I was reminded of just how my own will had been crushed by Brij Bhushan's power. Now he was going to exercise it all over again.

That was the moment I felt I was finally done with the sport, at least for myself.

I knew that if Brij Bhushan Sharan Singh's crony was going to become president, then even if I had wanted to, there would be no way for me to wrestle again. And even if for some reason they just forgot what our entire protest had been about, how would I justify returning? Because, if I had had to fight for one year, sleep on the streets for forty days and, at the end of it all wrestle under a federation headed by an associate of the same person who had led me to protest in the first place, then what was the point of it all?

I had no more expectations. I'd given the sport everything I had. I loved it more than I loved anything else. I had started coaching young girls. I was trying to develop in them the same love for the sport as I did. But if these were the type of people who were going to run the federation and be in charge of their lives, then how could I send young girls out into the same muck I had to wade in myself? I couldn't take that decision for them, but I could certainly make that call for myself.

I had already been thinking of my retirement after the 2022 Commonwealth Games. I was now thirty-one years old and nearing end of my career. I knew I would probably be in good condition for the Asian Games in 2023, and if I was still wrestling competitively, then maybe for even the next Olympics.

There is a tradition in wrestling that when you know you have wrestled your last match, you leave your shoes on the mat. It's not an Indian tradition, but it's always made sense to me.

Although they look like your regular high-top sneakers, wrestling shoes are very unique. Their soles are very thin. You can't wear them like you would your regular jogging shoes. The only place they really belong is on the synthetic mat.

They've always been special to me. It's when I bought my first pair of shoes that I actually felt I was a real wrestler. People would sometimes think my attachment to my shoes was a little extreme. If wrestling was a form of worship for me, then my shoes were one of the instruments of my devotion. That was what I truly believed.

They were as sacred to me as the Hanuman murti at the Chhotu Ram akhara.

The only time we wore our shoes was when we were going to wrestle. When we finish our practice, we take those shoes off and touch them to our head before we step off the mat. That's the only place you are supposed to wear them. In India, you will not see a wrestler wear his or her shoes to the washroom or any place where they think they'd get dirty.

When I went to the world level, it always struck me as odd to see some of the international wresters wear their match shoes as they stood in line outside the toilets. I couldn't ever get used to that. On the other hand, if we Indians had to visit the toilet, we'd always have a pair of open-toed slippers handy. We would wear them over our shoes when we went to the washroom. I just couldn't bear the thought of my wrestling shoes directly touching the washroom floor.

There was only one time of the year where my wrestling shoes would leave the competition or training hall, and that was on the eve of Diwali when we celebrate Lakshmi Puja. On that day, we Hindus worship the instruments of our trade. I've seen people worship books. I'd always put my wrestling shoes in front of the image of Lakshmi and pray over them. To a lot of Indian wrestlers that might seem a little too extreme, but I've always insisted on it. I started doing the same after I moved to Satyawart's home after my marriage, and although he found it odd in the beginning, he follows the same practice now.

After the Commonwealth Games, I had come to terms with my approaching retirement, but I wanted it to be on my terms. I expected to qualify for the Asian Games, and based on how I did there I'd have a good idea as to whether I was still good enough to wrestle with the best in the world. If I was, I'd try to qualify for the Olympics at the 2023 World Championships. If I managed to make it to the Paris Games, then after my final match, whether I won a medal or not, I would leave my shoes on the mat there. As it turned out, I didn't go to the Asian Games or the World Championships after that. I wasn't able to take the trials for those competitions, but I still had hopes that I would be able to qualify for the Olympics, and there I would go out the way I wanted.

At least, that's what I had hoped for.

On the evening of 22 December, after the federation elections, I knew I was never going to be able to get to Paris. We had already announced a press conference. I told the press just what I felt about what had happened. I said I didn't feel I would be able to wrestle any more. I wanted to make it clear that I would not be going back on my word at any point.

As I spoke I started tearing up but got the words out of my mouth. On that day I had been squarely beaten. I'd put in my best efforts, but I was nothing in front of the machinations of a man who was much more experienced at another kind of game than I was. Since I could no longer wrestle on his terms, I had to leave.

With that I took out a pair of blue Asics wrestling shoes. They weren't the shoes I would have worn in competition, but with our press conference just a few hours after the federation elections I didn't have time to get them. These blue ones were the ones I had with me in New Delhi. I'd been training in them every morning at Karnail Stadium, getting ready for what I thought would be a final shot at the Olympics. I took that pair and placed it on the table.

I announced my retirement from the sport and walked away from that press conference and from twenty years in the sport. I didn't expect anything to come of that gesture. It did get a few people excited on social media. For a few hours it trended on Twitter. I remember one channel came up with the headline '*Dabdaba joote ki nok pe*. (The fate of "power" resting on the tip of a shoe).' But that wasn't what I had planned. I just did it to leave the sport at least somewhat on my terms.

It didn't give me as satisfying a closure as I hoped it might. I knew that the federation was still going to be in Brij Bhushan Sharan Singh's hands. For a few weeks after I announced I had quit the sport, I'd just cry for no obvious reason. I knew that my career as a wrestler was over.

It's something I'm still coming to terms with.

27

Why I Continue to Fight

On 15 May 2024, the Rouse Avenue District Court in New Delhi ordered the framing of charges against Brij Bhushan Sharan Singh. That meant that the court told Brij Bhushan exactly what was the case that the police intended to prove against him. It was a small step in what will be a long road towards justice, but it came as a huge relief for me.

In essence, the court had found there was enough reason to proceed with the case. No matter what else happened, our case had merit. All those people who questioned us were now silent. And now, many more who had been afraid to stand with us felt they could come out in support of us.

Within a couple of days of the verdict, I was invited by JSW to attend a Delhi Capitals match of the IPL at Ferozeshah Kotla stadium in Delhi. Just a year before, Bajrang, Vinesh and I had tried to enter the stadium and take our protest to the IPL. The police had got wind of our plans and had refused to let us enter the stands. Now Satyawart and I were special guests. I had mixed feelings about this, of course. It would have been nice to get this sort of public support

Why I Continue to Fight

back then, during the time of our protest, but I also understood why that hadn't happened.

Things have been looking up for me in recent weeks. In April of 2024, I was named one of the 100 most influential people in the world by *Time*. I wasn't even aware that there was such a ranking or what it meant to be included in it until then. I got to go to New York and attend the gala ceremony, where there were plenty of celebrities and actors. What I really enjoyed about going to the States, though, was that it allowed me to attend the USA Olympic wrestling trials in Pennsylvania. At the end of the day, I still love wrestling!

After the court filed charges against Brij Bhushan Sharan Singh, I was on a call with Rebecca and I asked her what would happen next. She told me that all the women who were part of the case would probably have to come to the court and testify once again. I asked her if Brij Bhushan Sharan Singh would be in the same room as us, and she said he probably would. Once again that same old fear came over me. I asked Vinesh what she would do if she were in the same room as Brij Bhushan Sharan Singh, and she told me she'd probably spit out a few abuses.

She's a lot bolder than me. I feel I still hold back. Vinesh doesn't care at all. She retweets videos of Dhruv Rathee's where he speaks against the government. I've still not worked up the courage to do something like that. I know that this can be a very vindictive government. This matter could have been resolved many months ago, but it wasn't because there was no reason for the system to solve it properly. So many of the battles we fight have to be against the system itself.

I struggle to speak directly against the government even though I know the role they have played in this whole matter and just how much has been done to protect Brij Bhushan Sharan Singh. The government's hand is behind everything.

I sometimes think I'll just tweet 'democracy' followed by ten or twelve question marks. I start to type it out but then delete it.

I wish I could be a lot more outspoken, and maybe I will become so in time. Maybe I'll react strongly in the witness stand when I'm face to face with Brij Bhushan Sharan Singh. I know I'll tell the truth. Hopefully, it will be enough.

It's a situation that will be well outside my comfort zone, but I have no other choice. Just like it is in wrestling – once I have committed to a bout, there is no way I can back out of it.

Perhaps life would have been easier if I had kept my secrets to myself. I could have kept smiling, pretended that everything was okay and wrestled a bit more. I'd have probably gone to one more Olympics. Perhaps Satyawart, who had never gone to the Olympics, might have got a chance too. But I know that we would have been living a lie to keep smiling.

I'd been part of that lie for so many years. For all the years that I wrestled, I was essentially a prop to make politicians and the government feel good. Everyone wanted to be around me when I was winning medals. The prime minister would call me and other athletes to his home in New Delhi before we went for a competition, and after we returned he'd invite us for tea and a meal. They'd want to talk to us and get pictures taken with us

I'd met the prime minister many times. I'd met him before going to the Olympics and after I came back from the Games. I met him when I got the Khel Ratna award and when I got the Padmashree. He was always very polite. He'd always say namaste and ask how my training was going. Before I left for the Olympics, he shook my hand. He asked me what sport I played. I told him I was a wrestler and he told me I'd win a medal for sure. I'd been very impressed by him. Here was someone who had a genuine interest in me.

When it came down to it though, Brij Bhushan Sharan Singh was a lot more important to him than I was. He was so important that the government had to save him. It took me a long time to understand that the athlete is never the priority. What matters is just how the athlete can make you look. The PM uses sportspersons for promoting himself, and we were also very willing to be used.

I'm no longer willing to be part of that system, but I know that there are plenty of athletes who are more than willing to be so. It's a tragedy for us sportspersons – how our love for our sport can make us blind to the fact that we are being used. As a wrestler, I'd served my purpose to the government and now there are new influencers for it to find. Hopefully, less troublesome ones.

Right now, the wrestlers are proving to be very problematic, so the PM has started using Instagram influencers to promote himself. Sometime back, he invited a wrestler, Ankit Bainyapuria, to his house. Bainyanpuria became famous on Instagram for following the '75 Hard Challenge', where you train for an hour and a half, follow a diet and maintain a healthy lifestyle for seventy-five days. I couldn't believe that something like a seventy-five hard days' challenge could be so popular. I'd been doing that challenge from the time I got into wrestling! I wasn't doing it for seventy-five days. I'd been doing it for twenty years.

I have no regrets about the protest and how it went, no regrets about even our early mistakes. If I could do it again, I would probably try harder to ensure that Bajrang and Vinesh didn't agree to take that spot in the Asian Games team. We lost so much of our moral high ground at that point.

Knowing what I know now, another thing that I would do is to go ahead and immerse my Olympic medal in the Ganga. I wouldn't have tried so hard to protect it. It's just a medal.

I always thought that that medal was what defined me. I know now that that's not true. It is what brought me fame and it's something no other Indian woman has, but I've started seeing things in some perspective now.

Ever since it was first placed around my neck in August of 2016, I'd never lost sight of it. I always knew where it was. That was true until that day in Haridwar last year, when I gave it to Narender Tikait. It was with him for several days, after which he returned it to some of the coaches who too had gone to Haridwar. They in turn gave the medals to Jitender, who left them at Bajrang's home. As far as I know they are still there. In all these months I've never gone to Bahalgarh to take mine back.

It just never happened. At first it was just that our schedules didn't match. After the breakdown of the protest, I'd gone to the USA while Bajrang had gone to Kyrgyzstan to train for the Asian Games. He was barely home during that time.

But after that a communication gap developed between us, owing to what happened before the Asian Games, so I didn't really know how to go to his house and demand my medal back.

It's not that I don't care about that medal or that it's lost its importance to me. That medal is still one of my career's biggest accomplishments. Of course I know that I can just go and pick it up if I want to, but that's just not a priority any more. It's not that the value of the medal has diminished. But it's just that I'm seeing it's value more objectively now.

There are a lot of other things that have become more important all of a sudden. I have to devote myself to those.

Why I Continue to Fight

That Olympic medal is a reminder of the bouts I've fought in the past. But there is another bout that I have right now, which is probably a lot harder. It's not going to win me a lot of favours. There's no expectation that I'm going to get a lot of money. There is no guarantee that people will respect me. I know I'll never be appointed to any honorary position, like so many athletes. But I sleep peacefully every night because I know I am fighting for the daughters of my country and for a cause that I know is righteous.

Recently, I went to the Jaipur nationals and I felt proud to have so many girls come up to me and say they had taken up wrestling having been motivated by me. I felt such a sense of respect among them for me. That is an accomplishment I can boast about.

But all of this can be taken away just as easily. If my fight against Brij Bhushan Sharan Singh and the federation ends without victory, then all this progress will be lost. If we don't win, people might think our protest wasn't justified. Already, Brij Bhushan Sharan Singh's cronies are starting to regain control of the federation.

I am fighting for all the girls and women in wrestling, but I'm one of those women too. I have a personal stake in this battle. I am literally defending my own honour. I know that if I don't win this bout, all my previous accomplishments will not count for much. If Brij Bhushan takes over the sport completely, my izzat in wrestling will be lost.

As long as control of the federation is, directly or indirectly, in Brij Bhushan Sharan Singh's hands, I know I will never be honoured by it. Neither would I want to be. If Brij Bhushan Sharan Singh stays in power, why would they ever treat me, even though the first Olympic medallist in women's wrestling, as anything other than an enemy?

There are days where I feel really motivated and there are days where I feel tired. I know that win or lose, there is now at least some fear that's been placed in the minds of those in power over athletes. They will think a hundred times before harassing a girl or a woman. Because of our protest, it will be easier for other women to raise their voice if they have to.

Even at my lowest point, that's what gives me hope. When I was a young girl I didn't have the belief that I could fight back. But now I do. And the more I think about it, it seems almost a little funny to me that after all the crimes Brij Bhushan Sharan Singh got away with, it was going to be this quiet women, afraid of even raising her voice, whom he thought he could have his way with, who ended up being the one who was going to make him pay.

There's still work to be done, though. Every wrestling bout has two periods; when I think of this case I'm fighting, I feel I'm through the first period. I'm trailing at this point and the score is against me. The clock is counting down. But I'm not done just yet. I've won before from this position. I'm going to win again.